Embrace the healing, harmonizing, life-affirming powers of
vastu—the Indian precursor to feng shui

The Power of Vastu Living

Now you can follow the ancient principles of vastu in decorating
your house, apartment, studio, or loft. . . .
Identify your zones of tranquility and creativity in the office,
cubicle, or conference room. . . .

Discove

- how to eliminate mental and environmental turbulence in
  any room

- the primary importance of honoring and aligning Earth's five
  elements—space, air, fire, water, and earth

- which natural forces govern which rooms and areas within
  rooms—and how they determine furniture layout, color
  schemes, and lighting

- how to fine-tune the mechanics of your inner balance
  through such crucial details as the direction and placement
  of your bed

- the power of honoring and respecting the self

The Power of Vastu Living

WELCOMING YOUR SOUL INTO YOUR HOME AND WORKPLACE

KATHLEEN COX

Illustrations by Rachel Evans and Adam Charles Lee

FIRESIDE
Published by Simon & Schuster
New York London Toronto Sydney Singapore

FIRESIDE
Rockefeller Center
1230 Avenue of the Americas
New York, NY 10020

FIRESIDE and colophon are registered trademarks
of Simon & Schuster, Inc.

Designed by Jaime Putorti

Manufactured in the United States of America

10   9   8   7   6   5   4   3   2   1

Library of Congress Cataloging-in-Publication Data

Cox, Kathleen.
  The power of vastu living : welcoming your soul into your home and workplace /
Kathleen Cox ; illustrations by Rachel Evans and Adam Charles Lee.
    p. cm.
  Includes index.
   ISBN: 978-0-7434-2407-3
    1. Architecture, Domestic—India. 2. Architecture, Hindu—India. 3.
Architecture—India—Philosophy. 4. House construction—India. I. Title.

NA7427 .C69 2002
133.3'33—dc21
                                                      2001058540

For information regarding special discounts for bulk purchases,
please contact Simon & Schuster Special Sales at 1-800-456-6798 or
business@simonandschuster.com

For my mom and dad, who are my link to the past.
For Kia and Ryan, who are my link to the future.

Acknowledgments

I would like to thank dear friends—Sudesh Prabhakar, Sally Helgesen, Reniera Wolff, Christel Haesicke, Stanley Siegel, Peggy Price, Laura Rittenhouse, Robert Millman, Kathryn Kilgore, and Larry Estridge—along with many of my clients, who have introduced vastu living into their homes and workplaces. They have all helped me enrich the contents of this book.

I also want to thank my agent, Anna Ghosh, for her enthusiastic support. She set this project in motion and got it into the loving hands of my editor, Kim Kanner, whose wise advice turned the process of creating this book into a wonderful experience. Finally, I want to thank Adam Lee and Rachel Evans for turning my ideas into the diagrams and illustrations that grace these pages. All these people exhibit the Truth of the Vedas: Thou Art That.

Contents

⁘

List of Illustrations   *xi*

Welcome   *xv*

WELCOME TO VASTU LIVING   *1*

1   The Power of Space   *3*

2   Personalizing Vastu Living   *27*

3   Creating Your Spiritual Blueprints   *45*

4   The Power of Color   *62*

5   Resolving Conflicts in Your Home and Workplace   *68*

6   The Peaceful Zone of Tranquility   *101*

7   Southern Hemisphere   *105*

8   Final Advice Before You Begin   *108*

THE WELCOMING HOME   *119*

9   Decorating for Your Soul   *121*

10   Special Issues with Your House or Property   *141*

11   Special Issues with Your Apartment   *147*

12	Special Issues with Your Studio or Loft	155
13	Revere Your Transitional Areas—the Porch to the Terrace	162
14	Commemorate Your Kitchen	174
15	Nurture Your Dining Room	186
16	Honor Your Living Room	196
17	Treasure Your Study or Home Office	207
18	Love Your Bedroom	218
19	Venerate Your Zone-of-Tranquility Room	242
20	Purify Your Bathroom	249
	THE WELCOMING WORKPLACE	257
21	Vastu Living in Our New Work World	259
22	General Guidelines for the Company	264
23	Respect Your Office	278
24	Acknowledge Your Cubicle	286
25	Appreciate Your Part of the Pod	295
26	Cherish Your Reception Area	305
27	Recognize Your Conference Room	313
28	Give Thanks to Your Dining Area	320
29	Value Your "Silicon" Workspace	329
30	Bless Your Boutique	337
31	Consecrate Your Medical Suite	348
	Spiritual Blueprints	363
	Glossary	367
	About the Illustrators	369
	Index	371

List of Illustrations

1. Location of the Five Basic Elements in the
   Northern Hemisphere   18
2. Vastu Living Adjustments for the Southern Hemisphere   19
3. Location of the Five Basic Elements and Cardinal Directions   22
4. Vastu Purusha Mandala   47
5. Human Form   48
6. Square Spiritual Blueprint   50
7. Rectangular Spiritual Blueprint Oriented East and West   50
8. Rectangular Spiritual Blueprint Oriented North and South   51
9. Two Examples of Spiritual Blueprints for L-Shaped Spaces   52
10. Spiritual Blueprint for the Odd-Shaped Property   53
11. Bedroom before the Room Swap   72
12. Den before the Room Swap   73
13. Bedroom after the Room Swap   74
14. Den after the Room Swap   75
15. Misdirected Furniture   77

16. Redirected Furniture — 78
17. Weighing Down the Northeast — 88
18. Shiva — 92
19. Ganesha — 94
20. Lakshmi — 96
21. "Impossible" to Solve Problem — 98
22. Small Zone of Tranquility inside a Room — 102
23. Introducing Water into the Northeast — 127
24. Dramatic Southwest Elevation — 128
25. Correct Furniture Placement in the Vastu Living Space — 129
26. Celestial Display of Plants — 138
27. Correct Orientation for the Vastu Living Property — 144
28. Spiritual Blueprint for the House with Guest Cottage — 145
29. Head of the Bed in the South — 149
30. Head of the Bed in the East — 150
31. Achieving Balance in an Unhealthy Quadrant — 151
32. One-Wall Kitchen Before — 158
33. One-Wall Kitchen After — 159
34. Unhealthy Barriers — 160
35. Healthy Exchange — 161
36. Porch That Honors the Past — 166
37. Comforting Balcony — 169
38. Spiritual Blueprint for the Shared Terrace — 171
39. Example of a Toran — 172
40. Spiritual Blueprint for the Food-Preparation-Only Kitchen — 180
41. Spiritual Blueprint for the Eat-in Kitchen — 181
42. Peaceful Zone of Tranquility — 185
43. Appeasement to the Sacred Center — 189
44. Spiritual Blueprint for the Dining Room — 190
45. Spiritual Blueprint for the Dining Area Attached to a Room — 191

46. Purr-fect Zone of Tranquility   194

47. Speak-or-Else Living Room   201

48. Spiritual Blueprint for the Thoughtful Living Room   202

49. Orchid Appeasement (A) and Overweight North Wall (B) 203, 204

50. Spiritual Blueprint for the Study or Home Office   211

51. Remedy for the Desk Facing the South   212

52. Simple Zone of Serenity   213

53. Life-Affirming Zone of Tranquility   216

54 Keeping Calm in the Bedroom (A & B)   224, 225

55. Spiritual Blueprint for the Master Bedroom   231

56. Zone of Love   233

57. Spiritual Blueprint for a Child's Bedroom   235

58. Spiritual Blueprint for the Children's Bedroom for Two   236

59. Child's Zone of Tranquility   239

60. Sweet Something   241

61. Spiritual Blueprint for the Zone of Tranquility in the
    Northeast of the Home   244

62. Spiritual Blueprint for the Zone of Tranquility
    in the Other Quadrants   245

63. Painter's Delight   247

64. Spiritual Blueprint for the Bathroom   252

65. Spiritual Spa   254

66. Spiritual Blueprint for the Company with Financial Office
    in the South   269

67. Spiritual Blueprint for the Company with Financial Office
    in the North   270

68. Spiritual Blueprint for the Executive Office   281

69. Office Zone of Tranquility   284

70. Spiritual Blueprint for an Acceptable Cubicle   290

71. Selfless Zone of Tranquility   294

72. Diagram of the Pod _296_

73. Spiritual Blueprint for an Acceptable Personal Space in the Pod _299_

74. Intimate Zone of Tranquility _304_

75. Spiritual Blueprint for the Reception Area with Lightweight Furniture _307_

76. Spiritual Blueprint for the Reception Area with Heavy Furniture _307_

77. Spiritual Blueprint for the Small Reception Area _309_

78. Comfy Waiting Area _311_

79. Spiritual Blueprint for the Conference Room _316_

80. Appeasing the Sacred Center _317_

81. Spiritual Blueprint for the Company Canteen _323_

82. Spiritual Blueprint for the Company Dining Room and Cooking Facilities _324_

83. Food for Thought _327_

84. Spiritual Blueprint for the Silicon Team Workroom _332_

85. Sporting Zone of Tranquility _336_

86. Southwest Entrance Turned into a Positive Barrier _339_

87. Spiritual Blueprint for the Separate Dressing Room Area _340_

88. Spiritual Blueprint for the Boutique _341_

89. Vision of Joy _343_

90. Creative Sacred Center _346_

91. Creative Zone of Tranquility _347_

92. Spiritual Blueprint for the Medical Waiting Room _351_

93. Sacred Center of the Waiting Room _353_

94. Spiritual Blueprint for the Medical Examination Office _357_

95. Tropical View in the Examination Room _359_

96. Gyana Mudra _361_

Square Spiritual Blueprint _363_

Rectangle Oriented East-and-West Spiritual Blueprint _364_

Rectangle Oriented North-and-South Spiritual Blueprint _365_

Welcome

In 1985 when I left New York to spend a year in India, I had no idea that I was about to embark on a life-transforming experience. India stirred me—deeply. I was moved by its wise culture and profound spirituality. By 1990, I shifted my home to New Delhi, where I wrote large portions of several editions of a popular American guidebook for travelers to India. For nearly ten years, I set off on long explorations through nearly the entire Indian subcontinent. I traveled to do my work—writing on behalf of future visitors who would use the guidebook. But this was a half-truth. I also traveled to satisfy my own insatiable curiosity.

Rituals define daily life in India—from the moment of awakening in the morning until the moment of retiring at night. The traditional Hindu greeting of *namaste,* which is said with two palms held together out of respect for the recipient, is a blessing that honors the divine that exists within each of us. The burning of incense, its aroma floating through a home or a shop, is a lingering residue of the early-morning *puja* (prayer service) that begins each day. People slip off their shoes before entering a home. Every home, however humble, is considered sacred and pure. It is the shelter that protects the soul.

This unique culture gave birth to many healthy disciplines that continue to draw followers from every new generation. It is the source of yoga, which includes meditation, *ayurveda* (the science of life and longevity), and *vastu,* the holistic science of design and architecture that helps us organize our personal environments so that they replicate the harmony of the universe and maximize our inner peace.

I had never heard of vastu until I moved to New Delhi. It was 1992 and I remember the day. I was visiting a friend in her house, which she had just rearranged and redecorated. But something else seemed different about the room in which we sat, something that extended beyond the change in furnishings and the shift in the function of the room. The room was incredibly soothing—and to more than my eyes.

My friend told me that her home had been redone according to vastu. This was the first time that I heard this Sanskrit word. As she spoke about this unfamiliar science that reinforced a spiritual way of thinking and living, I realized that the room in which we were enjoying our tea had a subtle power that affected my soul. My entire being responded positively to the surrounding environment.

Once I heard about vastu, I started seeing the word everywhere. Vastu was undergoing a resurgence in New Delhi. Again and again, I found myself in a home or office organized "as per vastu"—the phrase used by its advocates. Vastu's effect on people was impressive: everyone relaxed and settled comfortably into a chair, a sofa, or on a cushion on the floor. Even when I entered an empty room and waited to meet a stranger, the effect of vastu welcomed me. I connected to the space. It filled me with a quiet joy.

This ancient science, which predates and inspired the Chinese tradition of *feng shui,* led me to a new journey of discovery. I wanted to learn everything I could about vastu. I read translations of two of the greatest codifications of this science: the eight-volume *Manasara Series,* which dates back to the tenth century, and the two-volume set of *Mayamata,* which dates back to the eleventh century. I studied with scholars of the great Vedic civilization, which originally practiced vastu thousands of years ago.

I revisited my favorite historic Hindu temple in a state that neighbored the national capital of New Delhi. This time I analyzed the eleventh-century shrine from the point of view of vastu. I saw how vastu guidelines, which were incorporated into the design, created an intentional spiritual and psychological impact. The entire temple promoted a single goal: to serve as a potent reminder to worshipers of the journey that leads to spiritual discovery and speaks of the goal of immortality that comes with the soul's liberation and reunion with the divine. At the same time, I saw that vastu did not hamper artistic freedom. Every vastu temple has its distinct "look" that represents a specific era and the environment in which it was built. Anyone who has visited India knows that this is true—the country has an amazingly diverse architectural legacy.

I also found the perfect vastu mentor, Sudesh Prabhakar, an architect who lived in New Delhi. By coincidence or fate, Sudesh worked only a block away from my home in this huge city of at least 12 million people. For years, we shared a small neighborhood, but I had never seen him at any of the local shops or walking down any of the narrow streets and lanes. Vastu brought us together.

Sudesh was steeped in spirituality and found great joy in life and in his passion—architecture. He practiced yoga and meditated. This lovely, wise man was initially skeptical about his foreign neighbor who wanted to learn about vastu. But finally he said yes, and he guided me on my journey to discovery.

When I returned to America in late 1997, I wanted to spread the word of vastu to a culture where feng shui had taken hold, where yoga and meditation were hugely popular, where stress overload took its toll on everyone I knew or met—and had even begun to invade my own life. Working inside my own apartment, which was organized as per vastu, I wrote the first book to be published on vastu in the United States, *Vastu Living: Creating a Home for the Soul.** I began to give lectures, seminars, and workshops, where questions extended beyond the scheduled hour. Audiences wanted to know more.

I established a Web site, www.vastuliving.com, and began to receive hundreds of E-mails, with more questions and more requests for specific advice. My first book had whetted the appetite, but I realized that new advocates and would-be practitioners of vastu living wanted more practical information to successfully transform their own homes and workspaces into healthy oases that honored the soul.

I wrote *The Power of Vastu Living: Welcoming Your Soul Into Your Home and Workplace* to address this need.

The Power of Vastu Living is divided into three sections. "Welcome to Vastu Living" provides the information that gets you ready to begin your practice of vastu living in your home and workspace. You'll learn all about the power of space and the power of color—how and why they exert a powerful influence on our well-being. You'll dip into vastu's parent philosophy and learn the three all-important principles that form the backbone of this science.

The teachings in this book are based on my Western adaptation of vastu, which I call vastu living. Vastu, like any other science, is not static. To ensure the survival of its core philosophy, vastu guidelines were intended to reflect the passage of time and the changes that influence the way that we live. This new adaptation reminds us that while vastu has a spiritual base, this base should not be confused with religious dogma, which is unalterable and immutable. Vastu living can benefit everyone.

---

*Kathleen Cox, *Vastu Living: Creating a Home for the Soul* (New York: Marlowe & Company, 2000).

The remaining chapters in "Welcome to Vastu Living" show how to create your own set of spiritual blueprints, which will help you evaluate your home and workspace, resolve conflicts that may exist in your personal environments, and incorporate my addition to vastu called the zone of tranquility, which adds a measure of peace to each room or space. This first section concludes with general tips and advice that will enhance your actual practice of vastu living—which begins with section two, "The Welcoming Home."

"The Welcoming Home" and "The Welcoming Workplace" provide extensive practical advice for the creation of specific vastu living environments. The chapters cover a wide range of rooms and areas that may exist in a house or apartment or company or other work environments. Each chapter includes drawings and diagrams to help you visualize what to do in each space or how to rectify a problem that may get in the way of your practice of vastu living. I provide guidelines for fixing up different rooms in houses and apartments, as well as a company office, cubicle, pod, medical office, "Silicon" high-tech environment, even a boutique. I address structural problems that may exist in many of our homes and workspaces.

Throughout these two sections, I provide tips from other Vedic sciences—a soothing therapy, a pampering technique, or a natural remedy. Following these tips can give an additional boost to your well-being or the well-being of the people with whom you share the space. Consider them teasers that I hope will trigger an interest in other highly beneficial Vedic disciplines.

Before you begin your journey through vastu living, let me tell you a fundamental truth about vastu that highlights its accommodating nature. Vastu is not an all-or-nothing science. We should do our best to follow all its guidelines, but many of us will find that we just can't fix some structural problems or limitations connected to our home or workspace. But, other remedies can do the trick and restore the balance and harmony inside an enclosed space and within us. In addition, if you can make your personal environments so that they are 51 percent as per vastu, it will put you on the winning side of vastu living. You and any guests who come to your home and workspace will feel a positive difference. Vastu living spaces are comfortable and inviting. They treat each of us, even if we are just visitors, with love and kindness. Vastu living environments nurture that most valuable part of us that we can neither see nor describe—our essence, our spirit, our soul.

Welcome to Vastu Living

There is a soul at the centre of nature, and over the will of every man, so that none of us can wrong the universe. It has so infused its strong enchantment into nature, that we prosper when we accept its advice, and when we struggle to wound its creatures, our hands are glued to our sides, or they beat our own breasts. The whole course of things goes to teach us faith. We need only obey. There is a guidance for each of us, and by lowly listening we shall hear the right word.

—Ralph Waldo Emerson
"IV Spiritual Laws"
Emerson's Essays and Representative Men, p. 83
Collins Clear-Type Press

1

The Power of Space

We live in a stress-filled time where rapidly changing technology is rapidly changing our lives. We've lost valuable old anchors that were connected to a slower pace, which contributed to our balance and stability. Many of today's "creature comforts" rob us of a deeper comfort that once accompanied a more manageable lifestyle.

The computer is indispensable and invaluable, but it has created an impersonal world where we commune with a screen and not face-to-face with the people who are important to us. The cell phone allows us to stay in touch but not in that "touchy-feely" way of personal communication. It easily disrupts a private moment and destroys the mood.

Our work has become so portable that we often do some work from our home. But we still remain chained to our desk, even when the real desk is miles away. Too many of us are trying to do fifty things at once, but not even a juggler can successfully kept fifty balls moving in the air. Our new lifestyle is leaving us frazzled, overwhelmed, and battling with stress.

The human body is programmed to handle a certain amount of tension and anxiety. When a situation or circumstance threatens us, our "flight or fight" mechanism goes into effect. Our brain releases neurotransmitters or "chemical messengers" that send a warning to our adrenal glands. The adrenal glands respond by releasing a combination of hormones that prepare our body to meet the danger. We become alert and sharply focused so that we can think clearly. During this heightened state of awareness, we actually perform better and are better prepared to get through the crisis.

But too many of us now live in a state of *chronic* stress where these lifesaving mechanisms attached to the flight-or-fight syndrome never shut down. This condition is threatening our health. We suffer from headaches, backaches, insomnia, indigestion, and chronic frustration. We feel overwhelmed, irritable, and moody. Our blood pressure has shot up and our immune systems struggle to keep us free of serious illnesses.

If you are saying, "Oh, but this isn't me," consider these statistics from recent studies. Stress causes the health problems of 43 percent of all American adults, and at least 75 percent of all our primary-care physician visits are due to stress. The number of workers in the United States who feel highly stressed on the job has more than doubled from 1985 to 1995, and nearly half of all working Americans are suffering from "burnout." *Burnout* is another word for stress.

Chronic stress makes us candidates for strokes, heart attacks, diabetes, sexual dysfunction (including infertility and miscarriage), anxiety disorders, and depression. Chronic stress is linked to at least three of the top ten causes of death: heart disease, cerebrovascular disease (strokes), and suicide. So if you accept the commonly held belief that stress is an unavoidable part of life, you are dancing with danger. If you suffer from chronic stress, your survival may depend on reducing your tension to a manageable level—no matter how complicated your life.

The majority of us attribute our stress to the conflicting demands that push and pull at us from every conceivable direction. We struggle to meet the demands of our job and the demands of our family and our home—and we usually sacrifice our own needs in the process. But there's another frequently overlooked factor that can contribute to our stress. How many of you understand that your home and workplace can be sources of discomfort, rather than comfort—that your home and workplace can feed your frayed nerves rather than nurture your soul?

If you walk into your home and there's no place where you can sit in serenity, if you walk into your home and find it impossible to unwind, if you walk into your home and it doesn't feel the slightest bit welcoming, then your home is contributing to your stress. If you go to work and feel unconnected to your workspace, if you feel tired or tense as soon as you sit down at your desk, if you gulp down cup after cup of coffee in order to stimulate your brain, then your work environment is a source of your stress.

But here's the good news. You can eliminate the stress that is attached to your personal environments. You can practice vastu living, which is the contemporary version of the world's oldest holistic design and architectural system, called *vastu*. This ancient science, which is connected to yoga and ayurveda, originated thousands of years ago in the land that we now call India. Through the practice of vastu living, you can design healthy spaces for living and working. Your home and workspace become a source of harmony, not disharmony. Through vastu living, you can reduce your stress. But before you learn about this powerful science, let's first learn about the power of space.

Imagine that it is a lovely day in late September. Imagine that you are taking a walk in the woods. The air is crisp. You breathe deep and fill up your lungs. You soak in the delightful aromas attached to the forest during this appealing time of year. A gentle breeze rustles the branches overhead and sends flickering shadows and bursts of sunlight that highlight the luscious colors of autumn. Delightful sounds remind you of nature's diversity—the chattering and fluttering of birds, the whir of insects, the crunch of pinecones, twigs, and withered leaves under your feet.

When we connect with nature, we grow silent and discover a deep inner calm that leads to a rare point of stillness. We turn inward and hear our inner voice, and we let its gentle words wash over us. We feel good to be alive. This communion between nature and our intimate self reminds us that we are not alone on this earth. We are connected to everything that surrounds us.

Now imagine that you are sitting in a typical doctor's waiting room. The room has far too much vinyl, molded plastic, and other synthetics. The only plants are fake. Chairs are positioned close together, and side tables are piled high with magazines and medical pamphlets. You pick up a magazine, flip through its pages, but fail to read an article or even study a picture. You may be sitting a few inches away from another person, but you don't initiate a conversation. Instead you shrink within yourself while you sit in this comfortless environment. And shrinking within your self is very different from consciously turning inward.

Some of you may think that this comparison is flawed. Your feelings inside the doctor's office have nothing to do with the environment. Before you entered the room, you were tense from worrying about the doctor's impending assessment of your health or the health of a loved one. Okay, maybe you did arrive feeling tense, but this feeling only reinforces the need for a nurturing environment in this particular space. A doctor's waiting room should be a calming oasis. The room is normally filled with people who are not feeling well and may be struggling with anxiety.

It is also conceivable that when we set off for a walk in the woods, we may be agonizing over a problem or grieving over a significant disappointment or loss. A stressful problem may even have willed us to go for a walk in this environment. Instinctively, we understand that nature is therapeutic—a source of solace that can heal us and improve our emotional well-being.

But let's resume this walk in the woods. Pretend that as you move through this world of nature, you come across a log cabin in a grove of pines. Its presence surprises you, but it does not offend you. The rough timber exterior is in harmony with its surroundings. But now imagine that you approach a small lake where a huge, modern house sprawls along the bank. The house is out of proportion with its landscape. A satellite dish sits on the roof, and power and telephone lines connect the house to another world and another pace. The building commands your attention, pulls you away from nature, and disrupts your mood.

Every day you are reacting to your surrounding environment. Think of how you feel when you are stuck inside a filthy subway car or stuck inside a crowded elevator or sitting in a movie theater with your knees jammed against the back of the seat in front of you. Even a hotel lobby, however grand, can be a source of discomfort. The décor can be so impersonal that you are unable to connect to the space. The lobby just isn't welcoming.

These examples reinforce the need to pay attention to the personal surroundings that *are* under your control. You owe it to yourself to turn your home and workspace into friendly retreats that are calming and life-affirming. The ancient science of vastu helps you achieve this goal.

THE POWER OF VASTU

Vastu, the science of architecture and design, is a Sanskrit word that means "dwelling" or "site." While the practice of vastu living is applied to buildings and interior designs, the word *vastu* also applies to the human body. Vedic scholars recognized that the human body is an example of vastu. And if you think about your body, it is a human-made dwelling and it does provide shelter. The body surrounds and protects that most important part of you—your essence, your spirit, your soul. Just as the home and workspace protect the physical body, the physical body protects the soul. This correlation helps us understand vastu—its philosophy and principles, and how they introduce harmony and balance into our personal environments.

Vastu and Its Sister Sciences

Vastu is related to yoga, which includes meditation, ayurveda, and all the other important Vedic sciences from the *raga* (Indian classical music) and Indian classical dance to *jyotish* (Indian astrology). Vastu, yoga, and ayurveda share the same spiritual philosophy and goal: to increase our well-being and inner balance so that we can free our mind of distracting thoughts and turn inward to connect with our soul.

While yoga and ayurveda focus on the body and the inner self, vastu focuses on the personal environments in which we spend most of our time. Vastu is the critical outer envelope. Our home and workspace need to be in harmony for us to experience internal harmony. If our home and workspace contribute to our stress, this undermines the benefits of yoga, meditation, and ayurveda. Ideally, we should practice yoga and meditate in a space organized as per vastu. It helps us stay centered and focused.

The Vedic Civilization

Vastu, which is the inspiration behind the Chinese tradition of feng shui, originated in the Indian subcontinent during the flourishing Vedic civilization, which many scholars and archaeologists now date back as early as 6000 B.C. The word *Vedic* comes from *veda,* a Sanskrit word that means "knowledge." Knowledge flows through the *Vedas,* which are the four Hindu holy texts. These extraordinary texts, which provide a philosophical and spiritual analysis of the creation of the cosmos and the creation of all existence, define the Hindu way of life and the rituals that accompany the Hindu religion.

The same issues that absorb many of today's scientists and philosophers—the formation and nature of the universe and all its phenomena, including humankind—intrigued Vedic scholars. They carefully observed the planets and conducted sophisticated studies to determine their influence on earth and its environment. Many of their discoveries in astronomy and the related fields of physics and mathematics predate those of their Western counterparts. Vedic scholars determined that the earth is not the center of the universe, but that the earth rotates around the sun. They realized that the earth is tilted in its rotation. They perceived that all phenomena are animated and contain energy, which emits vibrations.

The Vedic Philosophy

Vedic scholars incorporated these discoveries and theories into an extraordinary philosophy that wove together a potent blend of spirituality and science. The inherent order and harmony that they witnessed in their observations led them to conclude that a Supreme Creative Force, which was omnipresent, omnificent, and omnipotent, was behind the creation of the universe and all existence. This spiritual philosophy is at the heart of vastu.

THE THEORY OF ORDER AND HARMONY

Vedic philosophers recognized that all phenomena, from the tallest mountain to the smallest organism, achieve balance and harmony by following the natural rhythms that govern the universe. They saw rhythm in the rotation of the moon around the earth and in the rotation of the earth around the sun. They realized that these orbits lead to the orderly expression of time and the orderly passage of the seasons. They observed the rhythmic patterns that exist in the climate and the weather.

These ancient scholars understood that every object observes its own cycle of creation, preservation, and destruction. A baby is born, lives its life, and finally perishes to be replaced by new life. They understood why destruction is a positive part of this cycle. The natural decay that comes with destruction is reabsorbed into the surrounding matter and makes room for rebirth. Consider the decomposition of leaves and other detritus on the forest's floor. All this disintegration becomes compost and a nourishing environment that creates and supports new growth.

The Vedic scholars realized that all created forms observe a law of nature in which an intrinsic order ensures harmony and balance. This means that nothing is random in creation. Everything in the natural world serves a purpose and a function. The intended design of each created form also follows this rule. Every color, texture, shape, and size adheres to a predetermined order.

The consequences attached to the law of nature amplify its meaning and significance. If we disturb the order that is at the heart of this law, we create disharmony and imbalance. We can see this principle in action when oil spills into the ocean. The heavy chemical sludge damages the ecosystem—destroying animal and plant life. We can also observe this when we review the effects of global warming. When ozone-depleting gases, such as chlorofluorocarbons, damage the ozone layer that shields us from the full force of solar ultraviolet radiation, this destruction threatens our own body's protective shield. Melanoma, the most serious type of skin cancer, is increasing faster than any other form of cancer. Climatic patterns are also in disarray. Rising sea levels threaten vulnerable coastal areas. Low-lying islands, such as the Maldives, may disappear under the ocean.

Every aspect of the Vedic philosophy honors some part of the law of nature. Consider, for example, the concept of *karma* or the law of cause and effect. This is nothing more than the law of nature transferred into the metaphysical realm and attached to moral order. Simply stated, the law of karma says that we get back what we put out—if not today, then tomorrow. According to the law of karma, we are doomed to an endless cycle of rebirth on earth until our daily life is a model of unequivocal selflessness (as opposed to ego-oriented selfishness), at which point we achieve liberation or *moksha* and our soul is reunited with the Supreme Creative Force.

This same law is the underlying rule in every Vedic discipline from vastu to ayurveda. Vedic scholars realized that every man-made creation needs to observe this governing principle to ensure harmony with its own surroundings and with the individuals who occupy the created space. If a man-made creation disturbs or disrupts the natural order, harmony gives way to disharmony, which creates discord, friction, and imbalance. The well-being of everyone inside this environment suffers as a result. This law is also central to ayurveda, as you will see in chapter 2, "Personalizing Vastu Living."

THE POWER OF VIBRATIONS

Vedic scholars understood that energy exists inside every created form in the universe and that energy is the force behind animation. They realized that this energy pulsates and vibrates at a specific frequency or wavelength and that each example of matter has its own set of vibrations. The vibrations of objects interact with one another and always observe the law of nature. When the vibrations of each object maintain their original intensity, they create a positive interaction and there is harmony among the objects. When the interactions disturb the original intensity of the vibrations, there is disharmony.

Under normal circumstances, internal vibrations are usually inaudible unless they are extremely loud or piercing; they are also difficult to see. But we can feel the vibrations of a kitten when it purrs on our lap, and we can feel this purring stop with the sudden presence of a dog or when our own unexpected movement disturbs the kitten. We can also see and hear the vibrations of a stringed instrument. As the bow moves back and forth across a violin, it creates vibrations that cause the strings to quiver and create their specific sounds.

On occasion we can also witness the dramatic impact of negative vibrations. We know what happens when one of the tectonic plates, which make up the earth's crust, pushes too hard against an adjacent tectonic plate. All this "pushing" triggers an earthquake. Shock waves and intense vibrations cause the land to rip apart and buildings to topple.

Vedic scholars realized that this immutable law of nature extends to the interaction of a building's energy with both its surrounding environment and its occupants. A new building can block the flow of positive energies that originally moved through the surrounding environment. The design of the interior of a building can disturb the flow of positive energies that are connected to every occupant and compromise their well-being. Negative interaction leads to disharmony and imbalance and heightens feelings that are associated with disorder—an absence of calm, an increase in stress and depression.

These sophisticated observations led to the creation of the science of vastu and its set of guidelines that determine the healthy alignment and organization of a space. Vastu helps us observe the law of nature so we ensure order, not disorder, inside our home and workspace. We create havens that nurture our soul.

☀ THE DIVINITY IN ALL CREATION

The law of nature, which asserts that nothing is random in creation, reminds us that everything in the universe is interdependent, interconnected, and contributes to the whole. This is an expression of holism, but in Vedic philosophy, holism is imbued with spirituality. The ancient Vedic scholars believed that the essence or spirit, which animates every object, is connected to the Supreme Being, the Supreme Creative Force, or whatever word is used to define the mysterious cause of creation.

In the Vedic view of the world, this essence or spirit is divine; and the surrounding matter that contains this essence is worthy of our love and respect—every rock, every drop of water, every pulsating object, which, of course, includes every single one of us. This belief that the soul is part of the Supreme Creative Force is expressed in the Vedic phrase *Tat Tvam Asi*, or Thou Art That.

This phrase, Thou Art That, is the most important message of the Vedas.

By following the principles in vastu living, we create environments that are harmonious and calming. In these environments, we try to shut out the noise of the world around us and the clutter of thoughts in our mind so that we can turn inward; and in our search for inner calm, we observe silence and commune with that part of us that is connected to the divine—our soul. We discover how to celebrate our connection to the divine force that created the universe.

THE THREE PRINCIPLES OF VASTU

To put the Vedic philosophy of the karmic law of nature into practice, vastu asks us to do our best to adhere to three critical principles. We must honor the five basic elements, respect nature and all forms of existence, and finally, celebrate our self and our special identity. We must never forget that all creation is divine.

Honoring the Five Basic Elements

The Foundation of All Creation

Vedic scholars determined that everything in the universe is composed of the five basic elements of space (also called ether), air, fire, water, and earth.* They also determined that every object at the point of its creation is endowed with a unique configuration of these five elements, which governs its nature or constitution. In the human body, the configuration of the five elements decides our physical type, mental type, and emotional type. It governs how we look, think, behave, and respond to the world.

---

*Modern science accepts that all phenomena contain these five basic elements. But for Vedic scholars these elements were irreducible, whereas modern scientists have discovered a list of over one hundred elements, which is still not considered definitive.

So where are the five elements inside the human body? From the moment of conception, your body requires the element of space so that your physical structure can grow. The element of air pumps your blood through your system and keeps you alive. Digestive fire burns up the calories that provide you with energy. Two-thirds of your body is made of water. And the element of earth exists in your bones and in the minerals, such as the potassium and the zinc, that keep you healthy. By not disturbing the original configuration of these five basic elements in your body—the configuration that was established at the creation of your particular embryo—you maintain the internal harmony that ensures your well-being. This principle holds true for every object, including every architectural form, such as the home and the workspace.

The Five Basic Elements

In the practice of vastu living, each element has a predetermined location on the property that surrounds a building, then again inside the entire building, and finally in each room within the building. The location assigned to each of the five basic elements is not arbitrary. Sometimes the placement is determined by its relationship to the universe. Sometimes its location reinforces similarities between vastu and the human body. The body, as I stated earlier, is an example of perfect vastu.

Whether you live in a Victorian house or the smallest studio apartment, whether you work in a sprawling company or a tiny boutique, you must try your best to honor the proper placement of these five basic elements to create healthy vibrations within your home and workspace. These vibrations will interact positively with the vibrations in the surrounding environment and allow them to flow freely through the enclosed space. The proper alignment of the elements will also lead to a positive interaction with your own body's vibrations. The building's vibrations help you maintain an inner harmony that will enrich you and lead you to personal fulfillment.

The Location of the Elements

Space

The center of every vastu space, which can refer to the center of the property as a whole, the home, or the workspace, or each individual home, is dedicated to the element of space or ether. Lord Brahma, the Hindu god of creation, governs this area, which is called the *Brahmasthana,* or the place of God. Spiritual energies collect here and disperse in the form of positive vibrations that shower everyone in the enclosed space with good feelings (see Figures 1 and 2).

Space or ether is essential in creation; and in vastu, this center area is compared to the womb, which houses the embryo, and the navel, which is considered the center of your body. The womb and navel are fragile, so the center of a vastu space should be protected and not bear any weight. It should be left uncovered so that its beneficial vibrations are unobstructed and can move freely in every direction.

Air

The northwest quadrant of the property, the entire home, or the workspace, and of each individual room, belongs to the element of air. The northwest is the direction identified with the strong wind known as the northwester. In the Southern Hemisphere, the element of air and its deity are in the southwest quadrant (see Figures 1 and 2).*

Air represents *prana* or the life force. The human equivalent is your breath, which draws in the oxygen that gives you life. This quadrant belongs to Vayu, the Vedic god of winds, who provided the breath of life to the universe. Air represents movement, and Lord Vayu is said to be restless and prone to impulsive actions. These characteristics, along with fickleness, vacillation,

---

*The location of the elements in vastu living must be adjusted to accommodate the climatic changes in the Southern Hemisphere, where the sun rises in the east and sets in the west, but moves across the northern sky. These adjustments will be noted throughout the text.

and indecisiveness, represent the psychological properties attached to the northwest quadrant.

In vastu, when the northwest quadrant is used properly, the element of air motivates quick thoughts and bursts of creativity and action that can inspire a healthy change. Air's quality of restlessness can also be put to good use. If your kids watch too much television, you can use this quadrant to your advantage. By placing the television set in the northwest, the element of air prevails, and your kids grow restless and leave this quadrant, and the television set with it.

Fire

The element of fire resides in the southeast quadrant along with Lord Agni, the Vedic god of fire. The southeast is a logical location when you think about the movement of the sun. This fiery star is at its hottest point around noon when it reaches this midpoint direction. In the Southern Hemisphere the element of fire and its deity reside in the northeast quadrant.

Agni is the light of knowledge, the guardian of immortality, and represents the awakening of the soul. All these symbols are conveyed in the Hindu ritual of cremation. The fire that consumes the body liberates the soul. It enables the enlightened soul to escape the endless cycles of life and rebirth, putting an end to its earthly bondage.

The psychological characteristics of fire are warmth, passion, and emotional intensity. These delicate characteristics call for moderation and balance. It is unwise to have either an excess or an absence of fire in the southeast. Either extreme causes discomfort.

Your barbecue grill, outdoor generator, or any equipment associated with fire or electricity, gas, or oil that is kept outside belongs in the southeast quadrant of your property. Inside your home, the kitchen is normally located in the southeast quadrant. Within an individual room at home or work, electrical equipment, such as an entertainment system or air conditioner, belongs in the southeast.

Water

The northeast belongs to the element of water, which is calming, soothing, and reflective. The Vedic deity Isa governs this direction. Over a long period of time, the Vedic Lord Isa became the Hindu Lord Shiva, the god of destruction. In the Southern Hemisphere, the element of water and Isa are in the southeast quadrant.

When the earth revolves around the sun, its axis is tilted about 23½ degrees to the plane of the orbit, which causes the change of the seasons on our planet. Vedic scholars determined that cosmic energy flows into the atmosphere from the northeast because of this tilt. They also believed that positive power from the gods flows in from this same midpoint direction, so they called the northeast quadrant the gateway to the gods.

The northeastern part of your property should be left open and unblocked. And consider yourself fortunate if this quadrant is also the lowest part of your property or has a swimming pool or a pond. The water or the depression collects the cosmic energy, which is so healthy for you. Inside your home or office, your tall and heavy furniture should not be placed in the northeast where they can block out the spiritual power and cosmic energy.

This quadrant is ideal for a room that is used for contemplative activities, such as meditating, studying, writing, or painting. The northeast is also the recommended location for the zone of tranquility (see chapter 6, "The Peaceful Zone of Tranquility"). This zone, which celebrates nature and people or objects that are dear to you, is so calming and therapeutic that it belongs in every home and workspace.

Earth

The element of earth and its deity, Lord Pitri, are in the southwest quadrant. When the sun moves into the southwest, its intense heat can sap us of all our energy. The heavy properties connected to the element of earth serve as a healthy and protective barrier. In the Southern Hemisphere, the element of earth and Lord Pitri are in the northwest quadrant.

The physical characteristics of earth are strength and heaviness. And the symbolism associated with Lord Pitri, who is the Vedic god of ancestors, reinforces these characteristics. Lord Pitri reminds us that death is a natural part of the cycle of life. The remains of all organisms decompose and return to the earth to nurture and grow new life. Pitri also represents the strength that we acquire from the wisdom and knowledge left behind by the departed—a gift that we pass on to those who follow us.

The southwest should mirror the properties of the earth. It should be heavy and strong, so that it shields us from the sun's lingering heat and traps the cosmic energy and spiritual power that flows here from the northeast quadrant. The southwest is perfect for a rock garden; and if this quadrant has a natural elevation or a thick growth of trees, consider yourself lucky.

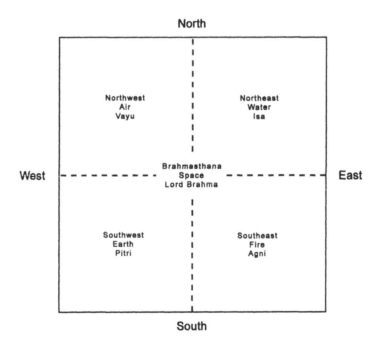

Figure 1: Location of the Five Basic Elements in the Northern Hemisphere

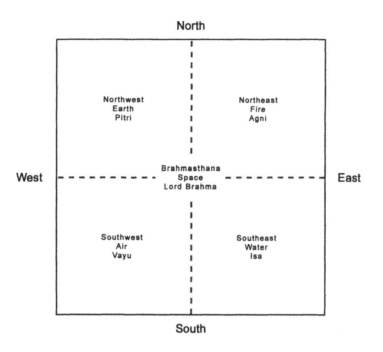

North

West

East

Northwest
Earth
Pitri

Northeast
Fire
Agni

Brahmasthana
Space
Lord Brahma

Southwest
Air
Vayu

Southeast
Water
Isa

South

Figure 2: Vastu Living Adjustments for the Southern Hemisphere

The southwest is empowering. Since you draw in the wisdom of our ancestors and the strength of the earth in this quadrant, this midpoint direction is good for the master bedroom or your workspace. The heaviest and tallest pieces of furniture also belong in the southwest area of each room so that they hold in the beneficial energy that comes from the northeast.

Do You Live in the Southern Hemisphere?

The text in this book is written for the Northern Hemisphere. Readers who live in the Southern Hemisphere should follow the spiritual blueprint above, which shows the effect of the earth's rotation below the equator on the practice of vastu living. Please note that four of the five basic elements, along with their properties, are in different locations in the Southern Hemisphere and that the guidelines governing the placement of lightweight and heavy furnishings, as well as other decorative suggestions regarding the elements, swap places. The properties associated with the cardinal directions (north-south-east-west) remain the same in the Southern Hemisphere. For additional adjustments, please refer to chapter 7, "The Southern Hemisphere."

The Role of Dualities

Light and dark, sunrise and sunset, hot and cold, wet and dry, good and bad, right and wrong, joy and sorrow, health and sickness, silence and noise, truth and deception: these are just a small example of the dualities that exist in the physical world and in the world of moral behavior. In the physical world, the presence of dualities creates the rhythms that govern the universe. The dualities that express the extremes in moral behavior help us understand the consequences of our actions and remind us to live in a state of moderation and balance. The dualities connected to the four cardinal directions of east, west, north, and south play an important role in vastu (see Figure 3).

East

The sun with its deity, Surya, reigns in the east. Lord Surya is often depicted as a charioteer with a chariot pulled by seven steeds. Each of these majestic horses represents one of the seven rays of the sun, which are displayed in all their glory each time it rises and sets. The sun dispels the dark of night, and its solar energy animates and sustains life. The sun and Surya represent the triumph of light over darkness and the power of enlightenment over ignorance, which enable us to distinguish good from evil and right from wrong.

West

Lord Varuna reigns in the west. He is the lord of the oceans, the lord of the night, who causes the moon and stars to shine, and the lord of rain. In other words, Lord Varuna governs in the absence of the sun. He represents the peace and quiet of darkness, which leads to the renewal that comes with the dawn. Varuna reminds us that action must be balanced by inaction and that the dark of night balances the light of day. Their coexistence creates rhythm and order. On a symbolic level, this deity fights against ignorance, which keeps us from seeing the light of truth. Ignorance is represented by the darkness of night, and Varuna's weapons are the celestial stars, which are under his control. Their light guides us along the path to enlightenment, personified by the sun that reappears at dawn.

North

The north belongs to Soma, the lord of the moon and the lord of health. A Hindu myth ties these two titles together. According to the story, Lord Soma was born from soma, the celestial plant that bestows immortality. An eagle supposedly took this plant from the heavens to grow in the mountains of the earth. So Soma represents the healing properties of herbs, many of which also thrive in the mountains and in the northern light.

Hindu legends also claim that the juice of soma is stored inside the moon, where deities imbibe it so that they can maintain immortality. As the deities drink up the soma, the moon grows smaller and smaller until the sun slowly replenishes the liquid and re-creates the full moon. Lord Soma protects us from the dangers that come with the darkness of night and the darkness of ignorance that interfere with our well-being, both spiritual and physical. Soma reminds us to take care of our body and to steer away from sin.

Lord Kuber, the lord of wealth and indulgence, also reigns in the north. He is usually depicted as a misshaped deity overburdened with too many jewels and ornaments. Just as Soma reminds us of the importance of good health, Kuber reminds us that if we overindulge and pay too much attention to material wealth instead of spiritual wealth, we become distracted from our responsibilities and

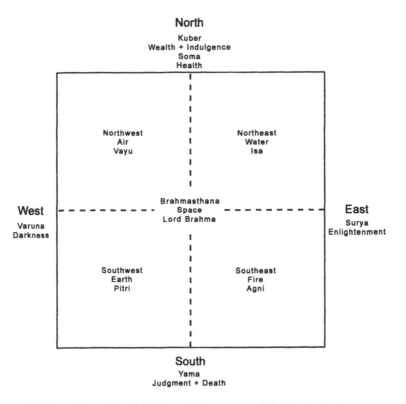

‑╬‑ Figure 3: Location of the Five Basic Elements and Cardinal Directions

duties. The consequences of our behavior are revealed through Lord Yama, who reigns in the south, directly opposite Lord Soma and Lord Kuber.

South

Lord Yama, who is the lord of judgment and death, reminds us to live responsibly. His presence encourages us to keep our eyes on righteous goals and our feet on the path that leads to enlightenment. Many fear this deity because of his power to determine the fate of the soul at the time of death. But Lord Yama is also the guide who takes the worthy soul into a higher and higher world until it escapes the endless cycle of life and rebirth and enters the world of immortality, which is free of all pain, all suffering, and all sorrow.

Respecting Nature and All Phenomena

Vastu asks us to show our respect for nature by bringing it into our home and workspace. The presence of nature comforts us and helps us relax. We are also connected to nature, and our respect for nature becomes an expression of respect for the self.

When you bring plants into your home and pay attention to their needs, they reveal their well-being in their beauty. Caring for them is also therapeutic and rewarding. Plants prove their value to us—day in and day out. They detoxify the air and remove impurities from our environment.

The presence of plants in your home and your workspace also reminds you of the world's great diversity. The leaves and flowers reveal a vast range of colors and shapes. Their individual needs also represent diversity: succulents thrive in sandy soil under a bright sun; peace lilies crave moist soil.

The different plants you grow and tend can also represent for you the rhythms of the seasons that govern the universe. These rhythms bring us feelings of comfort—the comfort that comes with predictability. In March, the bright green foliage in our home or something so sweet as the nubby growth on pussy willows brings to mind the renewal that accompanies the spring. The lush colors that are associated with summer speak of the harvest and nature's bounty. The bright, earthy colors of the autumn suggest the final burst of nature before its decay. Winter whites and evergreens suggest the everlasting quality of the cycle of life—the flow of year after year.

Many of us have environments that aren't healthy for plants. Some of us work in a cubicle that lacks natural lighting. Some of us travel too often and are unable to give plants the care that they require. But vastu's request to bring nature into the home and workspace is much more inclusive. You can introduce the presence of nature in a décor that uses natural fabrics—cotton, silk, wool, linen—and other natural materials—stone, wood, clay, woven grasses, and glass, which is made from sand. Organic products have the same positive effect on us as plants or a bouquet of flowers. They remind us of the powerful connection between all forms of existence.

Nature can also become the catalyst for creativity and inspiration. It brings a measure of tranquility that settles down the confusion of thoughts that rattle around our mind. Communing with nature can lead us to discover the elusive answer to a frustrating problem or see our way through a troubling dilemma. Nature can even help us empty our mind of all thought so that we can reach a point of stillness that lets us turn inward and connect with our soul. Our lives have become so busy that it is too easy for most of us to neglect this quiet and unseen aspect of our self. And when we forget to nurture our soul, it cannot nurture us. The absence of this interaction eliminates a powerful antidote to the stress that creeps into our life and becomes the source of much of our friction, unhappiness, and illness.

When we surround ourselves with nature and let it take us deep within ourselves, we experience inner calm. We can achieve an absolute stillness that leads to spiritual discovery and growth, and we can learn the truth in the Vedic message Thou Art That. We see that the essence of our being is part of that mysterious Supreme Creative Force. We see that the essence of every one of us is divine and that the Supreme Creative Force resides, as it always has, within us.

The realization of this truth is nature's greatest gift to you. It can transform your life. You become grounded, centered, and focused on what really matters. You see that the meaning of life is not about the acquisition of material goods and moving up the economic ladder. Life is about love, compassion, and forgiveness. You turn off that part of you that thrives on anger and frustration. You let go of the worries that turn into stress. You see that life's greatest rewards come from climbing up the spiritual ladder. Spiritual health brings emotional and mental health and—we all know the phrase—mind over matter. When your mind learns to truly love the self and not the ego, you try your best to keep the body, your temple, in the best of health to protect the divine presence that lives within you.

Celebrate Your Unique Identity

Let us think for a moment about our understanding of holism—how we respond to this word and how most of us practice holism in the West. The majority of us understand that everything in nature is interconnected and interdependent. We work to protect the environment and to save endangered species. But our notion of nature, when we think about holism, is oddly restricted to flora or plant life and fauna or animal life. Too many of us fail to extend the definition of holism so that it includes humanity.

How we ever came to accept this restricted view of holism in the West is difficult to understand. But maybe our machine-dependent culture has stunted our perception of our own value and we have lost sight of humanity's importance in the grand cosmic scheme. This is another reason why vastu has so much value today. This ancient science, which originated in a culture that is so different from our Western culture, reinforces the interdependence and interconnection that binds together all living matter. Holism is inclusive, not exclusive. A vastu living environment celebrates the individuals who use the space. It honors the people who live or work there.

A personalized environment has an astonishing impact on everyone who enters the space, even strangers who come to visit. When you walk into a room where the décor connects to the people who live in the home, you feel comfortable and at ease. The room speaks of love and respect for the divinity that resides inside each of us. Even if you don't connect to the individual objects that are on display, you feel the healthy connection that exists between the space and its occupants.

Harmony flows through the environment and has a positive effect on you. Conversely, environments devoid of personal objects are sterile. Think again of the doctor's waiting room that is filled with synthetics and devoid of character. Your body remains stiff and fails to relax. The absence of any personal connection between the space and the doctor becomes a source of discomfort.

Executive offices frequently fail to honor this third principle of personalization, and this oversight is often reflected in the demeanor of the person who works in the room. The room's sterility prevents everyone who enters from relaxing and feeling at ease. Conversations in executive offices are often stiff and stilted. The negative vibrations that flow through the sterile space interfere with productivity and prevent the creation of positive relationships with other employees and with customers. In your home, if your environment fails to celebrate your special identity, it will be impossible to relax. If you can't relax inside your own home, then you can't increase your well-being and realize inner calm. You fail to honor and love your soul.

2

Personalizing Vastu Living

❋

The celebration of your identity in vastu living goes much deeper than the incorporation of your personality and interests into your décor. The ancient Vedic scholars understood that no two people are alike. Each one of us is endowed with a combination of traits that sets us apart, and all these distinguishing differences create the diversity that brings wonder to our world.

But these differences also lead to different needs and preferences, and this holds true for your practice of vastu living. Before you plan any changes in your home or workspace, you first need to know what works for you, as a unique individual, and what doesn't. In Vedic terminology, you need to know your particular nature or constitution so that you can maximize the benefits of vastu and discover inner peace.

In India, vastu consultants use a Vedic form of astrology called *jyotish* to personalize the practice of vastu in the home and workspace. But the science of jyotish, which is connected to astronomy and mathematics, is extremely complicated and follows a system that is quite different from Western astrology. Jyotish also requires the precise time and place of birth to create a chart; and unfortunately, many of us don't know our exact birth time. This information isn't even available on many birth certificates. So vastu living uses an alternative Vedic science, ayurveda, to determine our particular nature or constitution.

❉ Ayurveda

Ayurveda is conceivably the world's oldest holistic health system. It was also the first health system to emphasize disease prevention and wellness. As with its sister science of vastu, ayurveda extends the meaning of wellness to include your physical, mental, emotional, and spiritual health. Ayurveda, which is also based on the law of nature, asserts that the harmony and balance that govern the universe also govern your personal well-being. In other words, health is a reflection of balance and order; disease is a reflection of imbalance and disorder.

The Five Basic Elements

As I mentioned in chapter 1, Vedic scholars realized that each one of us is born with our own configuration of the five basic elements and that our configuration of these elements is determined by a combination of factors that unfold at the moment of conception, such as the quality and individual properties attached to the sperm and the egg and even the condition of the uterus. In addition, Vedic scholars understood that usually one or two of three particular elements—air, fire, or water—is dominant inside our body and defines our nature, or, as it is called in the ancient Indian science of ayurveda, our *dosha* or constitution. It is the rare person who is born with all five elements in equal balance.

Staying Healthy

Ayurveda connects illness and disorders to the imbalance of the body's original configuration of the five basic elements. When the body's natural configuration of elements slips out of alignment, your immune system is compromised. You become vulnerable to disease. So to stay healthy, you need to pay attention to the characteristics that define your particular dosha or doshas. Once you have this knowledge, you can protect your health.

The Tridoshas

The three doshas, which are called the tridoshas, are *vata, pitta,* and *kapha.* Each one of these doshas represents one of the three forces of energy, described below, that govern all your body's physical and psychological functions. Once again, it is important to understand that your dosha or combination of doshas defines your nature and determines who you are physically, mentally, and emotionally. Your dosha determines how you relate to the world.

Pitta or Fire

The element of pitta or fire governs every aspect of your metabolism from digestion to absorption and assimilation. Pitta shares the properties of fire and the sun: hot, candescent, intense. The sun provides the earth with its heat and energy, and pitta performs the same function in your body. Pitta burns your food and creates the calories that give you energy. The sun regulates the earth's temperature; pitta regulates the body's temperature.

Individuals with a pitta dosha are generally intelligent and exhibit excellent judgment. These qualities reflect the symbols of enlightenment and clarity that are attached to the sun, which lights up our world after a night of darkness.

Excess pitta turns up your body's heat and creates fevers. Just as too much sun can burn your skin, too much pitta can cause prickly heat, acne, boils, and other skin disorders. Excess pitta also heats up the digestive process and produces acidity. This acidity irritates your intestines and can cause diarrhea, which is often hot and burning as it leaves the body. An aggravated pitta also exhibits emotional changes that we associate with fire and the sun. A fiery temperament replaces the pitta's generally warm personality. The natural pitta leader becomes a tyrant.

Vata or Air

The element of vata or air animates you. It is responsible for all the movement that occurs in your body. Vata controls your breathing, blinking, circulation, muscular and tissue movements, nerve impulses, the movement of food through your body, secretions, such as perspiration, and the excretion of waste products. Vata controls the flow of thoughts to your mind and ultimately governs the movements that convert your thoughts into action.

Just as pitta shares the properties of fire, vata shares the properties of air or the wind. The wind is subtle and always in movement. The typical behavior of individuals with a vata dosha mirrors this trait. They prefer activity to inactivity—mentally and physically. They grasp new ideas quickly and have flashes of insight that make them creative. If they are sitting, they tend to fidget. At night, they are restless sleepers who toss and turn. In general, the wind, unless it is a hot, tropical breeze, puts a chill in the air that often makes us feel cold. Vata exhibits this same property. Vata people often feel cold, especially in their hands and feet.

Just as a cold winter wind can dry your skin and crack your lips, too much vata inside your body can cause dryness—dry skin, lips, eyes, dryness in any part of your body. The wind can also unexpectedly change direction—a characteristic that shows up in vata behavior, especially when vata is overstimulated. Excess vata can lead to indecision, vacillation, and fickleness.

Vata physical disorders also relate to movement and carry the characteristics associated with air—cracking joints, dry skin, brittle nails and hair, constipation, gas, "nervous" stomach, insomnia and exhaustion, and any illnesses associated with the nervous system, such as tremors, panic attacks, and some forms of depression.

Kapha or Water

The element of kapha or water is your body's lubricant. It is wet, oily, and unctuous. Kapha creates heaviness and density, and a clammy kind of coldness that we associate with cold-weather rain. Kapha protects your joints from the friction and dryness that accompanies the movements initiated by the vata dosha. Kapha provides the mucus in your membranes and keeps moisture in your skin. People who are kapha tend to have oily smooth skin that is slightly cool to the touch.

Kapha, which is also the cohesive agent in your body that binds all your cells together, is responsible for your tissues and provides your body with its strength, sturdiness, and structure. When you injure your body, kapha is the healing force. When illness threatens you, kapha reinforces your immune system.

The kapha body is usually sturdy and often carries a few extra pounds on a normally strong frame. Kapha people move slowly, but they are endowed with endurance and grace. The kapha temperament is calm, forgiving, and good-natured. The kapha mind may take its time to grasp new knowledge; but once the knowledge seeps into the brain, there is good retention. The kapha memory is excellent.

The body and mind turn sluggish when kapha is off-balance. Kapha's normal characteristic of moving slowly and taking one's time is replaced by the absence of movement as inertia takes over. The kapha person, who may normally have trouble getting going in the morning, may now have trouble getting out of bed. Excess kapha leads to sinus problems, respiratory illnesses, colds, allergies, obesity, and lethargy—disorders that are easy to attribute to either too much or too little water in the body.

✳ Determining Your Constitution

So how do you determine your particular dosha or constitution? It's easy. Just take this Vastu Living Ayurveda Test, but please follow the "rules." There is no such thing as winning, and you'll only lose if you rush through and choose inappropriate answers that lead to an inaccurate conclusion.

The Vastu Living Ayurveda Test

When you read each of the following questions, please don't think that one answer is better than another. Accuracy in this particular test comes from honest self-reflection. Also take your time and think carefully about each question before you choose your answer. If you honestly believe that more than one answer to a particular question applies to you, circle them both. In other words, the test has twenty-five questions, but you can end up with more than twenty-five answers.

Just remember that the objective of the test is to create a realistic portrait of your body type, mental type, and emotional type. Since a few questions are about diet, you may even find that you need to keep a record of what you eat or drink over a few days before you decide the most accurate answer for you.

I have discovered that my clients usually benefit from having a close friend also answer the questions about the client. So invite someone who knows you well to answer the questions on your behalf. This second set of answers can clear up inconsistencies. A few of the questions about your

physical type or the quality of your sleep or level of thirst or food preferences are essentially objective and only your own answers will be valid.
However, other questions may lead to a different response from someone
close to you who has no bias and sees your behavior day in and day out.
Many of us tend to be rough on ourselves or to inflate our capabilities or
reactions. So this second set of responses may help you think more carefully
about your initial answers, and this process leads to a more accurate personal assessment.

If you share your home with a roommate or partner or share your workspace with a co-worker, ideally this person should also take the test and follow
the instructions provided above, including having a close friend answer the
questions that serve as the valuable cross-check. And if you do share your bedroom at home or your workspace, please don't worry if the two of you discover
that you have different constitutions. I will show you how to factor these differences into your practice of vastu living.

Plan to retake the test a few months after you have arranged your personal
environments according to vastu living. It's good to check and see how you
are doing.

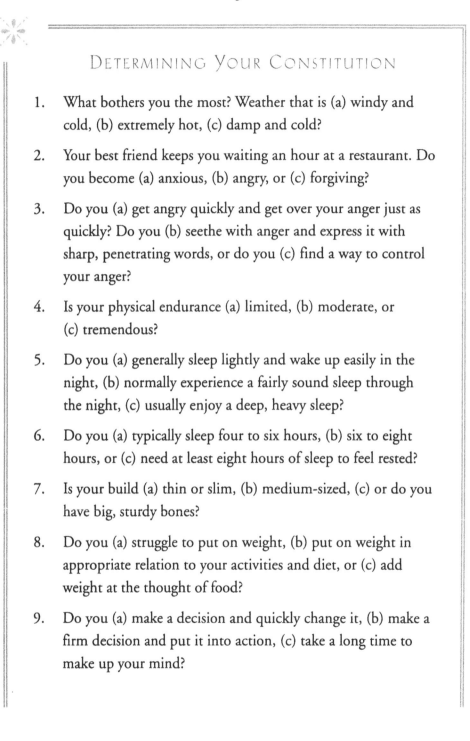

DETERMINING YOUR CONSTITUTION

1. What bothers you the most? Weather that is (a) windy and cold, (b) extremely hot, (c) damp and cold?

2. Your best friend keeps you waiting an hour at a restaurant. Do you become (a) anxious, (b) angry, or (c) forgiving?

3. Do you (a) get angry quickly and get over your anger just as quickly? Do you (b) seethe with anger and express it with sharp, penetrating words, or do you (c) find a way to control your anger?

4. Is your physical endurance (a) limited, (b) moderate, or (c) tremendous?

5. Do you (a) generally sleep lightly and wake up easily in the night, (b) normally experience a fairly sound sleep through the night, (c) usually enjoy a deep, heavy sleep?

6. Do you (a) typically sleep four to six hours, (b) six to eight hours, or (c) need at least eight hours of sleep to feel rested?

7. Is your build (a) thin or slim, (b) medium-sized, (c) or do you have big, sturdy bones?

8. Do you (a) struggle to put on weight, (b) put on weight in appropriate relation to your activities and diet, or (c) add weight at the thought of food?

9. Do you (a) make a decision and quickly change it, (b) make a firm decision and put it into action, (c) take a long time to make up your mind?

10. Is your memory (a) totally unreliable, (b) pretty good, (c) terrific—the envy of everyone?

11. If you had to choose a word to describe yourself in a social setting, would it be (a) vivacious, (b) intense, or (c) relaxed?

12. If you had to choose a second word to describe yourself, would it be (a) flexible, (b) ambitious, or (c) easygoing?

13. Do you (a) move quickly, (b) move at a moderate pace, or (c) are you happiest when your feet don't have to move at all?

14. Do you (a) eat whenever you feel hungry and whatever portion of food that feels right to you at the time? Do you (b) need to eat at specific times in the day and when you go off schedule, do you feel incredibly hungry? Are you (c) always ready to eat food but prefer small portions?

15. Do you (a) love to talk and find it hard to be quiet, (b) speak with intensity and usually say exactly what you think, or (c) exhibit restraint and choose your words with great care?

16. Does your desire for water (a) change constantly, or is it generally (b) high, or (c) low?

17. Is your disposition generally (a) unpredictable, (b) intense, or (c) calm and steady?

18. Does your energy (a) come in bursts, do you (b) efficiently manage your energy so that it gets you through the day, or is your energy level (c) slow but steady?

19. Do you walk (a) fast, (b) with a determined stride, or (c) at a slow, measured pace?

20. Do you (a) tend to jump into an activity and lose interest along the way? Do you (b) hate wasting time and work efficiently to achieve your goal? Do you (c) work at a slow but deliberate pace?

21. Do you (a) have the urge to buck the tide? Do you (b) like to be in charge, (c) prefer to be part of the team?

22. Do (a) your joints often ache or feel incredibly stiff? Do you (b) suffer from gastrointestinal disorders? Or are you (c) more apt to complain about respiratory illnesses?

23. Does (a) your skin get really dry? Do you (b) tend to get freckles, moles, or rashes? Or is your skin (c) usually moist and soft?

24. Do you (a) often get gas or constipation? Do you (b) often get diarrhea? Or do you (c) rarely suffer from bowel problems?

25. Do you find that you (a) perspire very little, perspire (b) a lot and can't wait to change your shirt, or (c) do you perspire a moderate amount?

✳ EVALUATING YOUR ANSWERS

When you and someone who knows you well have completed the test, compare both sets of answers. When they are different, recheck your responses to be sure that they are objective and represent an honest reflection of you. If you are certain that your response is truthful, discuss the question with your good friend to see what led to the different answer. If you are still convinced that your answer is correct, don't change it. But if you are persuaded to think otherwise, please make the change.

Now tally the total number of answers for each letter: *a, b,* and *c.*

Are the majority of your answers a? Then you are probably a vata dosha governed by the element of air.

Are the majority of your answers *b?* Then you are probably a pitta dosha governed by the element of fire.

Are the majority of your answers *c?* Then you are probably a kapha dosha governed by the element of water.

Are two letters high and close in number? Perhaps, you have answered eleven questions with *a* and nine questions with *b.* The number of answers with *c* is significantly lower. This means that the two elements represented by these two highest letters, *a* and *b,* combine to create your constitution. In this example, the test results indicate a vata-pitta constitution. We say vata-pitta because the number for vata is slightly higher. If the number for pitta were slighter higher, then you would have a pitta-vata constitution. The first dosha mentioned in any combination always represents the dosha that has the higher of the two nearly equal numbers. The dosha with the highest number also has a bit more dominance and influence in your body type, mental type, and emotional type.

You may also discover that you are one of the rare individuals who has a fairly even distribution among all three letters. This means that you are tridoshic in nature. No single element has a greater influence over the other elements. People who are tridoshic find it easier to maintain harmony and balance. If you are governed by one or two doshas, your body naturally exhibits a high level of either one or two of the dominant elements. This high level makes it easier for the dominating element or elements to slide into excess and create an imbalance that disturbs your well-being.

SPECIAL NOTE FOR "VATA" PEOPLE

If you discover that you have a vata constitution, please try to stick to your commitment to vastu living. In my practice as a consultant, many clients with a vata constitution dearly want to practice vastu, but they struggle to follow through with the guidelines that would increase the harmony inside their home and workspace. Their vata dosha causes them to vacillate, equivocate, and repeatedly change their mind.

LIKE INCREASES LIKE

Once you know your constitution, you can personalize your practice of vastu living in your home and your workspace so that you keep your dosha in balance. How do you do this? You adhere to the ayurveda principle of like increases like when you consider the location of the elements in vastu and their effect on your constitution.

These three words, which are the ayurvedic key to good health, are packed with wisdom and logic. In your practice of vastu living, you honor this principle in any space where you spend more than six hours at a stretch. This includes your bedroom and generally your workplace unless your job keeps you away from your work environment most of the day. Because these activities take up about two-thirds of your time, you don't want to sleep or to work in the same quadrant that matches your constitution. You risk triggering the negative consequences attached to the ayurvedic principle of like increases like: your constitution may become overstimulated and your health can suffer as a result.

Once you know your dosha or constitution, the principle of like increases like can help you create a home and workplace that keep you healthy—physically, mentally, and emotionally. And if you discover that you are sleeping or working in the quadrant that matches your constitution and you can't switch the location of your bedroom or workspace, vastu living is accommodating. You can restore the balance with the therapeutic properties of color or the healing side of nature, which are explained in chapters 4 and 5.

The negative consequences of like increases like should become a governing principle in your life. Once you know your dosha, you can make healthy adjustments in your diet when the weather changes. Each dosha connects to a specific season, and every dosha reacts to seasonal changes. If you pay attention to the effects of the weather and the seasons on your body, you can help ward away seasonal illnesses.

Ultimately, the principle of like increases like reminds you to pay attention to your dosha—always. In this next section, you see how to apply this principle in your practice of vastu living, how to maintain a healthy diet, and how to protect yourself each season.

❋ Honoring Your Dosha

Are You a Pitta (Fire) Dosha?

Pitta and Vastu

If you discovered that you are a pitta dosha, you have a lot of fire in your body. In your practice of vastu living, you observe the principle of like increases like by not sleeping in the southeast quadrant of your home or working in the southeast quadrant on your job. The same element of fire governs the southeast quadrant. If you spend too much time in this fiery quadrant, the fire inside you may heat up and boil over. You may suffer from pitta-related disturbances, such as skin rashes or an acidic stomach. Your passionate nature could turn into a ball of fire. You may become argumentative and overcritical. The leader in you turns into a boss.

Try to sleep or work in the southwest, which is the quadrant governed by earth, which can overpower fire. Earth also brings you strength and wisdom. Or sleep and work in the northeast, which is a calming quadrant governed by water. Water douses fire.

In the Southern Hemisphere, the unhealthy quadrant for anyone with a pitta dosha is the northeast, which belongs to fire, and the healthy quadrants are the northwest, which belongs to earth, and the southeast, which belongs to water.

Pitta and Diet

When pitta governs your body, you want to avoid eating too many pitta-aggravating foods, such as dishes that are hot and spicy, pungent (acidic or acrid), sour, and salty. You want to avoid drinking too many salty or acidic liquids as well as alcohol. Why should people with a pitta dosha limit their intake of salt? It speeds up the digestive process. Salt makes us salivate, and salivation stimulates digestion. Alcohol is not good for pitta because it intensifies the fire inside and outside of the body. It is literally a flammable substance.

Pitta Weather

Summer is hot and has the properties of pitta. This time of year can aggravate the pitta constitution and throw it off-balance. This is why most people with a pitta constitution don't like the hot, fiery weather associated with summer. But when the weather is hot, all of us should pay heed to the principle of like increases like and limit our intake of hot foods and hot beverages. During this time of year, we are all better off enjoying cold meals and cooling beverages. They make us feel more comfortable in hot, sticky weather.

Are You a Vata (Air) Dosha?

Vata and Vastu

If vata or air dominates the elements in your body, you can avoid imbalance by not sleeping or working in the northwest quadrant, which is governed by the same element—air. If you spend too much time in the northwest, the characteristics of this quadrant may turn your normally quick movements into restlessness. Your nerves may go over the edge and leave you rattled with anxiety. Little things may become big distractions; you just can't focus.

The solutions and remedies for an overstimulated vata dosha and overstimulated pitta dosha are the same. You try to sleep or work in the southwest or the northeast quadrants. The southwest quadrant of earth, with its strength and wisdom, holds down the element of air in the vata dosha. The northeast quadrant of water also dampens the element of air.

In the Southern Hemisphere, the unhealthy quadrant is the southwest, which belongs to air, and the healthy quadrants are the northwest, which belongs to earth, and the southeast, which belongs to water.

Vata and Diet

The properties associated with the element of air should serve as dietary reminders to vata people. They should limit their intake of bitter, astringent, or pungent foods and beverages that increase dryness, such as salads with leafy greens (they are brittle by nature), and foods that soak up the body's moisture, such as roughage and fiber. Salty foods, however, are good for vata people. They increase the body's secretions, which moisten the body.

Vata Weather

The windy, dry weather of autumn exhibits vata properties, so this time of year can bother people with a vata constitution. The wind, which dries out the leaves, aggravates the vata body. The skin loses its already limited moisture and becomes parched and flaky or brittle. Joints can stiffen up. During the autumn months, all of us should try to limit our intake of dry foods that are rich in roughage and sponge up our body's moisture.

Are You a Kapha (Water) Dosha?

Kapha and Vastu

If kapha or water rules over the other elements in your body, observe the principle of like increases like in vastu living by not sleeping or working in the northeast quadrant, which belongs to the element of water. If this is where you sleep or work, the characteristics of water may make you slower than sludge. You may be chronically exhausted. You may eat, eat, eat!—and gain too much weight. You may feel so malleable that you never even *think* of expressing your mind for fear of offending someone somewhere sometime.

Try to sleep or work in the southwest quadrant, where its element of earth gives you strength, or in the southeast quadrant, where its element of fire restores your energy. You can also restore your kapha constitution in the northwest. Its element of air keeps you on the move—mentally, physically, and emotionally. Just watch your focus in this quadrant. Don't let the element of air get the upper hand.

In the Southern Hemisphere, the unhealthy quadrant is the southeast, which belongs to water, and the healthy quadrants are the northeast, which belongs to fire, the northwest, which belongs to earth, and the southwest, which belongs to air.

Kapha and Diet

Kapha people should restrict their intake of sweet, salty, or sour liquids and foods that stimulate the water element. Sweets increase the property of heaviness, which is a prominent characteristic of kapha, and heaviness can turn into lethargy. Salt turns into saline when it enters the body and penetrates the body's tissues. Too much salt intensifies kapha heaviness and density. This can trigger an imbalance. Sour foods and beverages make us thirsty. A kapha body has an abundance of water and a slow metabolism, so an excessive intake of fluids can cause bloating or water retention, which is a common kapha disorder.

Kapha Weather

The damp cold of winter has the properties of kapha, so this is typically the least favorite time of year for people with a kapha constitution. The damp cold easily pushes the kapha dosha over the top. During this time of year, all of us should remember the principle of like increases like and avoid cold meals and cold beverages. Instead we should enjoy hot foods and beverages that warm up our body.

CREATING HARMONY FOR DIFFERENT CONSTITUTIONS THAT SHARE A SPACE

If you share your bedroom or workspace with someone who has a different constitution with its own needs, there are many ways to create harmony for both of you. First, see if you are sleeping or working in a location that is beneficial for both of you. If you are a vata, governed by the element of air, and you share a bedroom with someone who is a kapha, governed by the element of water, the ideal bedroom is in the southwest quadrant, which is controlled by the element of earth. Try not to sleep in either of the two quadrants that match the two constitutions—the quadrant of air, which reigns in the northwest, or the quadrant of water, which reigns in the northeast.

Let's continue with this example to see other solutions that can create harmony between conflicting constitutions. What do you do if your only bedroom is in the northeast quadrant of water, which is healthy for your vata but unhealthy for your kapha partner? You can place the bed in either the southwest or southeast quadrant inside the bedroom to offset the negative effects of like increases like. So when you are stuck with problematic room placement within your home or office building, try this second remedy of moving the actual bed or work desk to a safe quadrant *inside* the specific room.

But what do you do if there is no room for the bed in either of these two healthy quadrants *inside* the room? There are two remaining solutions: you can use the power of color or the healing properties of nature to restore the balance of a constitution that is being thrown off by the arrangement. These solutions are explored in depth in chapter 5, "Resolving Conflicts in Your Home and Workplace."

3

Creating Your Spiritual Blueprints

*

To put all this dosha knowledge into play in our homes and offices, we need to learn about the Vedic diagram called the *vastu purusha mandala*. The vastu purusha mandala is a spiritual blueprint that helps you follow the vastu guidelines. First, let's dissect this Vedic phrase to understand its significance.

The word *vastu,* which I defined earlier, means "dwelling" or "site," but *dwelling* refers to any created form or matter that is visible to us. Remember that your own body is an example of vastu. *Purusha* is the unseen energy or life-giving force—the spirit that exists inside every site and dwelling—in the largest sense of the word.

The *mandala* is a spiritual diagram. People who meditate often concentrate on a mandala to clear their mind of distractions, so that they can turn inward and focus on the spirit or the self. The mandala connected to vastu purusha helps you achieve the same goal. This spiritual blueprint shows you how to design personal environments so that their energy (purusha) creates vibrations that interact positively with your own vibrations. Your home and workspace increase your harmony and calm your mind.

Many myths tell the origins of vastu purusha. In one legend Shiva, the lord of destruction, was fighting an evil force when a drop of sweat fell from Shiva's brow to the earth. The moisture turned into a demon that threatened to devour the earth. Deities captured this cosmic spirit and held it down with its face pressed into the land. Lord Brahma, the creator who sits on the spirit's center or navel, named it vastu purusha and proclaimed that it must be honored at the start of any construction; otherwise, vastu purusha would create disturbance and disharmony. Nothing would go right inside the new structure.

The cosmic spirit is placed on a grid on the vastu purusha mandala and assumes a human form (serving as another reminder that each of us is an example of vastu). Vastu purusha is placed with its head tilted toward the northeast out of respect for the gods. And since each of the gods, who hold him down on the grid, represents an aspect of the perfect functioning of the universe, this respect also shows respect for the law of nature.

Vastu purusha's navel, which is the most fragile part of any body, is in the center of the blueprint and reminds you to keep uncovered the direct center of every space. His head, which also has many vulnerable organs, is in the northeast quadrant, which should be kept light and open so that the beneficial cosmic energy can flow through this midpoint area to the southwest quadrant. So on many levels, the placement of vastu purusha on the grid reminds you of the important principles in vastu (see Figure 4).

By appeasing vastu purusha in the design and organization of your home or workspace, you ensure a positive interaction between the vibrations of your environment and your own vibrations. You are also appeasing each deity that holds down this cosmic spirit; and through this act of appeasement, you acknowledge the law of nature and the three important principles in vastu that ask you to pay attention to the five basic elements, to show respect and love for all creation, and to celebrate the self, which is divine and connected to the Supreme Creative Force. The vastu purusha mandala is your guide to vastu

North

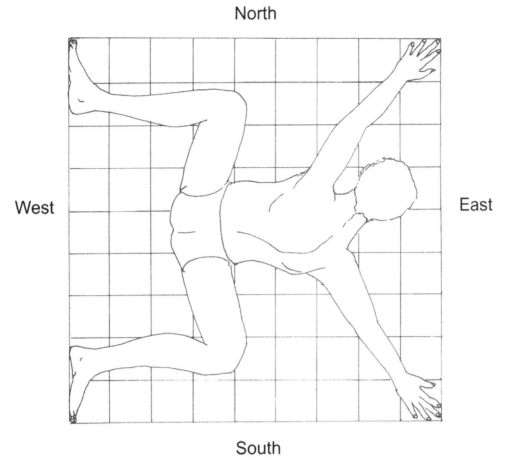

West

East

South

Figure 4: Vastu Purusha Mandala

living success. With this spiritual blueprint, you create constructions and interior designs that are holistic and harmonious. You create temples for your soul.

❋ THE IMPORTANCE OF THE SQUARE

The vastu purusha mandala can assume many shapes, but the square symbolizes the absolute harmony and balance that define the celestial world.

The four sides of the square create symmetry and balance. If we alter a side of the square, we destroy the symmetry and disrupt the balance and order. Vedic scholars also recognized that the human being represents a perfect square. If you extend your hands straight out to the left and right of your

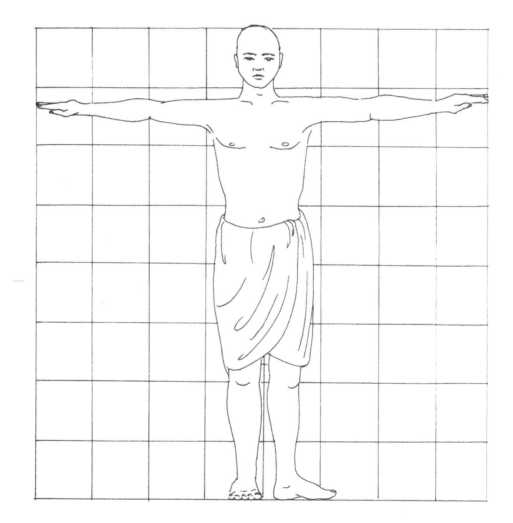

Figure 5: Human Form

body, the distance from the tips of your fingers on each hand equals the distance from the top of your head to the soles of your feet. The human form is proportionate and symmetrical. It mirrors the qualities of the universe.

CHOOSING THE CORRECT SHAPE FOR EACH SPIRITUAL BLUEPRINT

Now it's time to learn how to create your own set of vastu purusha mandalas or spiritual blueprints that determine the present level of harmony in your home and workspace: to see what works and what doesn't. The ideal shape of the spiritual blueprint is square, but many buildings and rooms are rectangular or even L-shaped, which is a combination of a square and rectangle. So *The Power of Vastu Living* provides three spiritual blueprints at the end of the book that you can copy for your use. One spiritual blueprint is in the shape of the square. The other two spiritual blueprints are rectangles, which are also square-based. One rectangle is for a property, building, or room where the front and back are oriented to the east and the west; the other rectangle is for spaces where the front and back are oriented to the north and the south. Make enough enlarged copies of each appropriate spiritual blueprint to cover all the possible layouts in your personal environments.

Your sample spiritual blueprints, which are shown below, do not include the cosmic spirit. Instead they demarcate the four important quadrants and the center of each space and identify the element that governs each of these five areas. The spiritual blueprints also indicate the cardinal directions (north, south, east, and west) along with their primary attributes. Each spiritual blueprint conveys the same information as the vastu purusha mandala shown in Figure 4, but these simplified versions give you room to make the notations that you need to include on each blueprint.

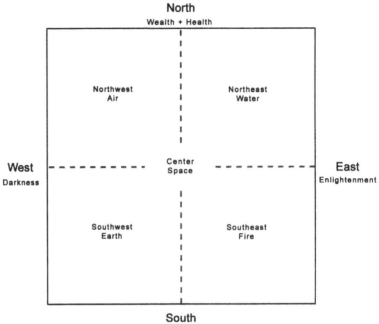

Figure 6: Square Spiritual Blueprint

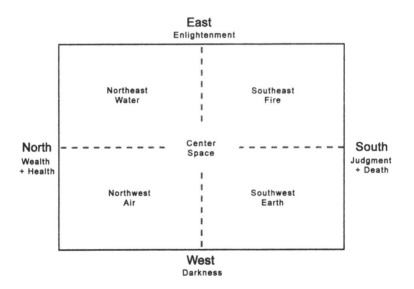

Figure 7: Rectangular Spiritual Blueprint Oriented East and West

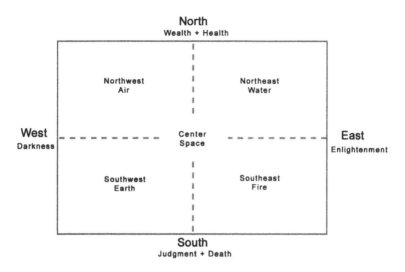

Figure 8: Rectangular Spiritual Blueprint Oriented North and South

WORKING WITH IRREGULAR SHAPES

An L-Shaped Space

If your home or workspace is L-shaped, use a square spiritual blueprint and the appropriately oriented rectangle to create the L-shape that matches the orientation of your space. Tape them together, but treat the quadrants of each spiritual blueprint separately. In other words, in this particular shape of home or workspace, you will use two sets of quadrants to cover the total home and workspace, and the space will be organized around two sacred centers. When you join the two spiritual blueprints together, please be careful to follow the actual orientation of the home to the cardinal directions. Also take care to join together the two spiritual blueprints so that their orientations match. The east of the square spiritual blueprint should line up with the east of the rectangle. The two figures below show two possible L-shaped blueprints.

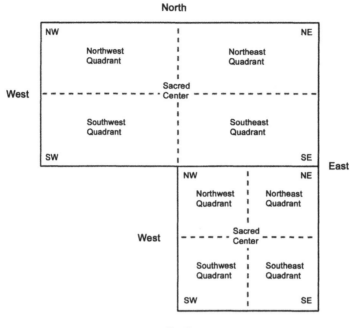

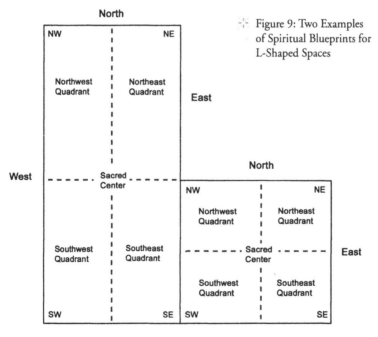

Figure 9: Two Examples of Spiritual Blueprints for L-Shaped Spaces

The Odd-Shaped Building or Property

Don't worry if your property, home, or workspace doesn't conform to a perfect square or rectangle. Many spaces don't. A home or workspace may have bay windows, balconies, or a veranda or porch that juts out on one side. Perhaps a few walls in a room even slant and create an angle that is greater or less than ninety degrees. This often happens in older apartment buildings. Just use the blueprint that most closely matches the overall shape—either the square or the rectangle. Do you have a round room or a circular home or workspace? A square fits perfectly inside the circle, so use the square spiritual blueprint for all circular shapes. Most likely the majority of your furniture has been placed so that it already conforms to an imaginary square.

You may also live or work in the countryside, where part of the property is

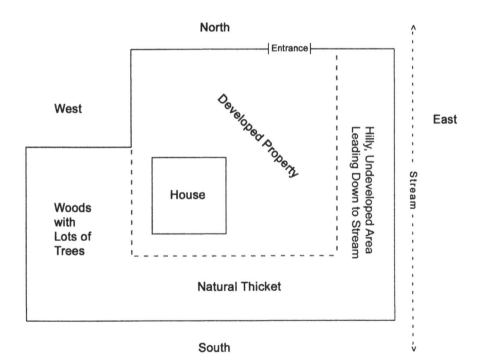

Figure 10: Spiritual Blueprint for the Odd-Shaped Property

undeveloped. It may have uncultivated fields, marshlands, or acres of woods. Vastu living blueprints only include the portion of a property that has or will be altered from its original state. If the land has been left alone, its vibrations have not lost their original intensity. The land continues to follow the law of nature, so it does not belong on the spiritual blueprint. So please remember that the blueprint for the property includes only the part of the property that has been or will be developed for use. This is the portion of your property where you must try to observe the vastu guidelines so that negative vibrations won't interfere with your well-being.

DETERMINING THE APPROPRIATE NUMBER OF SPIRITUAL BLUEPRINTS

You need to create a spiritual blueprint or layout for each of the following situations that relate to your personal environments and are under your control.

1. If you own property, you need to create a spiritual blueprint that shows the alignment of the property under use and the location and alignment of all the buildings on the site.
2. You need a spiritual blueprint that shows the placement of all the rooms in your home or workspace. If you have multiple floors, then you need to create a spiritual blueprint that shows the placement of rooms on each floor.
3. You need a spiritual blueprint of each individual room, on which you indicate the placement of windows, doors, furniture, appliances, and built-ins, such as cupboards and shelves, all plants, and all sources of water.

If you live or work in an apartment building or office complex, you do not need a spiritual blueprint that indicates the alignment of the entire building on the site. You can limit your practice of vastu living to the specific apartment or rooms that you occupy inside the building. You focus your attention on spaces that are under your control. If there are problems inside the building's lobby, you cannot do much to correct them.

If you live or work in a loft or open space that has few interior walls, note the location of each area, with its function, on your spiritual blueprint. For example, indicate the locations of each sleeping area, kitchen, dining area, work area, entertaining area, bathroom, etc. Then create a separate spiritual blueprint for each designated area that includes the placement of all your furniture and fixtures.

If you are planning to build a new home or workspace, you need to create spiritual blueprints before you proceed so that you can evaluate the architect's design. This is how you determine the extent to which your new home or workspace conforms to the vastu guidelines before you go to work to improve its harmony.

Spiritual blueprints can be extremely rough. You do not need to be an architect to create them. You can draw basic geometric shapes and then label each shape to indicate what it represents—bed, couch, kitchen stove, radiator, cupboard, closet. Just try to get the proportions correct. A small sofa should be indicated by a rectangle that is smaller than a large sofa. Every notation on your blueprint should attempt to approximate the correct proportion in relation to the other objects and the size of the space. Labels accompanying trees should include their approximate height. Other objects on the property, such as a swimming pool or a pond, should include their approximate dimensions. These details are important. Finally, write the words *window* and *entrance* at the appropriate points in your home and workspace or in each room.

Problems with spiritual blueprints occur when people improperly align their personal space within the cardinal directions. Some of my clients have also raced through their spiritual blueprints and put details into the wrong quadrant or overlooked items altogether. So please, be careful and go slowly when you create your blueprints. They are important to your practice of vastu living.

✳ Creating Your Blueprints

Please Remember . . .

Readers who live in the Southern Hemisphere should follow the spiritual blueprint below, which shows the effect of the earth's rotation below the equator on your practice of vastu living. Four of the five basic elements, along with their properties, assume different locations, and the guidelines governing the placement of lightweight and heavy furnishings alter. Place your lightweight furnishings in the south and the west; place your heavy and tall furnishings in the north and the east (see chapter 7, "The Southern Hemisphere").

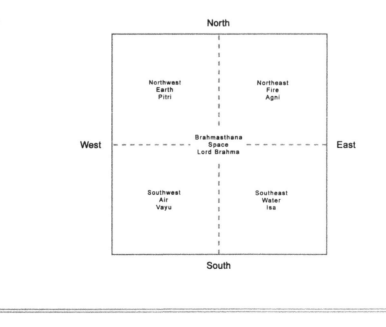

North

Northwest
Earth
Pitri

Northeast
Fire
Agni

West

Brahmasthana
Space
Lord Brahma

East

Southwest
Air
Vayu

Southeast
Water
Isa

South

Spiritual Blueprint of the Property

If your home or workspace has property, take your compass and walk around the exterior to determine the location and orientation of elevations and depressions on your site. Note the location of water sources. Do you have a swimming pool, fishpond, water fountain? Indicate all this information on your spiritual blueprint. Also include trees and shrubbery or anything on the property that may serve as a barrier, such as hedges or fences. Do you have a rock garden, sculpture garden, tree house? Include them.

> ## TO CREATE YOUR SPIRITUAL BLUEPRINT, YOU NEED THE FOLLOWING ITEMS:
>
> Metal measuring tape
> Compass that includes the midpoint directions of northeast, southeast, southwest, and northwest
> Pencil with eraser
> Red pencil
> Enough copies of the appropriate spiritual blueprints on which to write

If your home abuts a building on an adjoining property, make note of the building. Do you have an outdoor sauna, barbecue grill, generator? Mark them all down.

Determine the location of every building on your site, from a small shed to a large garage, and carefully place them on your blueprint. Determine the orientation of the entrance to your home and workspace by standing in your front doorway and looking out. What direction do you face? Correctly note this orientation. Finally, indicate the location of the property's driveway. Remember to try hard to maintain the correct proportion of everything on your property. Your shed should not be larger than your house on your blueprint.

Spiritual Blueprint of the Interior of a Building

To create the spiritual blueprint of the interior of your home or workspace, properly mark the location of every room inside your space. Or if you live or work in an open space, indicate every area that has a specific function—your work area, your dining area, your kitchen, your sleeping area, your living room area. Remember to include your bathrooms and laundry room if it exists. No room should be omitted, and show the location of all closets. If there are terraces, porches, verandas, balconies, mark them down. Also, indicate the location of each window and the entrances and exits in each room. If your home or workspace has multiple floors, you need a separate blueprint of each floor that shows the location and function of each room.

Spiritual Blueprint of an Individual Room

Room layouts are easy to create, but they include more information. Take your compass and stand in the middle of each room and match the orientation of the northeast on the compass with the northeast of the room. Now write down the furniture and room details in this quadrant on the northeast quadrant of the blueprint. Note all the windows, doors, closets, even plants. Include all your furniture, built-ins, bookcases, electrical appliances, and don't forget your computer or stereo, or fireplace if there is one. When you complete the northeast, rotate around the room and make note of all the details until you face the northeast again. Also be certain to indicate whether the direct center of the room is covered or uncovered.

Follow this same procedure in a loft or open space with few interior walls. Just create imaginary walls around each space that fulfills a specific function. Determine the northeast of this wall-less room and create a spiritual blueprint by using the same method for an individual room. The absence of doors and walls in vastu is often a plus, as you will learn in chapter 8, "Final Advice Before You Begin."

INTERPRETING YOUR SPIRITUAL BLUEPRINTS

After you create your spiritual blueprints, make a copy of the entire set and put it in a safe place to use as a future reference. As you read each chapter that shows how to incorporate vastu living into a specific environment, refer to the appropriate spiritual blueprint. When you see a problem, you may discover that a simple reorganization of the furniture inside a room or an actual room swap can significantly improve the vastu compliance of your home and workspace, and your well-being. Use a red pencil and make the intended change on your spiritual blueprint.

You can also check to see if the northeast is the most open quadrant on your property so that it maximizes the collection of the cosmic energy that enters the property from this direction. You can see if your property rises in the southwest to create the natural barrier that traps the cosmic energy that travels to this part of the property from the northeast. Your spiritual blueprints also show the degree to which each interior space is open on the north and the east and heavy on the south and the west. Openness in the north and the east encourages the healthy movement of the cosmic energy from the northeast to the southwest. Openness in the north and the east also helps us receive the healthiest rays of the sun. Painters have long recognized the inherent beauty of the light that comes from the north; they call it the painter's steady light.

Finally, your spiritual blueprints help you organize your spaces so that they conform to the personal needs associated with your constitution. They show you if your spaces are contributing negatively to the principle of like increases like that can overstimulate your constitution.

UNHEALTHY QUADRANTS FOR YOUR CONSTITUTION IN VASTU LIVING

CONSTITUTION OR DOSHA	NORTHERN HEMISPHERE	SOUTHERN HEMISPHERE
Vata / Air	Northwest (Air)	Southwest (Air)
Pitta / Fire	Southeast (Fire)	Northeast (Fire)
Kapha / Water	Northeast (Water)	Southeast (Water)

You can see the importance of these spiritual blueprints in this story about a dress designer in Brooklyn, New York. She contacted me when she was having trouble focusing on her work. Just a gurgle in a steam pipe in her large studio made her forget what she was doing on a dress pattern; and many careless snips of her scissors ruined many expensive pieces of fabric.

I asked the dress designer to take the ayurveda test to determine her constitution, and I also asked her to send me a blueprint of her studio. I discovered from her test results that she has a vata constitution, which is governed by the property of air. I also discovered from her blueprint that she was working in the northwest quadrant, which belongs to the same element—air—and exhibits the property of movement and fickleness.

In vastu living, this is not a good location for any dress designer who needs to do precision work; but it was especially bad for a vata designer. My client would work better if she placed her worktable in the serene and stabilizing northeast quadrant, which belonged to the element of water and was called the gateway to the gods. If she worked so that her table faced east, she would also receive lots of inspiration. I noticed on her blueprint that her dining area was in the northeast area of her studio. Her kitchen was in the southeast, and her bedroom was in a healthy southwest location.

When I visited the designer, I explained that even if she were not a vata, governed by the element of air, the northwest quadrant in a space could lead to the problems that she had described to me. The northwest of her studio was simply following the law of nature: the properties associated with the element of air made her mind wander. And since she has a vata constitution, the negative consequences of like increases like compounded her problem. She was spending too much time in the northwest quadrant. Her vata constitution was overstimulated: the results were expressed in her inability to focus on her work.

I advised the designer to make a simple correction in her studio: I asked her to swap the locations of her dining area and her work area. The switch was successful. The designer regained her ability to focus by working in the stillness associated with the quadrant connected to water, and her creativity improved by facing east when she worked at her table.

PROBLEMS: TO FIX OR NOT TO FIX

As you read the sections "The Welcoming Home" and "The Welcoming Workplace," please pay careful attention to your spiritual blueprints and take careful note of all the conflicts that exist between your personal environments and the vastu living guidelines. Try your best to create a home and workspace that observe the three important principles in vastu: honoring the proper location of each element, respecting nature by drawing it into your realm, and celebrating your unique identity. When you can't physically resolve a conflict between elements by moving around the furniture, there are other solutions. You will learn about them in chapter 5, "Resolving Conflicts in Your Home and Workplace."

4

The Power of Color

Have you ever seen a rainbow? Have you ever wondered how it was formed? The shimmering red, orange, yellow, green, blue, indigo, and violet, which produce the glistening arc that spreads across the horizon, are the seven visible rays of the sun. We see a rainbow when we gaze into rain or a waterfall or even a spray of water from a sprinkler or a fountain when the sun shines from behind us. The white light from the sun enters each water droplet and separates into the seven distinct bending bands of color. Like magic, the delicate rainbow glimmers for us to behold.

But the rainbow isn't magic, and its presence on the horizon teaches us many things. White light contains all the colors of the visible spectrum, and each of these seven colors has a distinct wavelength and frequency of vibration. Our eyes interact with the light's frequency of vibration and wavelength, and this interaction determines the color that we see. The color red, which is always at the top of the rainbow, has the longest arc, the longest wavelength, and the lowest frequency of vibration. Below red is orange, then comes yellow, green, blue, indigo, and finally violet, which has the shortest wavelength and the highest frequency of vibration. The color violet, which creates the shortest arc in the rainbow, also appears closest to the ground.

The law of nature, so central to the Vedic philosophy, shows us once again that even in this dazzling and seemingly miraculous display, nothing is random in its creation. Nothing is random in the order of its display of color, or in the properties attached to each color. And nothing is random in the effect that each color or the sum total of the seven colors, which is white light, has on life-forms. The predetermined wavelength and frequency of vibration attached to each specific color governs its effect on us.

The rainbow also reinforces this important point: the visible light that vibrates from the sun is energy. Energy, as we know, exists within all of us and sustains all creation. Each color, with its unique wavelength and frequency of vibration, produces a predictable level of energy: the shorter the wavelength, the higher the energy. This energy interacts with our own energy—or, as we learned in chapter 1, the vibrations of each color interact negatively or positively with our own vibrations.

☀ VEDIC AWARENESS OF COLOR

By reading Hindu mythology, we see that Vedic scholars understood that the sun's energy created the seven colors in the visible spectrum. In many legends, Lord Surya, the sun god, is portrayed as a charioteer on a chariot that is pulled by seven steeds. Each steed represents a single ray of color in the visible spectrum. The ancient scholars also understood that color has a deep influence on our well-being. The physical associations, along with the emotional and spiritual properties attached to each color, are commonly used to symbolize characteristics ascribed to Hindu deities and aspects of Hindu rituals.

Lord Vishnu, the Hindu deity of preservation, is the color blue. Blue, which is the color of the sky and the oceans, represents the heights and the depths of our physical world. In the metaphysical and spiritual realm, blue represents the infinite, the unending, and the everlasting. Emotionally, blue is cool, calm, reflective.

Yellow became the Vedic color connected to the knowledge of the Truth. Many Hindu deities, such as Lord Ganesha, the elephant-headed god, and Lord Krishna, wear garments that include the color yellow. In the physical world, yellow is equated with the sun, which is the source of all light. In the metaphysical and spiritual world, the light of the sun represents knowledge. The sun's light banishes the darkness that accompanies ignorance. The sun ultimately speaks of clarity and understanding.

White, which contains all seven colors, also contains all their characteristics and speaks of purity. Consider the sacred nature of the ash in Hinduism, which is often smeared on the forehead as a blessing from the priest at a Hindu temple or at the conclusion of a holy ritual. This blessing is rich with meaning. The fire flickers red, yellow, orange, blue, green—all seven colors dance in the flames. When the fire dies, it goes black and gives up its color. But the fire's residue is the white ash, which encompasses, once again, the seven colors of the sun's visible spectrum. So white and the blessing of ash symbolize the everlasting nature of the soul—its purity and its never-ending connection to the divine.

Color	Properties of Each Color
Red	In Hinduism, red is auspicious and represents the spiritual power that overcomes evil. Red motivates us, increases our vitality, and makes us passionate. It gives us power and courage that strengthens our conviction, confidence, and strong will. Red reinforces loyalty.
Orange	In Hinduism, orange or saffron represents the sacred fire that burns away impurities and signifies the quest for spiritual enlightenment. Swamis and others who choose a spiri-

tual life commonly wear this color. Orange increases our sensitivity, generosity, and compassion. It builds up our energy and our zest for life.

YELLOW In Hinduism, yellow represents the spiritual light that illuminates the Truth. Yellow stimulates our mind and intellect so that we acquire wisdom and clarity, which increases our inner strength and self-esteem. Yellow also increases our creativity and curiosity.

GREEN In Hinduism, rituals include green leaves from sacred plants to express the importance of nature. Green creates harmony, balance, and feelings of inner calm. Identified with nature, green has healing properties, which are therapeutic and stimulate our growth. Green is associated with renewal.

BLUE In Hinduism, blue represents the imperishable nature of the soul and the infinite presence of the Supreme Creative Force. Blue represents the cool side of nature, which we associate with the water and the sky. It inspires harmony, serenity, and calms down our emotions. It quiets our mind so that we can think clearly. It promotes integrity, trust, and faith.

INDIGO In Hinduism, indigo is frequently used in mandalas, which are visual aids to meditation. Indigo strengthens our intuition and imagination. It helps us turn inward so that we can understand the true nature of our soul and our connection to all existence. Indigo creates an inner balance that is stabilizing and reinforcing.

VIOLET In Hinduism, violet is also commonly used in mandalas. Violet inspires self-respect and enhances our creativity and inspiration. More spiritually potent than indigo, violet intensifies the experience of meditation. It provides us with inner strength and the wisdom to be mindful of our thoughts and actions. It guides us along the path to Enlightenment.

WHITE   In Hinduism, white represents purity and the nobility that comes with pure thoughts and pure actions. White, which contains all the seven colors, brings us peace and comfort. It purifies the body, the mind, the soul.

❋ VEDIC FINDINGS AND CONTEMPORARY RESEARCH

Western scientists can now measure the wavelength and frequency of vibration for each color in the visible spectrum. Their findings confirm the wisdom of the ancients that the warmer the color, the slower its frequency of vibration, and the cooler the color, the faster its frequency of vibration. Specifically, the warm colors red, orange, and yellow vibrate at a slower frequency than the cool colors green, blue, indigo, and violet. Geobiologists have also confirmed that the vibrations attached to a particular color interact with our own vibrations and create a response that affects our spiritual, emotional, and physical health. In addition, these scientists have discovered that some of the colors in the visible spectrum have a complementary color: a particular color will create a specific set of emotional reactions in us during the daytime, and a second color will create the same set of reactions in us at night.*

---

*The nighttime colors are from research published in the "Studies in Geobiology: Colours-Man-Building Interrelationships" in "Annual Report 1991-92," included in the annual research reports from 1989 to 1994, published by Sri Aurobindo Institute of Applied Scientific Research, Prabhat Poddar, director of Geobiology Research. Address: Academy House, 34 Marvadi St., Padmini Nagar, Pondicherry, 605012, India. The daytime colors are the seven colors in the visible spectrum and white, which contains all the colors.

COMPLEMENTARY COLORS

DAYTIME COLOR	NIGHTTIME COLOR
Red	Violet
Orange	Indigo
Yellow	Blue
Green	Green
Blue	Yellow
Indigo	Orange
Violet	Red
White	White

❋ USING THE POWER OF COLOR IN VASTU LIVING

When you know the properties associated with each color in the visible spectrum, you can use the power of color to balance the elements in your home and in your workspace. The power of color can even restore the balance to your dosha or constitution when a problem in your personal environment triggers the negative effects associated with the principle of like increases like.

The guidelines for the effective use of color in your practice of vastu living are explained in chapter 5, "Resolving Conflicts in Your Home and Workplace." The guidelines are easy to follow; but remember that when you want to get the full-time benefits of the properties connected to a color, you must also incorporate its nighttime complement, if there is one. And please listen to your body once you introduce colors into your environment. Pay attention to how you feel.

5

Resolving Conflicts in Your Home and Workplace

✳

You have personalized your plan for vastu living so that you can honor your special constitution or dosha. You've created your set of spiritual blueprints so that you can analyze your home and workspace. But before you begin your actual practice of vastu living, you still need to know about the accommodating side of this spiritual science.

As you enter each vastu-correct environment in section two, "The Welcoming Home," and section three, "The Welcoming Workplace," you will probably discover that all is not perfect with your home or workspace. This is to be expected. It's the lucky individual who doesn't have at least one troublesome area that is creating disharmony rather than harmony, imbalance rather than balance. But put away the crowbar; vastu living is *not* about demolition or destruction. Instead, vastu living offers four different methods for overcoming structural problems that block the flow of the cosmic energy and the spiritual power—four different methods for restoring the balance of the five basic elements inside your home or workplace—

four different methods for reestablishing the balance in your constitution.

So this chapter is all about solutions and remedies that can come to your rescue as you learn the vastu living guidelines. Let's learn how to use them, one by one. And please remember to refer to the charts below if you live in the Southern Hemisphere or if you realize that your constitution is out of sorts.

PLEASE REMEMBER . . .

Readers who live in the Southern Hemisphere should follow this spiritual blueprint, which shows the effect of the earth's rotation below the equator on your practice of vastu living. Four of the five basic elements, along with their properties, assume different locations, and the guidelines governing the placement of lightweight and heavy furnishings alter. Place your lightweight furnishings in the south and the west; place your heavy and tall furnishings in the north and the east (see chapter 7, "The Southern Hemisphere").

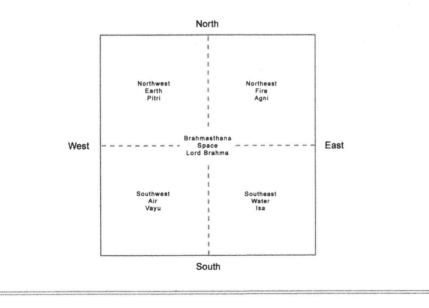

All readers should refer to these two charts to take good care of their constitution.

HEALTHY QUADRANTS FOR YOUR CONSTITUTION IN VASTU LIVING

CONSTITUTION	NORTHERN HEMISPHERE	SOUTHERN HEMISPHERE
Vata / Air	Northeast and Southwest	Northwest and Southeast
Pitta / Fire	Northeast and Southwest	Northwest and Southeast
Kapha / Water	Southwest, Southeast, and Northwest	Northwest, Northeast, and Southwest

UNHEALTHY QUADRANTS FOR YOUR CONSTITUTION IN VASTU LIVING

CONSTITUTION	NORTHERN HEMISPHERE	SOUTHERN HEMISPHERE
Vata / Air	Northwest (Air)	Southwest (Air)
Pitta / Fire	Southeast (Fire)	Northeast (Fire)
Kapha / Water	Northeast (Water)	Southeast (Water)

THE ROOM SWAP

The first solution involves the "room swap." This remedy in vastu living requires an obliging layout that allows you to swap the function and furnishings in two rooms. In certain situations, the room swap can be your easiest way to solve problems that occur in more than one personal environment. In addition, once you make the room swap, the exchange usually "feels" right.

Your newly organized rooms seem organic and everything fits like a second skin.

Let's examine a situation in which the room swap is an ideal solution.

A couple lived in a sprawling one-story home in New Jersey. The husband and wife spent little time in their bedroom despite its pleasant décor and ambience. They also tossed and turned and frequently woke up during the night. Their bedroom was in the northwest quadrant of the house, which is governed by the element of air. The restlessness associated with this element and quadrant made it a bad location for the couple's bedroom.

Worse, the couple's bed was placed against the bedroom's north wall (see Figure 11). The head is considered the north pole of the body, so the orientation of the bed contributed to the couple's restlessness. The two north poles repel each other and interfered with their sleep.

Their bed straddled the northeast and northwest quadrants but didn't cover the sacred center of the spacious room. Still, the bed was the heaviest piece of furniture in the room—and heavy objects belong to the element of earth, which governs the southwest quadrant. The bed, the element of earth, had been placed in both the northeast quadrant, the element of water, and the northwest quadrant, the element of air. In vastu, the south and the west of each enclosed space are supposed to bear the heaviest weight; the north and the east should be left relatively airy and open. So their setup violated important guidelines, but because of the room's built-in shelves, the couple couldn't shift around their furniture to correct these problems. However, they also had a problematic den.

Their den, which was almost the mirror opposite of the bedroom, was in the southwest quadrant of the couple's house (see Figure 12). The arrangement of its furniture also created conflicts with the elements. Their heavy sofa set, which belongs to the element of earth, was improperly placed almost entirely in the northwest quadrant, which belongs to the element of air. The

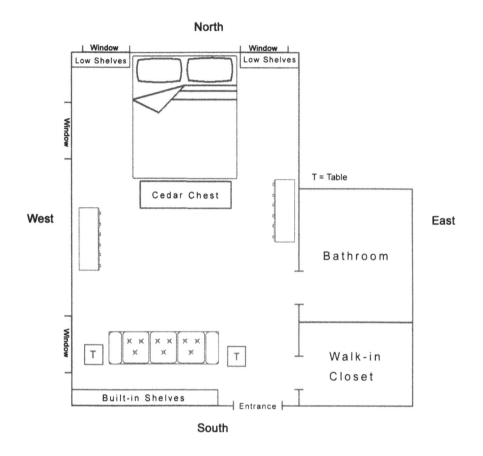

Figure 11: Bedroom before the Room Swap

den's two separate seating areas also had their backs to one another, creating an unfriendly environment. Their desk was oriented to the east, which normally encourages inspiration, but the person who sat there stared into a wall—an uninspiring view.

I drew two spiritual blueprints in which the furniture placement created harmony with the five basic elements. But because of the built-in shelves in the bedroom, the blueprints required a room swap. The couple needed to put

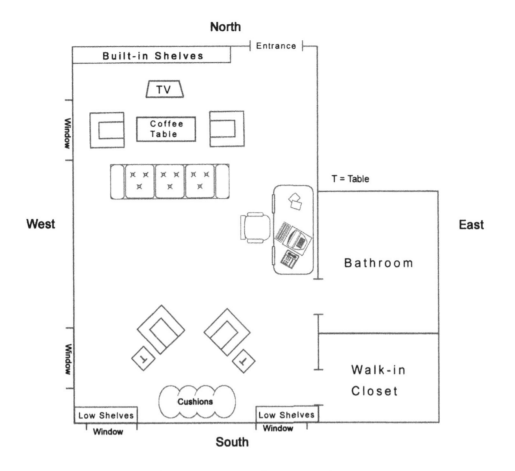

Figure 12: Den before the Room Swap

their bedroom in the southwest quadrant of the home and their den in the northwest quadrant.

Once the couple slept in the southwest, they were blessed with the properties connected to the quadrant's element of earth—wisdom and strength. They had escaped the restlessness attached to the element of air and could finally enjoy their bedroom. They also slept better because the head of the bed was against the south wall in between the low built-in shelves (see Figure 13).

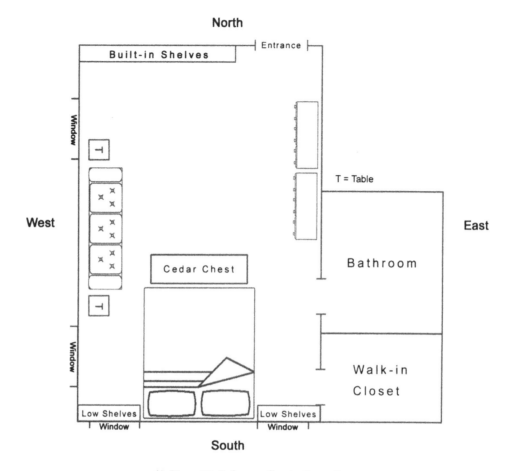

North

Built-in Shelves

Entrance

T = Table

West

East

Bathroom

Cedar Chest

Walk-in
Closet

Low Shelves

Low Shelves

Window

Window

South

Figure 13: Bedroom after the Room Swap

The couple slept with their head oriented toward the south instead of the north. They were able to get a good night's rest.

Their newly placed den was more vastu-correct (see Figure 14) and friendlier. The desk faced a window in the northeast, where an appealing view drew in the cosmic energy and spiritual power that enter this midpoint direction. Anyone who worked at the desk also benefited from the meditative properties associated with the northeast quadrant. Their heavy sofa and matching chairs

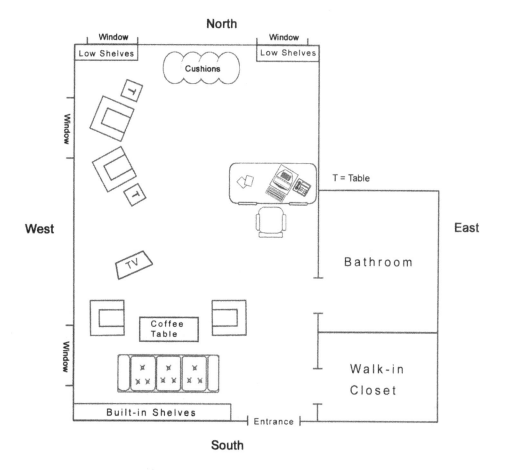

Figure 14: Den after the Room Swap

were shifted to the southwest quadrant. Anyone who sat in the sofa faced the healing properties of the north.

The two other cozy chairs were put in the northwest quadrant. Its element of air can disrupt the power of concentration, but one of the chairs faced the northeast. The serenity that is associated with this spiritual quadrant helps mitigate the restlessness. Anyone who sat in this chair could focus on this midpoint direction and be filled with peace and tranquility. The other chair faces east, which is a source of enlightenment that inspires healthy thoughts and conversation. The stack of cushions in the north also invites people to sit in the healing north or in the spiritually powerful northeast. Ultimately, no one sitting in the den—except for a person who may work at the desk—has his or her back to anyone else. The den became a people-friendly environment.

THE FURNITURE SHUFFLE

You can also resolve conflicts between the elements or conflicts that disturb your constitution through the thoughtful reorganization of your furniture within a room. I call this solution the furniture shuffle.

Let's see how a lawyer used this solution to solve his problem—chronic distraction.

This lawyer, who was a partner in a small firm, had a midsize office in the northeast corner of his company's modern new duplex. The attorney's office was cheery. Lovely morning sunlight poured through four windows in the north and the northeast. His workspace was also designed for efficiency with floor-to-ceiling built-in shelves and cabinets (see Figure 15).

But after the firm moved into this duplex, the young lawyer was anything but efficient at work. The heaviest object in the office was his desk. It belonged in the southwest quadrant, which is governed by the element of earth. Unfortunately, his desk was placed in the northwest quadrant, which belongs to the element of air. This element is all about get-up-and-go—in the wrong sense of the phrase.

The young lawyer kept losing his train of thought when he was on the phone or reading through a legal brief. He tired quickly and found himself taking quick catnaps in a chaise lounge that he had placed in the northeast quadrant of his office. The chaise was oriented so that he faced the southwest and not the northeast, which is the calming gateway to the gods that would have allowed him to still his mind and reenergize. The lawyer didn't realize that he worked in an unsupportive environment.

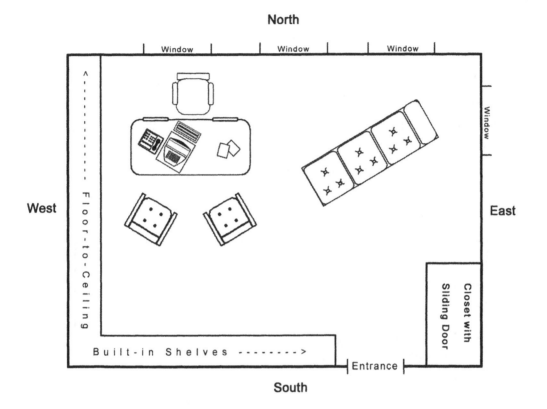

Figure 15: Misdirected Furniture

I showed the lawyer how to rearrange his furniture according to a spiritual blueprint that I sketched for him (see Figure 16). In this vastu-correct layout, his desk was in the southwest quadrant where it belonged. This restored the balance between the elements of air and earth. The lawyer could also sit with his back to the south. The properties of the southwest quadrant—strength and wisdom—would empower him and put quality back into his work.

The visitor's chairs were in the northwest quadrant of air. Their location was perfect since his visitors did come and go. The properties of movement associated with this element were in total alignment with the functioning of his office. His visitors also faced the south into the realm of Yama, the lord of judgment, who reminds us to live responsibly. This is sound advice that a lawyer would give to any client.

Finally, the lightweight chaise lounge was turned around so that my client stared into a northeastern window when he took a short break in his workday. The serenity and spiritual power connected to this quadrant would help him empty his mind of distracting thoughts so that he could turn inward. He would return to his work completely reenergized.

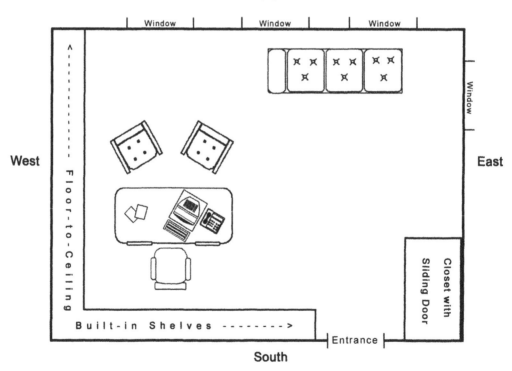

Figure 16: Redirected Furniture

THE PACIFYING APPEASEMENT

You may discover that some conflicts in your home or workspace defy physical solutions. Major appliances often create discord in the kitchen. The stove, with its property of fire, may not be in the kitchen's southeast quadrant, which belongs to the element of fire. The sink, which is connected to the element of water, may not be in the kitchen's northeast quadrant, which belongs to the element of water. The refrigerator, which is typically the heaviest item in this room, may not be in the southwest quadrant, which is assigned to the element of earth. Or the house may sit on top of the sacred center of the property where it holds down the spiritual energy that should circulate around the site. This causes a lot of weight to bear down on both the fragile navel of vastu purusha, who is the cosmic spirit of the land, and the holy realm of Lord Brahma, the Hindu god of creation.

Physically correcting the improper alignment of the elements in your kitchen can be expensive. You may need to rip apart the entire room—redirect water pipes, electric wiring, and possibly the gas connections. Reorganizing your kitchen may not even be an option. You may rent your home. Physically correcting a house that covers the sacred center is a ludicrous proposition. You would need to hire a crew from that rare breed of movers who jack up buildings to shift your house a ridiculously short distance into the southwest quadrant of the property, which is the preferred location in vastu living.

So what do you do when a problem in your home or workspace seems unfixable in your practice of vastu living? You draw upon the logic of the ayurveda principle of like increases like and restore harmony through the use of appeasements. And why do you pay attention to this principle? Because when a space is not vastu correct, most likely it has an effect on your well-being and your constitution. You need to restore its balance and harmony. It is also important to think of appeasements as offerings. When you make an appeasement, you acknowledge the presence of a problem in your home or workspace. You make an offering that pays respect to the offended deities and their elements and your own divine self.

Two types of appeasements can maintain or restore the harmony and balance: you can draw on the healing power of color and you can draw on the healing power of the divine. But before you learn how to use either option, let's first examine three typical problems that can occur in the practice of vastu living where either appeasement would work.

Three Problems

Conflicts between Two Elements

You can use appeasements to restore the harmony of a space after an element that belongs in one quadrant has been placed in a quadrant that belongs to another element. For example, your refrigerator, normally the heaviest object in the kitchen, rightfully belongs in the quadrant that belongs to the element of earth—the southwest of the kitchen. Instead the heavy refrigerator is in the northeast quadrant, which belongs to the element of water. Unfortunately, this is the only quadrant in your kitchen where the refrigerator fits; you cannot move it. But this arrangement violates an important vastu guideline: lightweight and low objects belong in the northeast of the kitchen so that the cosmic energies can flow into the room; bulky and tall objects belong in the southwest where they can trap these energies and keep them inside the kitchen. To restore harmony in your kitchen, you need to make two separate appeasements. You make one offering in the quadrant that belongs to the trespassed element: the element of water in the northeast, which has been disturbed by the presence of your heavy refrigerator, which should be the southwest with the element of earth. You make a second offering to the element of earth in the southwest, which is the correct location for the refrigerator. Both elements and their quadrants have been disturbed; both elements and quadrants are in disharmony; both elements and quadrants need to be appeased for you to rediscover inner calm.

Covered Sacred Center

You can use appeasements to restore the harmony when you are forced to cover the sacred center of a space and keep the spiritual energy from radiating through the area. In this situation, only one element and only one part of the space is affected—the element of space (ether) and the direct center of the affected area. You only need to make an appeasement to one element and its realm to restore the balance in the space and within your self.

Threatened Constitution

Finally, you can use appeasements when you have no choice but to sleep or work inside the quadrant that matches the element that governs your constitution and overstimulates it and jeopardizes your well-being. To restore your inner harmony, you make an appeasement to reduce the effect of the element in this quadrant that has disturbed your constitution.

GUIDE TO PLACEMENT OF APPEASEMENTS

TRESPASSING ELEMENT	VIOLATED ELEMENT	WHERE TO MAKE APPEASEMENTS	NORTHERN HEMISPHERE	SOUTHERN HEMISPHERE
Air	Space	In air quadrant and center space	Northwest and center	Southwest and center
Air	Water	In air and water quadrants	Northwest and northeast	Southwest and southeast
Air	Fire	In air and fire quadrants	Northwest and southeast	Southwest and northeast
Air	Earth	In air and earth quadrants	Northwest and southwest	Southwest and northwest

Fire	Space	In fire quadrant and center space	Southeast and center	Northeast and center
Fire	Air	In fire and air quadrants	Southeast and northwest	Northeast and southwest
Fire	Water	In fire and water quadrants	Southeast and northeast	Northeast and southeast
Fire	Earth	In fire and earth quadrants	Southeast and southwest	Northeast and northwest
Water	Space	In water quadrant and center space	Northeast and center	Southeast and center
Water	Air	In water and air quadrants	Northeast and northwest	Southeast and Southwest
Water	Fire	In water and fire quadrants	Northeast and southeast	Southeast and northeast
Water	Earth	In water and earth quadrants	Northeast and southwest	Southeast and northwest
Earth	Space	In earth quadrant and center space	Southwest and center	Northwest and center
Earth	Air	In earth and air quadrants	Southwest and northwest	Northwest and southwest
Earth	Fire	In earth and fire quadrants	Southwest and southeast	Northwest and northeast
Earth	Water	In earth and water quadrants	Southwest and northeast	Northwest and southeast

Using the Healing Power of Color

Review the Properties of Each Color

When taking advantage of the power of color, you use the properties associated with one of the seven colors in the visible spectrum or white to trigger a healing effect on your body. You simply introduce a therapeutic color or colors into your décor or place them discreetly into the areas in conflict. The vibrations attached to these colors neutralize the negative vibrations that are created when the elements in the space or within you are out of balance.

Whenever you have a problem in your practice of vastu living, just review this chart below, which lists the properties of the seven colors plus white, along with their corresponding nighttime colors (see chapter 4, "The Power of Color," for more details).

DAYTIME COLOR	PROPERTIES OF EACH COLOR	NIGHTTIME COLOR
Red	This color is the warmest of the seven colors and has the lowest frequency of vibration. Red is an effective energizer that motivates us, increases our vitality, and makes us passionate. Red endows us with power and courage that strengthen our conviction, confidence, and strong will. Red also reinforces loyalty. Too much red in a home or workspace can overstimulate us and make us anxious and aggressive.	Violet
ORANGE	Less warm than red and with a faster frequency of vibration, orange	Indigo

increases our sensitivity, generosity, and compassion. Orange builds up our energy and our zest for life. Too much orange in a home or workspace can overcharge us and make us tense, nervous, agitated.

YELLOW

Less warm than orange and with a faster frequency of vibration, yellow stimulates our mind and intellect so that we acquire wisdom and clarity, which increases our inner strength and self-esteem. Yellow also increases creativity and curiosity. Too much yellow can make us judgmental and turn us into overzealous perfectionists.

BLUE

GREEN

A cool color with an even faster frequency of vibration, green creates harmony, balance, and feelings of inner calm. Identified with nature, green has healing properties that are therapeutic and stimulate our growth. Green is associated with renewal. Too much green can create negative energy

GREEN

BLUE

Cooler than green and with a faster frequency of vibration, blue inspires harmony, serenity, and calms down

YELLOW

our emotions. Blue represents the cool side of nature, which we associate with the water and the sky. It quiets our mind so that we can think clearly. It promotes integrity, trust, and faith. Too much blue can make us feel cold and aloof.

INDIGO

Cooler than blue and with a faster frequency of vibration, indigo strengthens our intuition and imagination. Indigo helps us turn inward so that we can understand the true nature of our soul and our connection to all existence. Indigo creates an inner balance that is stabilizing and reinforcing. Too much indigo can consume our energy and make us tired.

ORANGE

VIOLET

Coolest of the seven colors and with the fastest vibration, violet inspires self-respect and enhances creativity and inspiration. More spiritually potent than indigo, violet enhances the effect of meditation. It provides us with inner strength and the wisdom to be mindful of our thoughts and actions. It guides us along the path to enlightenment. Too much violet

RED

can fill us with self-importance and disconnect us from the concerns of this world.

WHITE   The sum of all the seven colors, white brings peace and comfort. It purifies the body, the mind, and the soul.   **WHITE**

Assess the Problem's Effect on Your Well-Being

When you analyze your spiritual blueprints and discover that the organization of a space or part of a space violates the vastu guidelines or interferes with your constitution, you can restore harmony by taking advantage of the power of color. After you have identified the problem area, your next step is to analyze its effect on your well-being so that you can choose colors that provide the correct remedy. Does the vastu problem in the space make you feel overstimulated, agitated? Does it make you feel jittery and unsettled? Or is the space so empty of warmth and welcome that it makes you feel cold? Each response connects to one of the three doshas or constitutions—pitta (fire), vata (air), and kapha (water), respectively. This form of appeasement restores your harmony and the balance in your constitution as a way of resolving the vastu problem that exists in the space. You always use colors that reverse that all-important ayurveda principle of like increases like.

Pitta or Fire

When a space is overstimulating and intensifies the pitta or fire in your constitution or if you *are* a pitta and your pitta is aggravated and thrown out of balance, stay away from warm colors. To restore your inner harmony, make appeasements with the cooling colors of green, blue, indigo, and violet—or white, which is the sum of all colors in perfect proportion. Their calming properties douse the fire in the space and within you.

Vata or Air

When a room makes you jittery or fidgety and heightens the vata or air in your constitution, or again if you *are* a vata and your vata nature has gone over the top, don't select warm colors, such as reds, oranges, and yellows, for your appeasements. Warm colors stimulate your already active body and mind. Opt for cool colors that reinforce contemplation. Introduce green, blue, indigo, violet, or white into your décor. But please be careful: if you discover that you're developing a cold shoulder or cold heart, cut back on the blues.

Kapha or Water

When a personal environment is far too cool in the cold sense of this word and increases the kapha or water in your body, or if you *are* kapha and the element of water has weighed you down, choose reds, oranges, and yellows to restore your balance and inner harmony. The stimulating properties of warm colors provide you with fuel that can stimulate your mind in a deadened environment.

Color to the Rescue

Let's see how the power of color helped a graphic designer who was having trouble after she'd moved into her new work studio. After fifteen years of success, she was struggling with assignments and missing deadlines, and her career was heading unexpectedly south.

When I met the designer in her second-floor studio, she was a classic pitta, governed by the fire element. She was vibrant and self-assured despite her tailspinning career. Her worktable, which was against the east wall near the northeast corner, was neat and tidy. She faced east when she worked, but she was not absorbing the strength and inspiration that came with this direction. The northeast quadrant, with its spiritual power and cosmic energy, failed to calm her down or help her focus. A trespassing element had neutralized the beneficial properties that are associated with this quadrant.

My client's worktable was the culprit. Easily the heaviest object in her studio, the table was connected to the element of earth. It belonged in the southwest quadrant of her studio, not in the northeast, which belonged to the element of water. The conflict between two elements, water, which

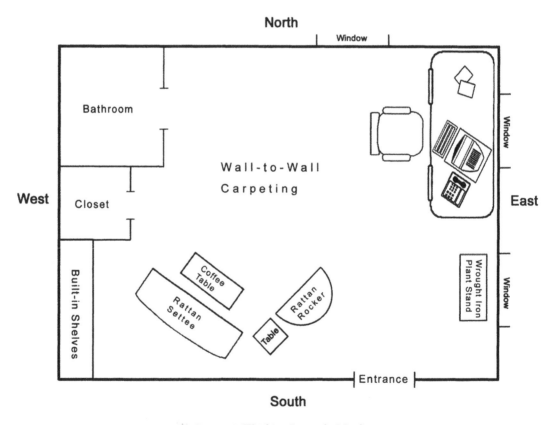

Figure 17: Weighing Down the Northeast

belongs in the northeast, and earth, which belongs in the southwest, had altered the studio's vibrations. These vibrations created a negative interaction with the vibrations connected to the designer, who spent so much time here.

The spacious studio had very little furniture: a lightweight rattan settee with matching coffee table and chair, a wrought-iron planter, and a set of built-in shelves. The designer could place her worktable in the southwest quadrant if she put the rattan furniture in another part of her studio. But the designer showed another quality of the pitta constitution when I suggested that she move around her furniture. She insisted that her worktable had to stay just where it was. She wanted to work in front of this eastern window, which had a view of the public garden adjacent to her building.

The garden and trees were lovely, and as an urbanite in New York City, she was indeed fortunate to have nature outside her window. The garden should have increased her well-being, but the conflict between the two elements of water and earth interfered with her harmony and disturbed her inner calm.

Instead we decided to use a clever mix of three daytime colors to resolve the conflict. She introduced blue and yellow into her environment, which allowed her to receive the benefits of each color. Yellow and blue have emotional properties during the daytime that are supported by each other during the night. Blue brings serenity and calms down fire, which is the element that governed her constitution; its complementary color is yellow. Yellow stimulates the mind and reinforces creativity; its complementary color is blue. She also introduced more white, with its properties of peace and serenity, into her studio décor.

The positive vibrations attached to these colors counteracted the negative vibrations that were triggered by the improper placement of the element of earth in the quadrant that belonged to the element of water. The properties associated with these colors, along with their vibrations, also interacted positively with the designer's vibrations so that she regained her inner harmony and could work creatively and efficiently once again.

And how did the designer actually incorporate these colors into her studio? To solve her problem, she needed to place these pacifying colors in the northeast quadrant, where the presence of her too heavy worktable had introduced the element of earth into the realm controlled by the element of water. She also needed to place the pacifying colors in the southwest quadrant to appease the element of earth, which had been introduced in the wrong part of her studio.

The designer bought two wool *dhurries* (area rugs) with blue and white geometric patterns, which she placed under her worktable and on the floor in the southwest quadrant. She put a yellow, blue, and white cushion on her work chair. She recovered the pillows on her rattan settee and rocking chair in a second fabric that was also yellow, blue, and white. She repainted the gray built-in shelves so that they were white. Finally, she hung a silk tapestry, which had a royal blue and vibrant yellow motif, on the north wall near her worktable.

Correcting a problem through the use of color can be dramatic and alter the visual impact of an environment, but it can also be subtle. You can use small paint swatches of your chosen daytime and nighttime colors and place them discreetly in the appropriate locations. They can be affixed to the underside of a piece of furniture or on the bottom of the wall behind an object in the troubled area. Success comes from introducing both the daytime color and the nighttime color into the part of the space that belongs to each element in the conflict.

Healing Power of the Divine

You can also calm down an overstimulated environment through the use of a second form of appeasement and select an object that represents the divine: a pacifying object from the world of nature or the celestial world of deities. The placement of these objects follows the same guidelines for the placement of healing colors.

Nature, in all its divine beauty and endless diversity, is calming, soothing, and an eternal source of inspiration. A beautiful plant or precious product created out of flora or fauna reminds us that the essence of all creation is part of the Supreme Creative Force. It is worthy of our love and respect.

When you surround yourself with reminders of your divinity, they serve as a powerful antidote to the disharmony that creates trouble in your space. Divine objects in your home or workspace act as balancing agents that restore your well-being and help you quiet yourself so that you can slowly realize inner peace.

If you choose to make an appeasement from the spiritual world, it can be an image of a deity or any symbol that is connected to your religion or any other religion that you respect. You can display a picture of the Buddha or a picture of His Holiness, the Dalai Lama, or one of the objects used in the practice of Buddhism: a prayer wheel, a small prayer flag, a *thangka* (religious wall hanging). You can honor a holy symbol related to Islam, Christianity, Judaism, or any faith that has special meaning to you.

Vastu living works for anyone living anywhere who chooses to embrace the principles of this science, but it is specifically based on the wisdom of the Vedas and Hinduism. Since every aspect of a Hindu god or goddess is symbolic and expresses the theories and beliefs of the Vedic philosophy and vastu, why not learn a bit about three popular deities? You may discover that a particular attribute or symbol appeals to your constitution or relates to an aspect of moral behavior that you would like to emulate. You can incorporate the deity or a symbol connected to the deity into your practice of vastu living.

Figure 18: Shiva

SHIVA

SHIVA, whose name means "auspiciousness," is the lord of destruction in the Hindu Trinity. Destruction, however, is part of the cycle of life and necessary for creation. Without destruction there can be no rebirth. And without the destruction of the body, there can be no liberation of the soul.

Shiva has a cobra coiled around his neck, which reminds us that this deity who has destroyed the evil within the snake can destroy evil thoughts and evil actions. Shiva also represents the everlasting bliss that emerges from the reunion of the soul with the Supreme Creative Force. In this context, the snake also represents time. Time has no meaning to Shiva. He is eternal. He reminds us to acquire the knowledge that makes us immune to the symbols attached to the snake. Only the body is bound by time—governed by the cycle of life and death. The ashes on Shiva's body represent the residue of the fire that consumes the body. The soul lives on.

Shiva, whose life reflects the path that leads to enlightenment, is the Supreme Teacher. If we follow his example, we discover the Truth. He is the lord of meditation, who has such perfect concentration that he can resist any distraction. His mind contains only pure thoughts. He is the lord of yogis, who has mastered control of his body. He has escaped the world of attachments that creates superficial needs, and he reminds us to let go of attachments as well. They interfere with our journey to self-discovery.

The crescent moon in Lord Shiva's hair represents the nectar of immortality that legend claims is kept inside Soma, the lord of the moon. Shiva's throat is blue from the deadly poison that he imbibed at the behest of deities. So Shiva is a compassionate god who reminds us to endure our own suffering and absorb the suffering of others. Shiva kept the poison in his throat. It never entered his stomach. The presence of the nectar and the poison within Shiva express the dualities that define our earthly existence, such as joy and sorrow, pleasure and pain, health and sickness. Shiva's calm demeanor reminds us that we should not let the dualities interfere with our inner harmony and inner peace.

Shiva's third eye in the middle of his forehead symbolizes wisdom. This eye looks out at the world and destroys ignorance and the evil that is caused by ignorance. The third eye reminds us to eliminate our own ignorance and the evil it inspires. Shiva's other eyes stand for love and justice. So Shiva is not only compassionate but also wise, loving, and just—four qualities that should exist within us all.

GANESHA

GANESHA, the benevolent elephant-headed deity, is the remover of obstacles and the god of auspicious new beginnings. He is worshiped first in any

Figure 19: Ganesha

Hindu ritual and before the start of any new undertaking so that his blessings will remove obstacles and assure success. Ganesha has the head and corpulent body of an elephant, but the elephant represents powerful symbols that explain why so many Hindus choose to pray to this deity above all others.

The elephant is considered the wisest animal in the jungle and it never forgets, which is borne out by its unchanging migratory path. An elephant will trample down any construction that gets in its way rather than alter its course. All these characteristics exist in Ganesha. His huge ears and head make him an intelligent listener who absorbs all the Vedic wisdom and retains it. His trunk has the power to uproot a tree and the sensitivity to pluck a single blade of grass. This level of discrimination makes it possible for Ganesha to remove all forms of obstacles that make us stray from our spiritual path.

Ganesha's power of discrimination is also expressed through his tusks, which represent the dualities that distract us in this world. One of his tusks is broken. This reminds us that we, too, must break through the world of dualities to move forward in our journey of true discovery and enlightenment.

Ganesha's large stomach accommodates his huge appetite, which symbolizes his ability to digest all of life's experiences. One of his four hands holds a rope, which he uses to draw us nearer and nearer to the truth. Another hand holds an ax, which he uses to sever the attachments that bind us to this material world. A third hand holds a sweet, which represents the joy that comes as we move toward enlightenment. The fourth hand is held in a *mudra* or pose that blesses us and protects us from the obstacles that get in our way.

And why is there a rat at the feet of Ganesha? The rat is his unlikely vehicle, which moves him around the celestial world. The rat, like Ganesha, is cunning and wise. It is also a nuisance that eats food, clothes—anything. The rat, which symbolizes gluttony, represents our own unending appetite for possessions and unnecessary desires. It symbolizes our ego, which eats up our good qualities and fills us with self-importance. But Ganesha has subjugated his rat, just as we must subjugate our ego and false desires. The rat looks up at

Ganesha. It will not nibble into the sweet that it holds in its paws until Ganesha grants his permission.

LAKSHMI

LAKSHMI is the goddess of wealth, who brings abundance to the world and helps sustain all creation. She is responsible for all the goodness that comes to

Figure 20: Lakshmi

us. But material wealth is misused unless we acquire the wisdom that leads to noble intentions and proper values. We need to use our wealth wisely; therefore, the wealth associated with Lakshmi includes inner wealth that leads to spiritual values.

We ask Lakshmi to give us the wisdom that we need on our spiritual journey. Her blessings endow us with self-control so that we can get beyond the superficial desires of the body that lead to acquisition and excess. Through the wealth that comes from Lakshmi, we provide healthy nourishment to our soul.

Hindu mythology claims that Lakshmi, who is the embodiment of beauty, first appeared when deities churned up the waters during a battle with demons over the control of the nectar of immortality. Lakshmi arose from a milky-white froth on a lotus throne. The lotus is a symbol of purity. Its roots grow in the mud at the bottom of the water, but its flower blooms above the surface in a display of beauty. The lotus symbolizes the soul that rises above the impurity in this world to move into the realm of enlightenment.

Images of Lakshmi show her sitting or standing in a lotus. Her four hands express the symbols attached to this deity. Her lower right hand releases gold coins, which represent the wealth that Lakshmi showers on all of us—physical wealth, mental wealth, and spiritual wealth. Her lower left hand is bent down in a mudra that offers protection. Her upper right hand holds a lotus. Because this lotus is on the right side of her body, it reminds us to fulfill our *dharma* or responsibilities. When we live a noble life on earth, we ultimately attain the goal of enlightenment, which is represented by the lotus held in her upper left hand.

Divine Resolution

Let's see how a graduate student used meaningful objects and colors to resolve conflicts in his small apartment. The student suffered from severe migraine headaches, his stomach was so acidic that he seemed to live on Tums, and he frequently broke out in hives. He is a pitta, and his fire dosha was in overdrive. He was clearly exhibiting the adverse effects of a lack of balance.

The graduate student lived alone in a small one-bedroom apartment. His bedroom was in the southeast quadrant, which is governed by the element of fire. It was an unhealthy location for his pitta constitution. His large bed spilled into the southeast quadrant of the room and covered the floor's sacred center (see Figure 21). This bedroom, where the graduate student spent every night, had disturbed his pitta's original balance. But the graduate student had to sleep in this room unless he wanted to doze on his sofa or inside his under-size bathtub.

A closet in the northwest, entrance in the northeast, radiator in the east,

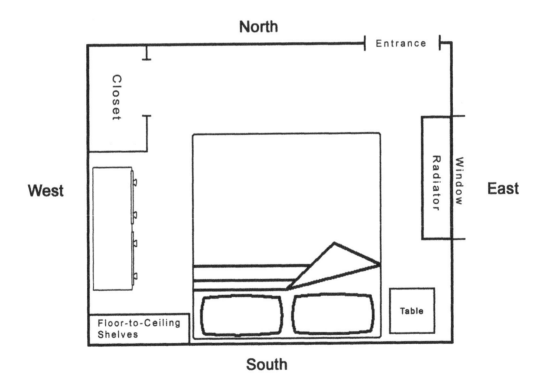

Figure 21: "Impossible" to Solve Problem

and built-in shelves in the southwest corner prevented the student from putting his bed in any other quadrant. He had to leave it against the south wall where it spilled into the problematic southeast quadrant of fire.

So the graduate student chose objects from nature and the world of the divine to soothe his overheated constitution. He bought a small aloe plant, which is medicinal and used as a cooling balm on burns and cuts, and placed it on his nightstand, which was close to the southeast corner. On the north wall overlooking his bed, he hung a series of three Indian miniature paintings of the elephant-headed deity, Ganesha.

The young student also draped a white Afghan made by his mother over the foot of his bed to placate the covered sacred center. These properly placed objects, which had special significance to him, restored the balance in his room. It would take time for his pitta to regain its original balance, but now he slept in a healthy environment that would no longer cause him harm.

Sincerity of Purpose

Vastu requires the same sincerity of purpose as yoga and meditation. If you can't master an *asana* (posture), awareness of both the error and the correct centering to achieve the posture keeps you striving to make the appropriate adjustments. In vastu living, if you can't change the location of your bed or stove, at least do your best to make sincere appeasements and to celebrate whatever aspects are right about your space. And some aspects will be right. I've never seen a home or workspace that is 100 percent wrong.

Ultimately, please understand that your offering or appeasement is your acknowledgment of the importance of universal harmony. It expresses and affirms your belief that harmony must prevail on earth, within your home and your workspace, and within your own physical form—the three sheathes that surround your unique soul. When you acknowledge the importance of living in harmony and balance, you move a gigantic step forward on your path to spiritual growth and self-discovery. Your symbolic appeasements aren't merely gestures, but sincere acts that carry deep significance.

For this reason, you must always take care to choose colors and objects from the world of nature or the heavenly realm of deities that have a profoundly positive effect on you or they won't balance the negative energies that have disturbed your well-being. Every appeasement must connect to you—mentally, emotionally, and spiritually. Only then can it restore your inner harmony. A successful appeasement always connects to your soul.

6

The Peaceful Zone of Tranquility

*

The zone of tranquility is a place of quiet beauty that *you* create to celebrate nature and your unique identity. It is a personalized place that displays a few objects that are filled with meaning. Your choices can symbolize an aspect of the divine or it can contain photos of people whom you cherish or a few collected mementos that remind you of significant moments in your life. Your zone of tranquility also honors something from nature—a lovely plant, dried flowers, a piece of wood, a terra-cotta tile, antique lace or silk, a collection of stones or seashells, a jute basket filled with pinecones—anything from the world of nature.

Your zone of tranquility can be an actual room in your home and workplace, or your zone can be so small that it takes up no more than a few inches and sits on top of a small table, a portion of a windowsill, or right on the floor inside a room that serves another function. Size has no bearing on the ability of your display to enrich the quality of your life, but its location is extremely important. Your zone of tranquility should always be associated with the northeast quadrant, whether it is in the northeast quadrant of the structure or in the northeast quadrant inside an enclosed space.

The northeast, which is the gateway to the gods, belongs to the element of water, with its properties of serenity, reflection, and introspection. The cosmic energy and spiritual power, two gifts that flow into this quadrant, also bless your zone of tranquility and enhance its power to improve your well-being. In the Southern Hemisphere, your zone of tranquility should be placed in the south-east quadrant, which belongs to the element of water in this part of the world.

Every zone of tranquility must be created with the utmost care so that it captures your attention and connects to you—immediately. It should be so inviting that you are compelled to stare into it and, in the process, connect to your vital essence, which is the core of your being and too easily neglected in the maddening rush of each day. This is the purpose behind the zone of tran-quility. While vastu environments restore and maintain the original harmony

Figure 22: Small Zone of Tranquility inside a Room

of the elements that exist within the environment and inside the body, your zone of tranquility reconnects you to your inner essence, which is formless and eternal—your source of pure energy that radiates unconditional love.

THE MESSAGE OF THE ZONE OF TRANQUILITY

Your zone of tranquility is your three-dimensional mandala or visual aid that helps you escape the material world. It leads you into the realm of self-knowledge, a term that we should reassemble to understand its importance—knowledge of the self. As you focus on your zone of tranquility, you can slowly learn to meditate: an invaluable practice that takes time to master, but delivers benefits even as you develop the technique. You train your mind to concentrate just on your breathing instead of the million thoughts that rattle around inside your head.

You forget about these thoughts as you feel the calming rhythm of your inhalation and exhalation and hear the sound of your breath as it moves in and out of your body. Your mind becomes aware of your diaphragm as it expands and contracts in consonance with the rhythm of your breathing. You feel an increase in positive energy as if it enters your body with each breath. You feel your inner turbulence, which you experience as tension and stress, seep out with each exhalation.

You relax, completely relax, and can reach that point of stillness where you forget all about your physical body. You can turn inward and connect to your self—that sacred part of you that you can neither see nor feel with your hands. In this moment of deep stillness and inwardness, you can hear your spirit's life affirming message. Your soul or spirit or essence is divine and expresses the Truth. This sheltered part of you, which is the animating principle that gives life to your physical body, is eternal and connected to the Supreme Creative Force. Only your body vanishes with death.

Reaching this level of self-discovery or self-awareness is the ultimate objective behind the zone of tranquility. The zone is our oasis where we take a quick break to unwind and rejuvenate during a busy day. It is our spiritual retreat where we try to spend at least fifteen uninterrupted minutes to turn inward and gather the positive strength that comes when we shed our ego and realize the true nature of the self.

We realize why we should believe the phrase "listen to your inner voice." Our soul should guide us through our life, not the transitory issues connected to self-importance and our ego that manipulate so many of us. Our soul teaches us the power of love and respect. When we escape our ego and extend love to the self and all existence, our life is transformed. We escape the world of negativity and negative thoughts.

If we listen to our inner voice, it protects us from becoming consumed by problems at work or at home that cause so much stress. These problems, no matter how severe they appear to us, are temporary. They are connected to the ego and have nothing to do with our essence. Yet we all let these problems balloon way out of proportion.

When we come to understand that it is our soul that defines us, we see the irrelevance of our title at work, the irrelevance of the address of our home and the name on the label of our possessions. All this connects to the ego and the material world. All this is temporary and fleeting. None of it has any value. We learn instead to focus on the issues of life that connect to our essence. We let our soul guide us so that our life is filled with meaning. We cultivate compassion, forgiveness, tolerance, and most importantly, respect and love for all existence. We understand that everything is divine. Everything is connected to the Supreme Creative Force.

If you can carry this Truth with you even when you are far from your zone of tranquility, you feel a positive change in the quality of your life. You have redefined your priorities. You are no longer vulnerable to the pressures that turn into tension and stress. You improve your physical and mental well-being and find that you live with inner peace and inner awareness. And this inner peace and inner awareness does not go away.

7

Southern Hemisphere

✻

The text of this book is written for the Northern Hemisphere. If you live in the Southern Hemisphere, you need to make some adjustments to the vastu living guidelines to reflect the climatic changes that occur below the equator and to maintain the logic of this spiritual science.

✻ POINT 1: SWAP FOUR ELEMENTS

First, you need to shift the location of four of the five basic elements on the spiritual blueprint to reflect the effect of the earth's rotation below the equator. The element of space doesn't change. It remains in the center of every enclosed space.

When you shift these four elements, you also shift their properties and their deities. They connect to the element, not to the location, and obviously their properties are constant: they never change. Air, which is governed by Vayu, always has the properties of movement and indecision; fire, which is governed by Agni, always has the properties of heat and incandescence; water,

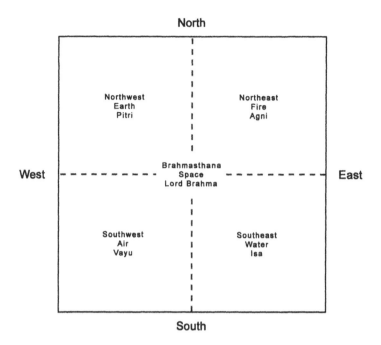

Vastu Living Adjustments for the Southern Hemisphere

which is governed by Isa, always has the properties of serenity and contemplation; and earth, which is governed by Pitri, always has the properties of heaviness and strength. So, please remember, the shift of the elements also shifts their properties and deities with them.

✳ POINT 2: THE CARDINAL DIRECTIONS

The properties of the cardinal directions (north, east, south, west) remain the same. The east is still connected to the sun and inspiration; the north is connected to wealth, indulgence, and health; the west is connected to darkness and the unknown; and the south is connected to judgment and death.

POINT 3: THE FLOW OF COSMIC ENERGY AND SPIRITUAL POWER

The cosmic energy and spiritual power always enter the quadrant that belongs to the element of water, which is the northeast in the Northern Hemisphere or the southeast in the Southern Hemisphere. Irrespective of its location, the quadrant that belongs to water is always called the gateway to the gods.

In the Southern Hemisphere, the beneficial gifts of the gods come into the southeast quadrant and flow in a wide arc to the northwest quadrant, which belongs to the element of earth in this hemisphere. Again, the location has changed, but the movement of the cosmic energy and spiritual power still flows from the element of water to the element of earth.

POINT 4: OPEN AND AIRY; HEAVY AND DENSE

This swap of four of the basic elements and the change in direction of the movement of cosmic energy and spiritual power require one final adjustment. In the Southern Hemisphere, you want to place lightweight and delicate furnishings in the south and the west so that you don't obstruct the flow of the gifts of the gods. Conversely, you want to put heavy, bulky furnishings in the north and the east to create barriers that trap these gifts and keep them in the room.

8

Final Advice Before You Begin

✳

Please understand that the creation of a vastu living space takes time. Vastu is not a quick fix, and hurried decisions often work against you and the creation of harmony and balance. Just as it takes a lasting commitment to get a neglected body into good physical condition, it takes a lasting commitment to get an imperfect space into vastu living condition. So, please think carefully and methodically about the decisions that govern every aspect of the design of your home and workspace so that your personal spaces fit you properly. They should honor your constitution or dosha and honor the law of nature so that they bring harmony to your soul.

✳ CLAIM YOUR SPACE

So often we live or work in a space and never claim it as our own. The rooms inside the house or apartment or the cubicle or office are just places where we happen to live and work and spend a lot of time. This attitude has broad implications that affect our well-being. When we live in an apartment or house and never embrace it as our own personal space, it cannot become our home. This is also true with our workspace.

Impersonal environments remain cold and unfriendly when you refuse to see them as an extension of your self. As a consequence, you do nothing to connect them to your identity, and this seals their fate: your home and workspace always feel uncomfortable. You view them as places of transition as your mind conjures up some great, unknown future place or recollects some dear lost place that is related to your past. You behave as if your current home or workplace is a stopover where you are momentarily stuck on your way to somewhere else. Unfortunately, extremely long moments are often spent in this unreal frame of mind.

I have worked with many people who have recently moved into a new home. They contact me because they feel out of sorts and totally out of place. They liked the house or apartment when they bought it or signed the lease, but once they move into the new accommodations, they become miserable. Almost all these clients feel better when they learn to let go of their attachment to their old space so that they can welcome the new house or apartment as their home. This is also true with people when they change their workspace—even when the change is made within the company and they stay inside the same building.

The failure to embrace a physical environment as your own home or workspace creates the shabby space that you imagine in your mind. You move into a house or apartment and have no interest or desire to organize it. You take forever to unpack your possessions or invent endless excuses for never putting things away. You tell yourself that you're going to give some of your stuff to a secondhand store or you're going to have your rugs cleaned, curtains rehemmed. You invent an excuse for every new pile of belongings and get more depressed as the clutter mounts—and during this time, you blame your feelings on the space.

If you don't connect to your home and workspace, you won't get any joy out of cleaning them either. Everything associated with the maintenance of these spaces turns into a chore, and you put off each chore until the last possible moment or forever. On some deep level, this is exactly the way that many people treat their body. They let themselves get out of shape and like themselves less and less. Still, they offer a million reasons why they can't reverse this process with a positive decision that could boost their self-esteem and their well-being—not to mention show love and respect for their own soul.

The building in which you live or work is also a living entity that is deserving of your love and respect. It is so important to remember that when we take good care of our home and our workspace, they take good care of us. When you claim your home and workspace as your own special spaces, you honor your self or your soul. It is at this point—when your attitude changes—that you find pleasure when you are inside your home and your workspace. You can even enjoy the *process* of keeping your home and workspace organized, clean, livable—living expressions of your self.

✳ GUIDELINES, NOT RULES

Guidelines are not the same as rules, which are usually rigid and inflexible. Vastu living is not about rigidity. Its guidelines are not the Ten Commandments inscribed in stone. Vastu guidelines to harmony and balance are not intended to put a stranglehold on artistic freedom. A vastu building should express the Vedic philosophy and its principles. This means that it should express its own nature and characteristics that add to the world's diversity. If vastu had hard-and-fast rules, every vastu building would look alike. There would be an absence of artistic freedom and an absence of creativity.

If you look at India's architectural legacy, which many consider unrivaled in the world, you see an astonishing diversity. Much of India's great architecture was built according to vastu. The majority of its historic Hindu temples, Hindu palaces, Hindu forts, and even many of the subcontinent's stunning old cities are vastu-correct. They adhere to the vastu guidelines. Yet every one of these monuments is distinct and contributes to India's remarkable display of aesthetic virtuosity. Each monument gives free range to artistic creativity. Each building is beautiful—an expression of the elegant rhythm and proportion that defines vastu.

☀ NOT AN ALL-OR-NOTHING SCIENCE

Hindu temples, which are built to follow the vastu guidelines, are homes for the gods and should exhibit perfection. The gods deserve nothing less. But we are mortals and imperfect. This distinction will probably play out in your practice of vastu living. Few of us are able to follow all the vastu guidelines and create a home and workspace that are 100 percent as per vastu.

Adhering to the proper placement of each of the five elements on the property, inside the building, and inside each room is often impossible. You may rent an apartment or own a condominium or cooperative inside a multistory high-rise. Your kitchen may be in the northwest quadrant of air and not in the southeast quadrant of fire. But as I've mentioned, few of us are able or even inclined to rip out the kitchen and its appliances to relocate them in another part of our home. Our landlord will boot us out if we are tenants and try to make an improperly located kitchen vastu-correct.

Creating a 100 percent vastu-correct space may even be difficult with an undeveloped site for the home or workplace. It's hard to find the perfect property, where every aspect of the land conforms to the vastu guidelines, your budget, and other requirements, such as location and size. You may find a suitable piece of land, but the southwest and not the northeast is the lowest quadrant on the property. Vastu compliance should never be your reason to reject a site. Your particular requirements should govern the selection of the property for your home or workplace.

So let this be one of your most important vastu guidelines: as long as you can make your home and workspace at least 51 percent vastu-correct, you are on the winning side. Your home and workspace will increase the well-being of your body, mind, and soul.

✳ Not a Quick Fix

Please don't think that, the minute you swap your bedroom with the kid's bedroom or shuffle around furniture and make changes in your décor, you will feel a powerful transformation change your life. Vastu doesn't work that way. It is not a magic bullet; nor does it operate with the speed of a bullet.

Once you establish harmony and balance in your environments, it takes time for the healthy vibrations in your space that now mesh with your own vibrations to restore your body, mind, and soul to good health. Think of it this way: you have been damaging your body and inner being over an extended time. Healing takes time to undo the damage, especially when you follow natural healing. So before you can reap all the benefits of vastu living, your entire system needs to detoxify.

You may also discover that your constitution or dosha requires special attention in your practice of vastu living. You need to listen carefully to your body signals to determine if the changes in your environment are working. You may need to make some adjustments or do some fine-tuning over time.

When you choose to practice vastu living, you initiate a journey to self-discovery that continues well after your home and workspace are in harmony and in balance with your self and your constitution. Once you have increased your level of tranquility so that you calm down, relax, and de-stress, try to continue your journey and aim for that point of stillness that lets you turn inward. Try to learn to commune with your soul, which is a part of the Supreme Creative Force. From here, transformation turns into transcendence. You move beyond the universe into the world of enlightenment.

✳ THINK CAREFULLY BEFORE YOU BEGIN

Before you start to move furniture around in your workspace or home and change the accents in your décor, carefully work out your plans in advance. Be certain that your changes not only honor the vastu principles and guidelines but also appeal to your eyes and soul. Far too often, hasty decisions, especially in your décor, are made without consideration for aesthetics. So when you think about reorganizing and redecorating, keep in mind the function of each space and the aesthetic "look" that you want to flow through each area.

Throughout section two, "The Welcoming Home," and section three, "The Welcoming Workspace," I provide design tips that may help you achieve the right effect in your home or workspace and each area within the space. But in general, you should view this need to create a visually appealing aesthetic as an extension of the law of nature, which reminds us that everything is interconnected. Vastu living conveys this principle from room to room and space to space within each environment.

✳ BE CAREFUL WITH RENOVATIONS AND ALTERATIONS

If you decide to make structural changes to your home or workspace, please remember that changes to a structure upset the preexisting vibrations. If you add a room or an extension to your home, this addition will create a new set of vibrations. You want these vibrations to be healthy and not a source of harm. So please plan changes so that they observe the three vastu principles: honoring the proper placement of the five basic elements, respecting nature, and celebrating your unique individuality.

For example, have you decided to erect a new wall that blocks the northeast or are you removing a door or window that was close to the northeast corner? You may want to modify your design so that your new space continues to draw in the positive energy that should flow into this spiritually powerful quadrant. The change in your design then rewards you with healthy benefits.

Sometimes structural changes can improve the harmony within an environment. If you are creating a big room out of many small rooms, this will allow for an easier flow of positive energy throughout your space. Or if you plan to add a sunroom in the northeast, this will increase the flow of positive cosmic energy and the beneficial sun rays into your personal environment. Your new sunroom in the northeast becomes a healthy addition. Conversely, be cautious with additions in the southwest. If you add an open and airy room, the cosmic energy and spiritual power, which should be trapped inside a space, will have an easy exit and float right through your home to somewhere else.

Also be careful when you shift around your furniture in an enclosed space. Try to remember that the north and east of each area should be relatively open and airy. You want to receive the healthy sun rays and you want the positive energy to move in its arc to the obstructing southwest quadrant of the space. For example, you don't want to place a towering china cabinet, even if it's a gorgeous piece of furniture, in your dining room against the north or the east wall. It will block the positive energies or sun rays. Perhaps you can shift your dining-room table toward the east and make room for the china cabinet against the western or the southern wall, where it conforms to the vastu guidelines and doesn't destroy the positive vibrations that should exist in every space.

When you follow the vastu guideline of lightweight or delicate furnishings in the north and east quadrants and heavy or tall furnishings in the south and west quadrants, you discover a special quality about vastu and India's design sensibility. We, in the West, tend to favor a symmetrical arrangement of furnishings. We often align a sofa so that it's in the absolute center of a wall, whether we push the sofa close to the wall or move the sofa out into the room.

Or we divide up the room's heavy furniture and arrange it so that it is evenly dispersed in the north, the south, the east, and the west.

But when you follow the lightweight-vs.-heavy furnishings guideline, an appealing asymmetry defines your home and workspace. This asymmetry follows the law of nature, which rarely exhibits perfect symmetry. Study a flower or a leaf or a stone, or just study your face in a mirror. It is not symmetric. When we organize a room to allow for airiness in the north and the east and place our heavier furniture and tall plants, such as indoor palms, in the south and the west, we introduce a design that appeals to us immediately. We let go of symmetry and embrace this new approach that mirrors the world of nature. This design aesthetic is another effective way to honor nature inside your home or workspace.

INCORPORATE VASTU LIVING INTO YOUR MOVE

How many times have you moved from one place to another and allowed exhaustion or confusion to dictate the *temporary* placement of occasional pieces of your furniture or heavy objects in an empty spot in a room in your new home or workspace? At the time, you had every intention of putting this chair or table or heavy ceramic object somewhere else, but to this day it sits where it was initially placed on moving day.

A *temporary* placement can create a problem with your practice of vastu living. It may go against an important guideline and create negative vibrations and disharmony in your personal environment. In addition, removing the object, years later, could mean the reorganization of a lot more than one piece of furniture.

So before you pile your possessions or let someone else pile your possessions into the moving van, try to map out the organization of your furnishings in each new room. Creating a spiritual blueprint for each room before the move decreases the stress that occurs on moving day and also minimizes the lugging and lifting that continues long after the movers have left. By determining the location for big, bulky furniture or heavy, fragile items in particular, you simplify your move and your practice of vastu living.

PLEASE REMEMBER . . .

Readers who live in the Southern Hemisphere should follow this spiritual blueprint, which shows the effect of the earth's rotation below the equator on your practice of vastu living. Four of the five basic elements, along with their properties, assume different locations, and the guidelines governing the placement of lightweight and heavy furnishings alter. Place your lightweight furnishings in the south and the west; place your heavy and tall furnishings in the north and the east (see chapter 7, "The Southern Hemisphere").

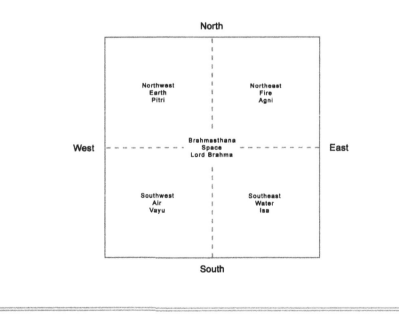

Now you are ready to let vastu living into your personal world. Take out your set of spiritual blueprints. And as you read each chapter in section two, "The Welcoming Home," and section three, "The Welcoming Workplace," try your best to follow the vastu guidelines so that harmony flows through your environments and you center your self and honor your soul.

The Welcoming Home

Your vastu living home welcomes you with gentle warmth that touches all your senses, even your sixth sense, which some say connects to the inner voice that belongs to your soul. Nothing is haphazard about the décor in your vastu home and the arrangement of each space. Every room or area honors the five basic elements, shows respect for nature, and unabashedly celebrates the unique identity of everyone who lives here.

Your home, which becomes a conscientious expression of the three vastu principles, achieves a level of comfort that puts everyone at ease. Your mind unwinds even when you are engaged in activities. Your body feels calm even when it's in motion. This is because you are surrounded by harmony, not chaos; order, not disorder; mindfulness, not emptiness. You rediscover inner peace inside your vastu living home. It becomes the temple that honors your soul.

9

Decorating for Your Soul

✳

Rhythms regulate the universe. They even govern the proper functioning of your body. Consider the rhythm of your breath, pulse, heartbeat, or the continuing cycles attached to digestion, sleep, or the processes that create your bodily secretions. Think of how you respond to the sun's daily journey, the waxing and waning of the moon, the arrival of each new season. Think of how you react to the rhythms that flow through music. You may clap your hands, tap your feet, or start to dance.

When a rhythmic pattern is disrupted—say, for example, the sun fails to shine for a number of days, with a gloomy sky—it can darken your mood and disturb your well-being. If your heartbeat suddenly races, you may feel it and suffer a pang of anxiety. Vastu understands the importance of rhythm, and in your practice, you consciously establish rhythms in your décor where they increase the flow of harmony around and within you.

Creating Rhythms through the Three Vastu Principles

When you let the three vastu principles guide your decisions in the arrangement of your furnishings, you set in motion three important rhythms that move from corner to corner and from room to room. The assigned location of the five basic elements encourages the placement of delicate and lightweight furnishings in the north and the east, bulky, tall furnishings in the south and the west, and a protected sacred center, which remains uncovered and unburdened by weight. This unchanging orientation of the elements creates a spatial rhythm that flows through your home. The other two principles of vastu, which honor nature and celebrate your individuality, add their own repeating rhythms.

These three rhythms create cohesion in your home and remind you of the interconnectedness and divinity that bind together all creation. Each room and area contributes to the whole in the same way that each note contributes to the musical scale and each instrument contributes to the symphony. The symphony played inside your vastu living home commemorates the principles of vastu.

Rhythm in Color

The selective use of color establishes another rhythm that you carry from room to room in your vastu living home. First, you select a few colors that are healthy for you (refer to the color chart in chapter 5, "Resolving Conflicts in Your Home and Workplace"), and then you work them into various aspects of each room's décor. The presence of these colors can be subtle and understated. They can appear quietly in the pattern of the fabric on the covers of throw cushions that line the back of your sofa. They can show up in the table linen in your dining room. They can repeat again in the wallpaper in your bedroom or on your shower curtain in the bathroom. Or the colors can make bold statements that grab your attention. A creamy white room frames a forest green wall. A collection of dark blue glass adds a dramatic accent to a trio of shelves. Rhythm expressed through color creates a continuum that turns your individual rooms into a harmonious and interconnected environment.

Rhythm through the Dualities

Light and Dark

The vastu living interior also introduces rhythm by honoring the dualities that govern the physical world of nature, especially the dualities attached to light and dark and their metaphysical equivalent of enlightenment and ignorance, which govern the world of moral order. You play with light and shadow inside your home through the use of candles, dimmer switches on electrical lighting, and through your choices in window treatments.

Blinds and drapes can moderate the sun's presence inside your home so that you receive the energizing sun of the morning and block out the harmful rays that arrive by noon. You can manipulate sunlight so that it creates a bright path that subtly shifts across the floor and highlights different objects and even changes their appearance throughout the day. Bright light accentuates the edges of an object; muted light softens them.

Your interior lighting can duplicate these same effects and mirror the qualities and properties that you associate with the light of day and the dark of night. Flickering flames in your fireplace or from candles in sconces on your walls create a lovely dance of shadows. This interplay between light and dark appeals to your soul. You become absorbed in this duality, which is also expressed in the flickering stars that brighten the sky at night. The flames and the stars inspire serenity and calm. You feel that all is well with your world.

Old and New

Another important duality that you can acknowledge inside your home connects to the rhythm of life: birth and death, new and old. You can honor the cycle of earthly existence with a worn-out object that you may be inclined to discard, injecting it instead with new life by recycling it. An old family chair that is too rickety to bear even the weight of a small child can become an attractive base for a display of pictures that chronicles the stages of your life. You can mix new and old together: a modern abstract painting can occupy center stage in a display of nineteenth-century artwork; a futuristic table with minimalist lines can show off an old, weathered box filled with bits of broken tile.

Décor Follows Function

The décor in your vastu living home always complements the room's function. So think about the activities that take place inside a room before you make changes that can alter its mood or ambience. Ask yourself, is this room a public space where we spend time with our guests, is it a center for quiet activities, or is it a private space? A décor that is at odds with a room's function is like a video with a mismatched sound track. Just imagine a home study that has a busy pattern in the wallpaper and chairs that are so formal that your body can't relax. Your eyes won't focus on what you are trying to do; your body's discomfort breaks your concentration. You may be sitting in your study, but you're unable to study anything. The study's ambience collides with function. A lack of harmony spills onto you. You don't feel at ease inside this space.

Suggestion 1
Create the Appropriate Ambience

Public space or room? Think light, cheery, or comfortable.

Quiet space or room? Think understated and subdued.

Private space or room? Think intimate and personal.

Then let the correct ambience flow through the entire room or space.

✳ GUIDELINES AND TIPS

Draw in the Cosmic Energy and Spiritual Power

Take out your spiritual blueprints, walk through your entire home, and examine the layout of your furnishings. Check to see if the north, the northeast, and the east of each space are relatively open and airy so that you receive the maximum benefits of the cosmic energy and spiritual power, which come into each northeast quadrant. On the appropriate blueprint mark with a red pencil any trespassing heavy or bulky furniture that violates this principle. These big items belong in the west, the southwest, and the south. Ignore stray side tables or small accessories that may connect to these large pieces; they will not cause trouble in the southwest. (If you live in the Southern Hemisphere, follow the spiritual blueprint on page 116, which shows the correct location of the elements below the equator.)

When you follow this guideline, your furnishings become your ally. They allow the cosmic energy and spiritual power to flow, unobstructed, from the northeast to the southwest, where your heavy furnishings act as barriers that keep these gifts from slipping away. The cosmic energy and spiritual power can then circulate around the space.

This arrangement of furnishings inside a space or room also establishes an asymmetry, which repeats from room to room. This aesthetic sensibility is extremely appealing to your spirit and your body. Asymmetry flows through nature. Examine a leaf, a seashell, your two feet. You relate, if only subconsciously, to this vastu theory of design. Asymmetry feels natural, whereas symmetry feels forced and contrived (see Figure 25).

Northeast Blocked? Southwest Open?

Many of your rooms may not have windows or a door in the northeast to let in the cosmic energy and spiritual power, or your rooms may have windows or a door in the southwest that allows these positive forces to escape. Still, symbolically honor these gifts from the gods. While you may not be able to receive their benefits in a particular space, you should appease the deities for this "fault" in the physical structure and still orient the furniture according to Suggestion 2, below.

Add Water in the Northeast

You can heighten the positive effect of the cosmic energy and spiritual power by reinforcing the element of water in the northeast and the element of earth in the southwest in a room or enclosed space. Consider placing a low, terra-cotta vase filled with water and floating flower petals or a small fountain where water splashes onto small pebbles in the northeast quadrant. These objects represent the element of water, which rules over this quadrant, and help retain these gifts from the gods. The use of water can also be incorporated into any appeasement that is offered to this element (see Figure 23).

Add Weight to the Southwest

If money permits, consider the construction of an elevated platform in the southwest quadrant of a room and cover it with contrasting flooring to create an aesthetic statement that draws your attention. The elevation adds height and weight, which are properties of the element of earth. The elevation also helps to hold in the cosmic energy and spiritual power.

SUGGESTION 2
RESPECT THE GIFTS
FROM THE GODS

To welcome the cosmic energy into your personal environments, place lightweight, low, and delicate furniture in the north, the northeast, and the east of each room so that these areas are relatively airy and open. Place heavy, tall, and bulky furniture in the south, the southwest, and the west of each room to create a relatively dense barrier to hold in this healthy energy.

Figure 23: Introducing Water into the Northeast

This dramatic change in a room can also be an appeasement to restore harmony in a space that has doors and windows in the southwest (see Figure 24).

Honor the Sacred Center

Please try hard to keep the center of your rooms open and clear of furniture. This is the sacred realm of the element of space and Brahma, the lord of creation, who

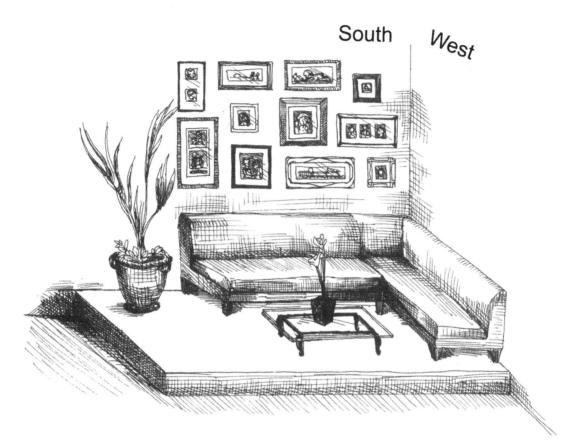

Figure 24: Dramatic Southwest Elevation

releases spiritual vibrations that circulate throughout the room. These positive vibrations increase your well-being and shower you with blessings.

Avoid Clutter

Let the openness in the north and the east and the center of a space act as a positive reminder to keep things simple. Clutter works against the vastu living

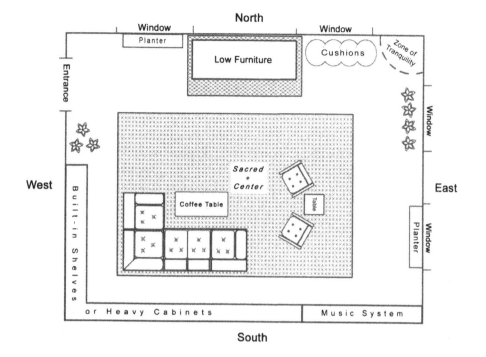

Figure 25: Correct Furniture Placement in the Vastu Living Space

SUGGESTION 3
LESS IS MORE

Don't overload a room or space with too much furniture and too many objects. You want the divine message of unconditional love and respect to shine through your décor.

décor. Your eyes get entangled in a room that has too much stuff. You are unable to see and feel the lovely rhythms contributing to the vastu principles that celebrate your connection to nature and your unique identity. When you sit in a vastu space, you want the significance of these principles to help you free your mind of the mental and emotional clutter that is associated with the ego and its needs, which create stress and tension. Your environment should not distract you from the quiet message that flows through your home and honors your all-important soul and its connection to all existence and the Supreme Creative Force.

SUGGESTION 4
DON'T BE UP
AGAINST THE WALL

Protect the positive vibrations that emanate from your soul. Remember to keep all the seating areas and beds inside your home four healthy inches away from a wall.

Protect Your Positive Vibrations

Scientists have discovered through sophisticated photographic studies that your energy produces an aura or halo around your body. When this aura is disturbed, it upsets your positive vibrations and inner harmony. So please don't interfere with your aura and consequently your well-being. Try to keep beds, chairs, sofas—any furniture in which you sit or recline—about four inches from the wall.

Circular or Square-Based Furniture

Your vastu living décor can include square or circular shapes. But each shape has a different influence on your emotional and physical well-being. When you sit at a square or square-based table (such as a rectangle), its shape conforms to the celestial world and the human body. The energy of the square is static and unmoving. Your body tends to relax when you sit at a square dining table. You are more inclined to eat slowly and enjoy your time sitting at the table.

When you sit at a circular or circle-based shape (such as an oval), its energy is dynamic. The circle is in constant motion and mirrors the properties of a wheel. The circular shape is conducive to animation, including quick thoughts and quick actions. If you eat at a circular table, you tend to eat quickly and the conversation can be more spirited and lively. So when you choose your dining tables, in particular, please keep these properties in mind. If you chose a circular table, try not to gulp down your food in the rush to finish your meal. Your digestive system will thank you when your food is thoroughly chewed and mixed with important enzymes before it is swallowed.

Guidelines for Specific Furnishings

Window Treatments

Attractive window treatments commonly used in India and other parts of Asia are now available in the West. Created from natural fibers, not synthetics, these designs are ideal choices for the vastu living home. You can choose from vertical or roll-up blinds and shades that use wood, reeds, or grass instead of plastic slats. Many grass blinds are often bordered or completely lined in delightful fabrics. You can also find natural-fabric shades that hang flat inside the window frame and create a tapestry-like effect. If you have windows in the south and the west of a room, heavy versions of these natural blinds or shades can help retain the cosmic energy and spiritual power that might otherwise rush out of the southwest quadrant.

If you prefer curtains or drapes, why not layer them so that you can regulate the intensity of the sunlight that enters the room? A sheer underpanel of organdy lace or voile, which acts like a filter, softens the light when your drapes are open. Closed drapes offer complete privacy and a peaceful ambience. Again, choose natural fabrics, such as raw silk or cotton or linen.

Floor Coverings

When you consider floor coverings, try to avoid "fake" and go organic. A jute rug, wool kilim, cotton dhurrie, or silk carpet that sits on top of a wood or tile floor is so much more appealing than wall-to-wall carpeting, which is often created out of synthetic fibers. Area rugs can accentuate specific room areas by creating a space within a space. They add color and texture, which enhances your décor. Area rugs are also practical. You can send them out for a good cleaning or just shake them outside to eliminate surface dirt and dust or occasionally hang them on a railing or fence or clothesline to eliminate musty odors. Even if you live in an apartment that comes with wall-to-wall carpeting, consider buying inexpensive area rugs or mats to add nature and warmth to your space.

Book and Music Collections

If you have shelves filled with books or racks stacked with CDs, DVDs, tapes, or a grand record collection of old LPs, 78s or 45s, try to organize them in an identifiable order, either by subject or alphabetically. These collections typically draw the attention of your guests. Books or CDs that are placed helter-skelter discourage anyone from picking out a book and leafing through its pages or looking at a back of a CD. You inadvertently deprive guests from an acceptable form of snooping. By sharing your books and musical or video tastes with your guests, they may discover mutual interests or something new that can broaden their horizon. Music and books are remarkable cultural unifiers.

Also try not to use empty space above books or collections of music as another set of shelves for keys, spare change, or restaurant flyers. Also avoid creating barriers near the front edge of your shelves. Fragile glass felines grouped near the edge of a shelf are land mines that can even deter you from grabbing a book or recording that brings you pleasure.

Musical Instruments

What would we do without musical instruments? An instrument, including the human voice, fills us with joy, brings us to tears, and leads us to an inner calm where the mind stays focused in the moment. Music can bring us to that point of stillness where we can escape the turmoil that often robs us of our harmony and well-being. Studies have shown that plants thrive in a home that plays classical music. Pregnant women insist that soothing music appeals to their baby in the womb.

In many religions, such as Hinduism and Buddhism, sound or vibration is considered the primordial force that initiated creation. The sound is identified with a sacred word: in Hinduism the word is *aum* and in Buddhism, it is *om.* These words, which are not too different in construction from the powerful word of affirmation *amen* in Christianity, represent the articulation of the full range of expression. The sound of the *a* in *aum* originates in the back of the throat. The sound connected to the *u* in *aum* also begins in the throat but moves through the mouth and onto the lips. The sound connected to the *m* is created by the lips pressed together and leads to silence. The concluding silence that accompanies this sacred word is as meaningful as the articulation of *aum.**

In India, every musical instrument, including the human voice, is accorded great respect. People are careful not to bump a musical instrument with their foot. This is considered an impure gesture that dishonors the instrument and its beauty. Shouting, which can damage our voice, is disrespectful to others and to the self. Shouting abuses our vocal chords.

In vastu living, try to mirror this behavior inside your home. Take good care of any musical instrument, including your voice. Try to speak softly at home. Over time, you will start to observe this practice everywhere. You dis-

---

*See *Vastu Living: Creating a Home for the Soul* for a full explanation of the significance and symbolism attached to the word *aum* and each of its letters.

cover that a gentle voice and gentle response help you stay calm and composed. Disengaging from moments that lead to anger reduces your tension and protects your inner harmony.

Treasures from the Past

Gifts passed down from generation to generation in a family represent a vital link between the past and the present and the future. They represent continuity and evolution—the cycle of life. Since family heirlooms connect you to your ancestors, they belong in the south or the southwest quadrant of an enclosed space. The south belongs to Lord Yama, the Hindu god of death and judgment. The southwest belongs to Lord Pitri, who governs the world of ancestors.

By placing objects that connect to your ancestors, including pictures of deceased relatives, in the south and southwest of a space, you commemorate their collective wisdom. Their wisdom is invaluable and enriches your appreciation of life's experiences and your understanding of this world. Your ancestors also connect to the love that led to your own creation and the love that leads to the subsequent generations who will carry on your family name. You gather inner strength from the presence of these objects, and when you gaze at them, try to be calm for a moment to feel their link to your soul.

Paintings, Pictures, Mirrors

You want your vastu living home to reinforce positive thoughts. Yet many of us too willingly hang pictures, paintings, or photographs that express the dark side of human nature. When we look at these images, their negativity can interfere with our well-being. So be careful about the art that you display on your walls. Consider the emotions that an image stirs inside you before you incorporate it into your décor.

Place works of art in the north, the east, or the west so that you can absorb the inspiration and harmony that radiates out from positive images. Please remember that the southwest and the south belong to the departed, who deserve this honored place that speaks of the past and their wisdom and strength.

Did you know that the shape of your mirrors can influence your feelings? Circular or oval mirrors are dynamic. Their energy, which is in constant movement, stirs you up when you gaze into them. Square-based mirrors reflect static energy and help you concentrate on your appearance when you are getting ready to step into the world.

In vastu living, you can also use mirrors on a wall that doesn't have a window. The careful positioning of a mirror on a windowless wall can reflect a window on the opposite side of the room. Your trompe l'oeil creates the feeling of openness.

Entertainment Systems and Computers

Your stereos, televisions, computers, and other equipment that use electricity or batteries technically belong in the southeast quadrant and its element of fire. While this equipment may help you with your work or bring you pleasure, it should not become the focal point in any room. Televisions and computers are passive and prevent interaction. They discourage communal activities and shared experiences that bind family and friends together.

If you use a computer for work, try to place the screen so that it faces the north, the northeast, or the east—the three directions that enhance productivity through inspiration, wealth, and health. Please remember that wealth and health extend to your spiritual, physical, and material well-being. If you or someone in your home watches too much television, place it in the northwest quadrant. The properties associated with the element of air, which governs this realm, create distractions and restlessness. A television addict loses interest and wanders away.

Money, Jewelry, and Other Valuables

Vastu says that you should keep your valuables in the north, which is governed by Kuber, the lord of wealth. But vastu originated before the time of banks and high crime rates. Ignore this rule and keep your valuables in a safe place that is known only to you. Instead, honor irreplaceable objects that have sentimental value to you in the north: your child's first pair of baby shoes or baby handprint, an embroidered wall hanging created by your great-grandmother, mementos that speak of valued moments in your life. Expensive cars, fat paychecks, and gadgets with fancy bells and whistles are worth less than any object that gives joy to your soul.

Respect Nature

Plants inside your home quietly remind you of the rhythms that govern the world of nature. Each plant observes its own life cycle. Some plants close up their leaves at night. Some plants rest in the winter, then shake off their slumber with blooms that open in the spring. Each season conveys a distinct look and significance. The green foliage of spring celebrates renewal and birth. Summer's array of color pays tribute to the annual harvest and nature's bounty. The fiery hues of fallen leaves are reminders of the decomposition that accelerates in the autumn and in the autumn of your life. The evergreens that continue to thrive in the winter speak of eternity and the everlasting nature of your soul.

Plants add warmth to a home that is as comforting as a heavy quilt on a cold wintry night. We instinctively connect to nature, and incorporating it into your zone of tranquility, in particular, helps you relax and unwind. When you focus on the individual leaves or the delicate petals that create each flower, you see that each part of the plant contributes to its overall beauty. This recognition of interdependence and interconnection reminds you of the Truth that binds together all existence. Nothing lives in a vacuum; no one is truly alone. We are all part of the Supreme Creative Force.

Your choice of plants for your home and their placement inside a room or space should never be random. In the natural world, each plant species grows in a beneficial soil and climate that provides the appropriate conditions that enable the species to survive. The plants that you select should appeal to you and reveal your personal preferences, but the appeal should be reciprocal. Your home must be able to cater to the needs of each plant. You want them to flourish, not wither up and die. After all, plants do you so much good. They produce oxygen inside your home and help rid the air of impurities. Many plants offer physical and emotional first aid. The juice of the aloe soothes a burn; marigolds and violets are good for your skin; and so many herbs become healthy teas or soothing topical potions. And every plant inside your home is good for your soul. Nature calms your emotions and helps you beat back tension and stress.

The Meaningful Display of Plants

Plant arrangements inside each room should express your intimate connection to nature as well as your unique creativity. It's easy to overlook small plants in a room if they are placed individually on a table or any other surface. Instead put different species that share the same needs into a huge terra-cotta planter or an old metal tub where they create a microversion of the natural world. Select greens and show off the diversity expressed in different leaves from delicate wisps to sturdy reeds, their subtle variations in hues, and their unique patterns of growth. Separately, each plant may escape notice; but grouped together they become a distinctive garden that highlights their individuality. Indoor palm trees can stand alone; but even their beauty is enhanced when you surround them with smaller plants that can survive under the shade of the umbrella-like fronds.

You can also arrange plants so that they slowly increase in size from the extreme right and left with your tallest plant in the center. This plant, similar to the spire on a church or a temple, points toward the firmament and speaks of formlessness and eternity (see Figure 26). Symbolically, the display honors the Supreme Creative Force and its connection to your soul. You can use a diverse selection of flowering plants and greens to achieve this effect, or you can focus on a specific plant classification, such as cacti, or choose a group of medicinal plants and also pay tribute to their beneficial properties.

Organic Products

If you travel too much and can't offer plants the care that they deserve or you lack adequate lighting, you can express your respect and love for nature with organic objects. Celebrate an aspect of nature that brings you special pleasure. If you enjoy the autumn months, honor this particular season. Place an earthen-colored linen mat on a table in a room and cover the center with a

Figure 26: Celestial Display of Plants

cluster of dried flowers that bloom this time of year. Add three low, yellow candles in glass votive cups on the southeast corner of the mat. Their location pays tribute to the element of fire and its connection to purity. The candles and the preserved dried flowers speak of the rebirth that follows destruction.

You can express your love of the forest and fill a bushel barrel with pinecones, acorns, and chestnuts. You can honor the seashore in the northeast corner, which belongs to the element of water, with a dramatic piece of driftwood or a sandy-colored vase filled with thin reeds that come from a salt marsh, or a large seashell filled with sea glass.

The important point to remember is to consider organic products that come from nature instead of synthetics whenever you are about to make a purchase for your home. A rattan wastebasket is worthy of a prominent place in a home whereas a plastic wastebasket is an eyesore, usually tucked out of sight. Glass, which is made from sand, and clay pots for plants evoke the earth, whereas plastic pots evoke, well . . . nonbiodegradable plastic. A carved wooden box for pens and pencils is much more expressive than a Lucite container, and the wooden box normally won't crack if it drops to the floor.

Celebrate Your Unique Identity

Your vastu living décor should fulfill the analogy made earlier in this book that your home is the temple for your body and protects your soul. Always choose furnishings that

SUGGESTION 5 INVITE NATURE INSIDE YOUR HOME

Here are three more suggestions to spark your imagination:

Fill an old glass milk bottle with wood, metal, and glass buttons.

Take a glass fishbowl and fill it with water and tiny hand-blown glass fish.

Hang a collection of antique silk scarves on a hook mounted on a wall.

are made of natural materials and feel good to the body and appeal to the eye. Make explicit choices in your décor that consistently connect to your life or the life of anyone who shares the space with you. A vastu living home always celebrates the unique identity of the people who live here.

Look at the objects that you display in each room: your photos and pictures on your walls, your collections of knickknacks, all your "attention-getters" that sit on a surface or the floor or hang from a wall or the ceiling. Can you actually describe the special meaning of each—how it fits into your life or the life of someone who lives in your home? If your mind draws a blank, then quite likely this particular object is just taking up space. It is clutter.

Repeat this exercise every time you are about to buy something and add it to your home. Of course, many objects that you purchase serve an important purpose or utilitarian need, but all too often we succumb to an impulse. Something catches our eye as we head toward the cash register or as we walk through a garage sale or amble around a flea market. But what catches your eye doesn't always speak to your soul. It may fail to celebrate your special individuality or honor the beauty in nature. So before you part with your money, be sure that what you are about to buy adds something other than clutter to your vastu living home.

SUGGESTION 6
INCLUDE A DOSE
OF TLC

Treat everything in your home that celebrates your special identity or the identities of those who share your space with loving care. Your décor speaks of what you love and cherish and represents the true wealth in your life.

10

Special Issues with Your House or Property

✳

✳ THE ORIENTATION OF ENTRANCES

Many vastu consultants insist that the cardinal direction of the entrance to your property or the cardinal direction of the entrance to your home seals your fate. They claim that the orientation of the property and the home has the power to reward you and make everything go your way or to ruin your life. But two of the most important ancient texts on vastu do not support this assertion. These well-respected texts say that an entrance in any direction is acceptable.* And if you flip through an illustrated reference of historic Hindu temples that are built according to vastu, you will see shrines that face the north or the south or the east or the west. Each direction has positive merits. So please don't believe that the orientation of the entrance to your property or

---

*See *Vastu Living: Creating a Home for the Soul* for the actual quote from the eleventh-century text, called *Mayamata*, Vol. 1, that reinforces this comment and for additional information on this work and the tenth-century texts by Manasara.

the entrance to your house guarantees wealth and health or hardship and misfortune.

A driveway or entrance to your home that is located in the north or the east of the northeast quadrant, however, does have a healthy benefit that is worth noting. This alignment enables the cosmic energy and spiritual power to flow freely into your property and your home. These gifts are extremely beneficial to you. They increase your well being.

Significance of Each Orientation

If you live in a house, take out your spiritual blueprint and check the orientation of the entrance to your property and home. While these entrances don't seal your fate, their orientation does relate to the symbols and characteristics attached to the specific deity or deities who govern the particular realm. These symbols and characteristics are worthy reminders. These deities, as I explained in chapter 1, represent the important dualities that govern the universe and our moral behavior.

Does your entrance face east? An eastern entrance receives the blessings of Surya, the lord of the sun. This deity represents enlightenment, inspiration, and creativity. Does your front door open to the west? This is the realm of Lord Varuna, who is the lord of the oceans, the night, and the rains. The west is showered with the peace and quiet that come with the night—that period of time that allows for the sun's renewal. Lord Varuna also reminds us to dispel the darkness that comes from ignorance.

Does your house face north? This cardinal direction belongs to Soma, the lord of the moon and health, and Kuber, the lord of earthly wealth and indulgence. An entrance that faces this direction looks out at wealth and health, but Lord Kuber reminds us that too much indulgence, which is often a by-product of excess wealth, can be costly. Indulgence can make you forget your responsibilities and obligations and can destroy your good health.

Does your front door open to the south? A southern entrance faces Yama, who is the lord of death and judgment. Lord Yama keeps us mindful of the responsibilities and duties that create an honorable life. If your house faces the south, this is not dangerous to your well-being or the well-being of anyone who lives with you. It does not augur an impending, unexpected death. The house that faces the south reminds us to lead a responsible and loving life. The cultivation of compassion, caring, and unconditional love leads to profound inner peace.

Also evaluate the entrance to your home or any room inside your home. Only temples, which are homes for the gods, have an entrance cut into the center of a wall. Entrances to homes and rooms for mortals should be off center—set inside one of the four quadrants, not in the direct center of a wall. We are imperfect, and this alignment for a door suits us best.

❋ IDEAL PROPERTY IN VASTU LIVING

In vastu, you are lucky if your home is built into the southwest quadrant of your property. Your house is heavy and belongs in this quadrant, which is governed by the element of earth. Unfortunately, many architects in the West prefer to place the house in the precise center of the property, which means that the house covers the sacred element of space, which is governed by Lord Brahma. This placement holds down the positive energy that emanates from this realm. It deprives you of its spiritual benefits.

You are doubly lucky if there is a water source or depression in the northeast quadrant, which collects the cosmic energy and spiritual power that enter your property or home from this midpoint direction and travel to the southwest. Your luck comes in threes if there is an elevation behind your house in the south or the west of your property. This elevation retains the cosmic energy and spiritual power and keeps it flowing inside your property. Finally, the perfect vastu living site has an open airiness in the north and the east, and heaviness and density in the south and the west. (If you live in the Southern Hemisphere, follow the spiritual blueprint on page 116, which shows the correct location of the elements below the equator.)

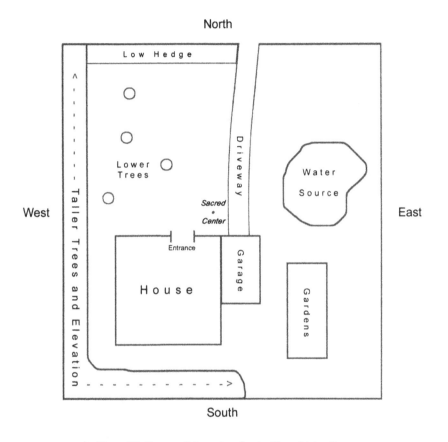

Figure 27: Correct Orientation for the Vastu Living Property

❖ THE MULTISTORY HOUSE

Having lots of space is obviously an advantage for most people, and it certainly creates no difficulty in your practice of vastu living. Look at your spiritual blueprint that you created for each floor and treat each floor separately.

This means that you honor the assigned location of the five basic elements on each floor, and, of course, within each room and enclosed area.

❊ THE HOUSE WITH A GUEST COTTAGE

If you have a cottage or separate dwelling on your property, just create a square spiritual blueprint around your second dwelling. If possible, try to orient the dwelling in the southwest quadrant of this blueprint. Then see how well you honor the elements within this square. Perhaps, you can add a small fishpond

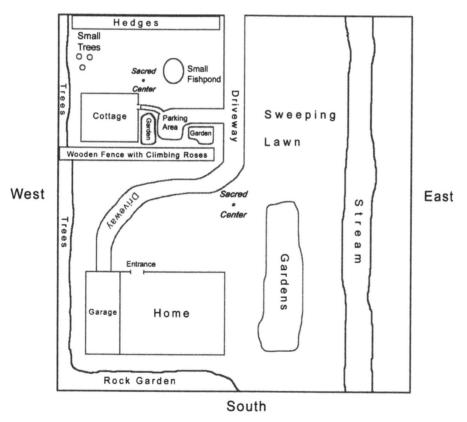

❊ Figure 28: Spiritual Blueprint for the House with Guest Cottage

or birdbath in its northeast quadrant and a wooden fence with climbing roses in the south and the west. In other words, create a vastu living environment around this building, and, of course, inside each enclosed area inside the building.

And how do you treat the entire property that has a house and a separate dwelling? Create one spiritual blueprint that contains both structures. In other words, you end up with a blueprint within a blueprint (see Figure 28).

11

Special Issues with Your Apartment

If you live in an apartment, condominium, or cooperative, please take out the spiritual blueprint that you created for your entire home. Most likely these three realities prevail: you have no control over the entrance to your building; you have no control over the entrance to your apartment; and unless you can do a massive alteration inside your apartment, you probably don't have any control over the layout of the rooms inside your home.

But, as I explained in the preceding chapter, please don't believe that an entrance to your apartment or an individual room can have a negative impact on the quality of your life. Just be aware of the symbols attached to each direction and their significance (see page 142) and focus your practice of vastu living on the issues that are within your control, which can influence your harmony and inner peace. (If you live in the Southern Hemisphere, follow the spiritual blueprint on page 116, which shows the correct location of the elements below the equator.)

✳ APARTMENT CHALLENGES

You may think that physical constraints inside your apartment, especially built-in impediments, will interfere with your practice of vastu living. You may worry that your space is too limited—one or more of your rooms or areas may serve more than one function. Or you may think that inadequate sunlight, which prevents the introduction of plants into your home, or your less than inspiring views of a bleak building shaft, signals vastu living doom and gloom. Not so. Let's examine a few common apartment problems so that you can see that vastu living works in even the most challenging environment.

Coping with Cramped Space

Many apartments test our ability to do without, especially apartments that are in metropolitan areas where demand exceeds supply and the rent for an average-size apartment can exceed a monthly paycheck. Please commit this line to memory: no matter how cramped your living quarters, they can be converted into a vastu living apartment that is more than 51 percent correct.

The Dual-Personality Room

By night, it's your bedroom; by day, it's your home office. How do you introduce vastu living into a room that serves more than one function? Especially when the two functions connected to the one room take up most of your time—the time that you work and the time that you sleep. It is true that you need to be careful with the locations of the bed and the desk in your dual-function space. The negative principle of like increases like can cause trouble in your heavily used environment and severely agitate your constitution.

Let's assume that your bedroom and office share a single space in the southwest quadrant of your apartment or any other quadrant in your apartment that is healthy for your constitution (see page 70 for healthy vs. unhealthy quadrants for your dosha). In this situation, you have two excellent options. You can place the head of your bed against the south wall or against the east wall. If the head of your bed is in the south, then you can orient your desk so that you face east—the source of inspiration—when you work (see Figure 29). If the head of your bed is placed against the east wall, then you can place your desk in the southwest and have your back to the south or the west. With this choice, you gather the wisdom and strength of the southwest quadrant when you sit at your desk (see Figure 30).

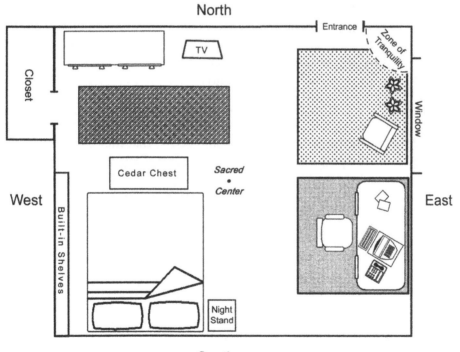

✴ Figure 29: Head of the Bed in the South

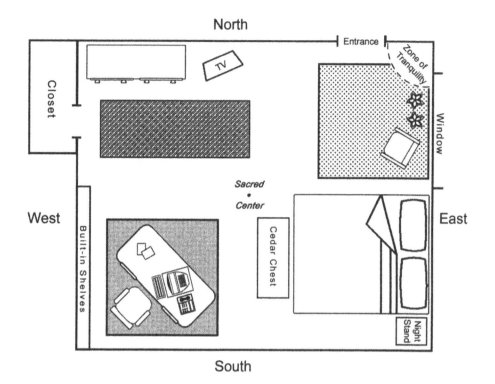

Figure 30: Head of the Bed in the East

Once you have oriented your desk and bed so that they contribute to your good health, organize the remaining furniture in your room—remembering that lightweight and delicate furnishings belong in the north and the east and that heavy and bulky items belong in the south and the west.

If your bedroom and office are located in the quadrant attached to the element that governs your own constitution, you can still organize this double-duty space so that you benefit from vastu living. Let's say that you have a vata or air constitution. This element controls the northwest quadrant of your apartment, which may also be the location of your bedroom. Try to put your bed in the southwest of the room, with your head facing the south, and your desk in the northeast quadrant, with your back to the west or the south. The element of earth, which is heavy and strong, helps induce a deep sleep at night; and the element of water helps you stay serene and focused when you work in the northeast. Both of these orientations also counteract the negative effects of like increases like—receiving too much air that would overstimulate your constitution.

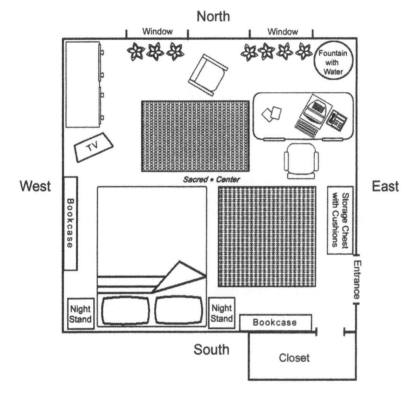

Figure 31: Achieving Balance in an Unhealthy Quadrant

The Dual-Personality-Room Guideline

The key to successful vastu living in each situation remains the same: First, consider the activities that take place in your room that serves more than one purpose. If you sleep and work in a single room, then you are spending the majority of your time in this part of your apartment. To avoid triggering a problem, you'll need to organize the actual areas so that their alignments are healthy for you. It is important to sleep well at night to work successfully the next day. Working well in a home office usually means staying focused and finding positive inspiration. Again, your primary consideration is to avoid orientations that can upset the balance of your constitution when like increases like.

Unhealthy Quadrants for Your Constitution in Vastu Living

Constitution or Dosha	Northern Hemisphere Unhealthy Quadrant	Southern Hemisphere Unhealthy Quadrant
Vata or Air	Northwest (Air)	Southwest (Air)
Pitta or Fire	Southeast (Fire)	Northeast (Fire)
Kapha or Water	Northeast (Water)	Southeast (Water)

Many other rooms that have dual functions are easier to turn into vastu living environments. If your living room is also your home office, where you sit many hours in a day, then first organize the office area of this room so that it doesn't interfere with your constitution. Once your desk is placed in a healthy location, then organize the rest of the room according to the elements and the principle of heavy objects in the south and the west and lightweight and delicate objects in the north and the east.

Finally, when a room with two functions creates a vastu living conflict that cannot be resolved through furniture rearrangement, please remember that you can solve problems with appeasements discussed in chapter 5, "Resolving Conflicts in Your Home and Workplace." To be successful with this method, carefully examine the nature of your conflict and determine whether it interferes with your well-being. Then, use either appeasing colors or therapeutic plants and objects to resolve the conflict or conflicts in your "dual-personality" space. The offering that you make to the offended elements and their deities restores the balance in your constitution. Your problem room becomes a positive vastu living space.

When More Is Less

Many of us live in an apartment that is the essence of compromise. We have given up natural light or a view for more interior space or an extra room or eat-in kitchen or a second bathroom. We may choose to save a few hundred dollars a month and live on a lower floor in the back of the apartment building where we need a periscope to catch sight of the sky. Or perhaps we are slightly more fortunate and live in a space where a sliver of the sun warms up our apartment a couple hours of the day.

The extra something that you often choose over natural light or a view can come with an emotional price. It's tough to live in an environment where you rarely see the sun or the world outside. Your environment is prisonlike. It accentuates feelings of alienation and loneliness. You miss the sight of the sun, the view of nature outside your windows, your connection to the outer world.

So how do you solve the problems that come with an absence of sunlight or view of nature? Once again, you follow the all-important principle of like increases like. Only this time, like increases like means that you do everything in your power to bring nature and light into your space so that your apartment, which seems dreary and unwelcoming, speaks of the rhythms of your daily life and the rhythms that govern the world in which you live.

You imitate the warmth and light of the sun in your space through the use of colors that speak of the sunrise and sunset—the palest shades of yellow, green, white, pink, lavender, even the faint glow of coral. You choose these colors because of their association with the sun, but in hues that won't aggravate a fiery temperament. You introduce the outer world of nature through the presence of organic substances and the avoidance of synthetics throughout your apartment. You can bring in jute, sisal, natural fabrics, wood, pottery, tiles, papier-mâché, dried flowers, fresh flowers, potpourri, brass, copper, pewter, silver, iron.

You draw the outer world in and surround yourself with images that speak of life beyond your viewless home. You may not be able to look at the world through a window, but you can look at the world right on your walls. You use all these solutions to reestablish the natural balance that was lacking in your apartment and made it feel dreary and isolated. You re-create this balance in your space so that you can reclaim your own harmony and balance. When you are surrounded by the world's beauty, you feel the connection—a connection that also celebrates your shared divinity.

12

Special Issues with Your Studio or Loft

❋

Do you live in a studio or loft? If you do, please take out the spiritual blueprint for your entire home and refer to it in the course of this chapter. In open spaces, from the small studio to the huge loft, the lack of walls allows the positive cosmic energy and spiritual power to move freely inside your space. This is a boon that should make it relatively easy for you to convert your studio or loft into vastu living interiors that increase your well-being and harmony.

But a couple of issues in your open-walled space can interfere with your practice of vastu living. Your small studio may have so little space that the five basic elements can be as crowded together as you and anyone else who shares your home. (If you live in the Southern Hemisphere, follow the spiritual blueprint on page 116, which shows the correct location of the elements below the equator.) Your huge loft may have left you craving intimacy. Up went new walls that are now unexpected barriers to vastu living. . . .

The Kitchen Compressed into One Wall

Do you have an efficiency kitchen? This is usually the most common vastu-related problem in the studio: the kitchen is usually anything but efficient. Your refrigerator, sink, stove, and small counter are usually jammed into one studio wall. Your "kitchen" may have about two or three feet of linoleum or tile flooring that juts into the rest of your studio to demarcate the space. Your kitchen cabinets may fill up much of the wall behind the appliances. Your small dish rack may take up your entire counter. Your efficiency kitchen may be the challenge that extinguishes the joy that should accompany cooking.

So how do you introduce vastu living into an efficiency kitchen, which is little more than an idea of a kitchen? First, you need to understand that your kitchen appliances are related to different elements and that each appliance belongs in the location that is governed by its element. Your sink is connected to the element of water and belongs in the northeast quadrant. Your kitchen stove, which belongs to the element of fire, should be in the southeast. Your refrigerator, which is normally the heaviest kitchen appliance, belongs to the element of earth in the southwest. Even if your efficiency kitchen is in the southeast of your studio, which is generally the best quadrant for a kitchen, the various locations of these appliances that line one wall are usually in conflict with vastu.

Complications related to the elements in your one-wall kitchen are often compounded by a second problem. You prepare your meals—your sustenance—in your kitchen. This environment should be so pleasing to you that you take your time and prepare your food with love. But your efficiency kitchen may be anything but pleasing. So how do you introduce vastu living into this difficult environment?

Let's consider an efficiency kitchen that belonged to an aspiring actress. Her one-wall kitchen was on the west side of her studio. Half of it fell inside the southwest quadrant, and the other half fell inside the northwest quadrant of her studio. Only the refrigerator, which was in the southwest, was properly placed in this one-wall arrangement. In addition, when the young actress stood at her kitchen sink, she had no lovely view; there wasn't even a window in the wall. She stared into a spiritually dead space (see Figure 32).

We solved the problems connected with her efficiency kitchen through color and the use of appeasing objects that can calm down the misplaced elements and restore the inner harmony of the actress. We used color judiciously because too many colors would have overwhelmed the décor in the rest of her small studio. And when we introduced objects, we also kept them subtle or small so that they would not throw off the balance in the "look" of her space.

Essentially, we concentrated on creating an attractive *ambience* inside her efficiency kitchen. It was important for her to enjoy the time that she needed to spend here to create healthy meals. We placed a lovely cotton area rug from the 1940s on the floor in front of her kitchen sink. The pale blue flower border seemed like an offering to the sacred center that belongs to Lord Brahma, whose element is space. The rug also added warmth to the old linoleum floor.

We hung three yellow plates—each one decorated with a lovely blue bird—on the north wall. The blue picked up the color of the rug beneath her feet. Birds, which come and go, also served as a good appeasement to the element of air, which had been violated by the presence of the sink with its water in the northwest quadrant. The yellow also added a cheery touch to this part of the studio, and the blue in the plate is yellow's nighttime complement. On the northwest corner of her sink, we added a simple clear-glass bud vase where the young woman keeps a single white bloom that speaks of purity as an offering to all the elements in her mixed-up kitchen.

Then we made the most important change to her tiny, windowless environment. We added a piece of folk art—a lovely Mexican, silver-edged mirror as a backdrop to the sink. This became her clever connection to her zone of tranquility. The mirror captured the northeast of the studio, which belongs to the element of water and is the proper place for her zone. Her special display in the northeast of her studio honored objects from nature and cherished objects that filled her with joy. When the young actress stood at her kitchen sink preparing her meals or washing her dishes, she could focus on her lovely Mexican mirror and see her contemplative zone of tranquility behind her. She relaxed (see Figure 33).

Figure 32: One-Wall Kitchen Before

⁎ Figure 33: One-Wall Kitchen After

⁎ BREAKING THE FLOW

Have you added interior walls to your loft that stop the free flow of positive energy and spiritual power in the formerly open area? A software programmer moved into a beautiful rectangular loft with a bank of windows on the north and the east. The previous owner had hung ceiling-to-floor velvet drapes to demarcate the living room, home office, and large bedroom (see Figure 34).

The programmer liked the idea of movable "walls" that he could open and shut at whim. He also liked demarcating these areas for reasons of privacy; but he hated the heavy, green drapes when they were closed. He felt claustropho-bic—nearly smothered in all the dark velvet. The curtains also stopped the flow of the important cosmic energy and spiritual power in his loft. These gifts of the gods, which entered the northeast quadrant, couldn't reach a portion of the space, including his all-important office and bedroom.

We removed the drapes, but I honored the programmer's desire to physically define the space and suggested that he replace the drapes with carefully placed Japanese screens made of blond wood and rice paper that didn't extend from the floor to the ceiling. The screens were so delicate that they didn't feel like barriers that sliced up the loft. He had his open loft, but he also had his privacy (see Figure 35).

The screens were so appealing that they became an attractive addition to the space. Sunlight, which streamed through the abundant windows in his

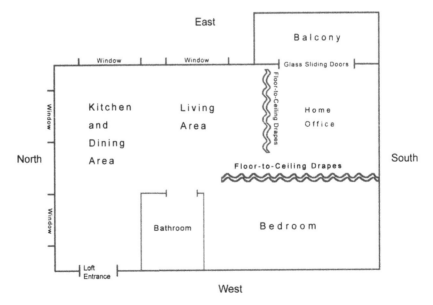

Figure 34: Unhealthy Barriers

loft, filtered through the rice paper in each screen. Since plants thrived in this environment, we created lovely arrangements in front of the screens that separated his living room area and office. The programmer placed a tall plant and large stone rabbit on the side of one screen near the east wall and grouped three indoor cypresses in tall stoneware pots against the far end of the other screen. The white rice paper in the screens was a stunning backdrop that allowed the delightful play of sunlight and shadow in the course of the day. In addition, when the programmer wanted to close up the screens, the placement of his tributes to nature didn't get in the way or need to be moved.

The programmer had established the boundaries between his bedroom and his home office, but where the harsh drapes had made an unfriendly statement, the screens and the plants were far more subtle and blended into the surrounding environment. They became a part of the whole; not so, the drapes, which had stood out like an eyesore. Finally, the cosmic energy and spiritual power moved freely, once again, through the attractive, naturally warm space.

Figure 35: Healthy Exchange

13

Revere Your Transitional Areas — the Porch to the Terrace

WELCOME TO THE VASTU LIVING TRANSITIONAL AREA, WHICH COVERS YOUR PORCH, BALCONY, TERRACE, VERANDA, EVEN A TWO-STEP STOOP. MAKE CERTAIN THAT YOU HAVE CREATED A SEPARATE SPIRITUAL BLUEPRINT FOR ALL OF THESE SPACES, HOWEVER SMALL, THAT PERTAIN TO YOUR HOME. YOU WILL WANT TO REFER TO YOUR BLUEPRINT OR BLUEPRINTS AS YOU READ THIS CHAPTER.

Have you ever seen one of those quintessential moments in an old movie where a couple enjoys a private moment sitting on a porch swing or on a stoop in the early evening as the sun goes down? From young teens to the young-in-spirit, these film characters always look so peaceful in this place at that moment—soaking in the silence, the loveliness of the hour, and the good feeling that grows within them. It registers on each face that fills the screen.

But these moments occurred in films that were made decades ago. And in this age, we operate at such a fast pace that too few of us take the time or believe that we even have the time to enjoy our porch or veranda or even our minimalist stoop. Does this sound like you? Do you race into your home or into the world outside and hardly feel your feet move up and down the steps? Is your mind wrapped up in a rush of thoughts about where you are going or where you have just been? Are you far from the present where you are right now?

If you are lucky enough to have a terrace or balcony or veranda or porch attached to your home, cherish it and enjoy it. It is an invaluable intermediary space that connects the public world to your private world—the outer world of the universe and all creation to the private world of your home, which connects to your unique self. Unfortunately, the fast tempo of our modern world has made many of us oblivious of our intermediary spaces, so how can we appreciate their value—their stunning ability to help us make a harmonious transition from one world into the other?

On a deep level, your porch and veranda, in particular, are the secular versions of the threshold to a temple. When you step onto your porch, you should remind yourself that you are about to enter the sanctity of your home, which is the temple for your body and soul. Your veranda and your porch are your transitional zones where you should shake off your outer-world concerns along with the dust on your shoes before you step inside. In India, many people follow a lovely custom where they remove their shoes before they step inside their home. This gesture, which is followed at every temple, extends respect to the home—nothing impure should ever sully this sacred space.

All your transitional zones, including your terrace and your balcony, should exhibit comfort and peace. They should have the power to slow you down so that you linger awhile. You want to follow the example of those couples in the old movies and soak in the deep pleasure that comes from watching the world go by you from your safe harbor. These environments quietly teach you how to disengage so that you can spend time with your interior self.

The Spiritual Blueprint for Your Transitional Area

Examine your spiritual blueprint or blueprints and focus for a moment on the orientation of each of your transitional spaces. Is your porch or stoop or balcony or terrace on the north, south, east, or west of your home? Let the orientation of each space inspire positive thoughts that connect to its location. If your porch is oriented toward the east, you can focus on the power of the sun and its symbols of clarity and enlightenment. If your veranda faces the south, you can concentrate on the deep satisfaction that comes from fulfilling your responsibilities and duties. If your balcony faces west, you can revel in the peace and quiet that comes with this direction. If your terrace faces north, you can offer blessings to the healing properties and the gift of wealth that come from the north and remind yourself of the perils of indulgence.

Once you are aware of the significance attached to each orientation, begin your practice of vastu living with the studious interweaving of the three vastu principles into each of your transitional areas. Honoring the five basic elements, nature, and the self maximizes the flow of harmony in each transitional space. You will want to spend time here. Your objective is the creation of environments that disengage you from the tangle of thoughts that distance you from the present moment and keep you from going deep within so that you can discover inner calm. Even if your transitional space is a stoop, still try to observe the assigned location of the five basic elements in each of these separate spaces, try to honor nature, and try to celebrate the self. Here are three very different examples of successful transitional spaces. (If you live in the Southern Hemisphere, follow the spiritual blueprint on page 116, which shows the correct location of the elements below the equator.)

The Porch or Veranda

One of my most enjoyable consultations included a porch makeover. This transitional area, which faced south, had become a well-used storage space— in other words a mess that cluttered the front porch of a renovated country home. This storage area, which extended from the southwest corner to the direct center of this south-facing home, held a heap of firewood, a mountain of bricks, an old awning that buried a porch swing, a self-generating compost pile, and an un-coiled garden hose.

The homeowners, a computer programmer and an attorney, loved antiques, and they loved renovating their house. Many of their decisions were instinctively vastu-correct. But by the time they thought about the front porch, the husband's "programming" skills and the wife's talent for creating whimsy had shut down. The mess was overwhelming.

With little effort, we were able to clean up the porch and pay tribute to the symbols attached to the south—duty and responsibility and the cycle of life that includes death and rebirth. We focused, in particular, on honoring antiquity, which also connected to the couple's interests. We redefined their porch environment by exposing the historical construction connected to this hundred-year-old house and by adding antiques and secondhand finds.

After moving out the clutter, the couple washed down the porch's wide-wood-plank floor. Its rough-hewn design was perfect for the south, where it reminded them of the people who had built this home in an earlier century. The husband removed layers of paint and stained the natural oak finish of the floor. He also honored the sacred center of the porch with an old braided rug, which had been placed at the far end of an upstairs hallway where it was unseen and underappreciated.

His wife placed a natural-coir floor mat close to the front door so that visitors would clean their shoes before they entered the home. The long garden hose was coiled and placed into a Victorian holder mounted on the outside of the porch near the northeast corner. This sensible location was close to the outside faucet, which was appropriately placed in the sacred northeast, the quadrant that belonged to water.

A strong sun, which flowed onto the porch, explained the presence of the tattered awning. But rather than rehang the awning, the couple decided to celebrate nature. They used plants to create a natural barrier across the front of the porch, which faced the south and needed, symbolically at least, to hold in the cosmic energy that would enter the porch from the northeast and collect in the southwest quadrant. They planted various climbers in the ground on the south side and the west side of the porch. They planned to entwine the plants around the wooden porch railings.

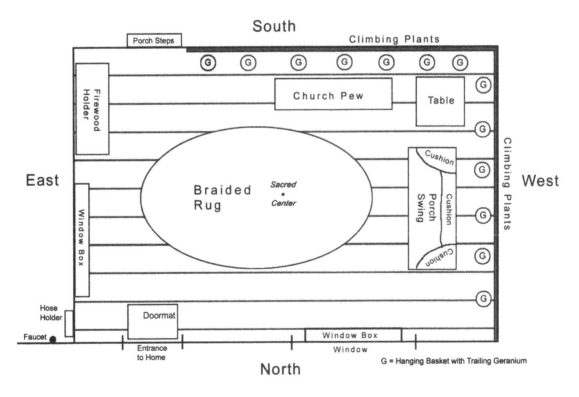

Figure 36: Porch That Honors the Past

Jute baskets, which held red, trailing geraniums, hung from the porch rafters and added height to the barrier. A firewood holder was placed in the southeast corner of the porch, an appropriate location. The logs would be used in the fireplace to warm up the house, so the holder honored the element of fire, which ruled over this quadrant.

The couple put an antique church pew against the southern railing near the southwest and placed a small wooden table in the southwest corner. They reclaimed the old, slated porch swing and rehung it near the porch railing in the west where it overlapped into the northwest quadrant. The swing's gentle movement honored the element of air that governed this realm. In addition, the back of the swing was to the west so that the couple faced east as they rocked back and forth. They gazed into three healthy directions as they enjoyed their transitional space and celebrated the calm of their country-home porch.

The Balcony or Terrace

A consultant lived in an apartment in a modern row house in Chicago. Her apartment, which faced north, had a front balcony, which was entered through glass sliding doors. The balcony was large enough so that my client could sit there, not just stand at the railing, and look down at the busy urban street.

But the consultant didn't use her balcony. A high-rise apartment directly across from the row house blocked much of the light that flowed into her space. The rays that flowed from the limited sun highlighted the heavy metal railings on her modern balcony. This transitional environment looked so severe and cold that the young woman didn't even *consider* using her balcony—even though it had been *the* selling point that had made her decide to move in.

Vastu living easily transformed this outdoor space so it became usable and soothing—a place where she sat and read or did nothing but gaze into the sky or watch the world go by below her. First, my client put down a sisal rug in a honey brown color that left a wide border around the edge. It created a warm contrast with the dark paint on the cement floor.

Since her balcony was due north and had a strong connection to the northeast, we decided to make these two directions her focal point. We placed three wood window boxes filled with low-growing plants—holy basil, which is sacred in India, and nasturtiums, which are a tasty addition to any salad—on the north railing. On the northeastern corner of the floor, we placed a stone birdbath, where the water honored the element of the northeast and collected the positive cosmic energy that flowed from this direction into her balcony and her apartment (see Figure 37).

We placed a bird feeder on a stand in the northwest to respect the element of air. The birds, like the wind, would come and go. In addition, the idea of inviting birds to the balcony pleased the young woman. Her mother had always kept canaries in her home. The young woman didn't like the idea of caged birds, but these visiting birds connected to her past and their chatter brought her fond memories and pleasure. She also loved taking care of a few of the creatures that shared her world.

In the southwest, we set up a portable wood-framed-and-canvas beach chair, which she had picked up at a flea market for trips to Lake Michigan. Her trips were so infrequent, she had to dig the chair out of a closet. We positioned her chair so that when she sat on her balcony, her back was to the southwest, which filled her with wisdom and strength, and she faced into the serenity of the northeast.

In the southeast corner, she attached a wall sconce where she could place two large candles, which paid respect to the element of fire that governed this quadrant and added some light in the night. The center was left empty, paying homage to Lord Brahma and his sacred realm. On the floor in the west below the railing we placed a rectangular, wrought-iron trivet that held three terra-cotta pots. Each one contained a begonia, which added color and height from the west to the southwest.

In this transitional area, the power of vastu living as a decorative tool was also apparent to the client. What was an unused space that required endless sweeping with nothing in return was now beautiful and inviting. Her balcony became a special transitional area and served its purpose well.

This vastu living design that the young woman used so successfully on her balcony can work just as effectively on a large terrace. All you need to do is increase the proportion of used space—create a seating area, for example, that would include a bench, chairs, and a table that are all positioned so that everyone faces a healthy direction. Again, your goal is to use the orientation of the transitional space for your inspiration. If the terrace faces east, then you can

✳ Figure 37: Comforting Balcony

create a theme around the sun. If it faces west, then focus on a message that evokes the setting sun and the rising moon and the companion stars. Use gentle, peaceful colors in your choice of plants. If the space is toward the southwest, think about using wood and wrought iron, which evoke solidity and the earth. Irrespective of the direction, always try to honor each of the five basic elements, nature, and yourself or the self of each individual who shares your transitional space.

The Shared Terrace

When you share a terrace with other people, please remember that this space was still built with the same function in mind as with a private terrace. The terrace is supposed to be used, not admired from a distance. Create an environment that makes you want to spend time here. Most shared terraces are divided into individual spaces for the use of each apartment or living space. Occasionally a shared terrace lacks a physical demarcation. But barrier or not, simply create a spiritual blueprint that includes only that portion of the shared terrace that belongs to your home. By marking off the boundaries on your blueprint, whether they physically exist or not, you know the proper location of the elements and can honor them individually (see Figure 38).

To incorporate nature into your space, try to introduce lots of plants if you have adequate sun and let their presence reflect your unique identity. Consider selecting blooms with colors that relate positively to your constitution. If you have a fiery or pitta constitution or tend to be extremely active, choose serene colors, such as white and shades of blue with its complementary color of yellow. If you tend to be sluggish and take a long time to motivate yourself, pick colors that are fiery and inspirational, such as red with its complementary color of violet and orange with its complementary color of indigo.

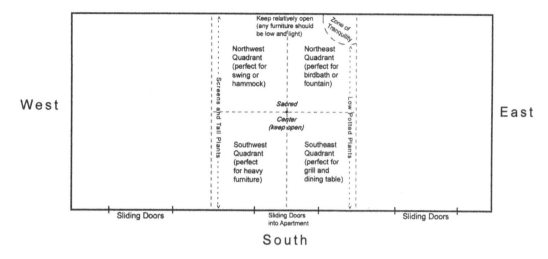

Figure 38: Spiritual Blueprint for the Shared Terrace

If your terrace lacks adequate sun, perhaps you can copy the example of the young woman in Chicago and draw birds to your terrace with a feeder or birdbath. If the presence of birds means too many pigeons and complaints from your neighbors, consider including a lovely stone image of an animal that connects to a garden—the trespassing rabbit, for example. And always concentrate on the use of organic products on your terrace; stay away from the unhealthy use of synthetics.

No Transitional Area?

Even if you lack a porch or terrace, you can symbolize the actual threshold that leads into your home. During the Christmas season, mistletoe is hung over the doorway in the hope of getting a kiss from someone who walks under the holiday sprig. In India, Hindus hang a *toran* over the threshold that leads into their home—not to receive a kiss, but to receive blessings from the gods every time the door is swung open. The toran, which can be an elaborately embroidered fabric banner that is decorated with Hindu symbols or just a few auspicious mango leaves threaded onto a simple string, showers goodwill on the home and on each individual who steps under this sanctified threshold.

Figure 39: Example of a Toran

❊ Your Zone of Tranquility

Try to create an appealing zone of tranquility in the northeast quadrant of any transitional space. The northeast belongs to the element of water, which is soothing and reflective—this explains why it's also called the gateway to the

CREATE YOUR OWN TORAN

Take dried basil leaves (or mango leaves if they are available). Both these plants are sacred and auspicious. Thread them on a simple cord along with some dried white flower blossoms— white symbolizes purity and serenity. Attach the ends of the cord to each corner of the entranceway. Be sure to hang the toran high enough so that it won't get caught in the door.

gods. (In the Southern Hemisphere, your zone of tranquility belongs in the southeast quadrant.)

The zone's special display draws your attention and encourages you to spend time in your special transitional space. Your display can be extremely simple. Collect a few objects from nature—stones, pinecones, shells, even broken bricks—and place them in the northeast quadrant of your terrace where they become the stationary backdrop to a clear glass vase that is filled with water and floating candles. When you want to shoo away the thoughts that race through your mind, bring out a cushion covered in colors that are healthy for you and sit and focus on your quiet zone, which accentuates the importance of this meditative transitional space.

14

Commemorate Your Kitchen

WELCOME TO THE VASTU LIVING KITCHEN. PLEASE TAKE OUT YOUR SPIRITUAL BLUEPRINT FOR THIS IMPORTANT SPACE AND REFER TO IT AS YOU READ THIS CHAPTER.

If you own any cookbooks, look at their titles. How many of them contain the words *fast* or *quick* or *instant?* Does this same preference for speed also define your typical eating pattern? Do you wolf down a breakfast compressed into the shape of a candy bar? Do you guzzle down a liquid-energy lunch? At dinner, do you order in or eat out to wrap up this kitchen-avoidance routine?

If you must cook in your kitchen, do you see the preparation of meals as one more job that must be done day in and day out? Or if you live alone, do you create instant meals? You empty a can of soup into a pan, scramble a few eggs, or microwave a frozen meal in three or four minutes. Do you consume your meal just as quickly while you read the newspaper, watch the news, or talk on the phone?

Far too many of us have decided that we just don't have time to cook. As a result, we rob ourselves of the joy that comes with cooking. And there is an unfortunate parallel here: too often the shortcuts that we take in preparing our daily nourishment indicate a similar lack of attention to our body, mind, and soul.

Vastu living can't churn up extra minutes in your day, but it can help you establish a healthier attitude about your kitchen, which is one of the most important areas in your home. Vastu can help you establish an enticing ambience, no matter your kitchen's size or its deficiencies, so that you will want to spend time there. You will come to cherish your kitchen.

⁂ RECLAIM THE JOY OF COOKING

I remember my grandmother busy at her kitchen counter and stove as she prepared family meals. She loved cooking and made everything from scratch with as many fresh ingredients as possible. She made cooking so much fun that all her grandchildren loved to pitch in to create the communal Sunday meal. We loved to knead dough with our fingers, cut vegetables with grown-up knives, or lick a bowl until it was empty. She would pick one of us to be the food taster, one of us to set the table in our own creative way, and one of us to ring two silver bells that called everyone to the huge dining room table.

Every meal began with a blessing. It wasn't overtly religious in its language. My grandfather was guided by humor, but he always offered heartfelt thanks for his special family and the wonderful food that we were fortunate to share. As we ate our carefully prepared meal, classical music played quietly in the background—and usually an entire recording of a symphony played before we finished eating. We ate slowly, told stories, and enjoyed the love that bound us all together. Mealtime was precious—savored like the food.

Yes, this memory sounds as if it were pulled out of an ancient time capsule—nothing more than history, which is impossible to re-create in this day and age. But to stay physically, mentally, and spiritually healthy, you need to reclaim some of the essential rituals that were once identified with the kitchen and mealtime. You need to rethink your attitude about cooking and eating so that you can reconnect these activities to deeper meanings associated with nourishment. When you prepare and eat a meal, you need to remember that this is an important time to wind down and enjoy the company of others, or just your own company if you are eating alone.

❋ CLEANLINESS IS GODLINESS

Everything about your vastu living kitchen should reflect order, not disorder. In other words, clutter is your kitchen's worst enemy. Clutter creates a visible chaos that makes you avoid the kitchen, or it complicates to the point of disaster every feeble attempt to cook. So the first step in the creation of a vastu kitchen is this reality check: Do you search through a drawer to find a wooden spoon or paring knife? Do you half-empty a cupboard to locate your rice or flour or a box of cereal? Are your pot holders a visual chronology of your last ten meals?

If you answered yes to any of these questions, then you need to clear out clutter and organize your kitchen. Try to get rid of anything that you don't use or that looks like a haven for bacteria. Clean everything that you choose to keep. Consider hanging frequently used utensils above your counter or keep them, like flowers ready to be plucked, in a container that is always within reach. Organize your pots and pans and baking paraphernalia so that you can easily find them.

Since many ingredients are fragile and lose their flavor or nutritional value over time, arrange your stored food so that you can find each item and use it. You can organize everything according to links that bind various ingredients together—spices; rice, pasta, and pulses; baking goods; cereals; soups. Since buried food becomes wasted food, display perishables in labeled dark glass or terra-cotta containers or metal boxes on open shelves where you can see them. Just choose a container that is airtight and dark so that it keeps out excess light.

Your vastu living goal is to create an efficient kitchen that is so clean and free of distractions that you surrender to the rituals attached to cooking. You get into the rhythms that accompany the preparation of a meal—the staccato of the chop-chop of spices, vegetables, and fruit, the subtle changes in the aromas released by your ingredients during cooking, even your motions that are connected to cleaning up your kitchen before you sit down to eat.

Kitchen cleanliness also relates to the purity of the ingredients that go into a meal. While organic food can be expensive, it reduces your intake of dangerous chemicals. The long-term bodily harm from these chemicals can cost you dearly over time. Fresh ingredients are also versatile. You can use fresh spices as garnishes or lightly cook vegetables so that they retain their nutritional value and create a crunchy taste. You can become more creative in your presentation of fresh produce on the plate.

Most importantly, choosing fresh ingredients helps you eat according to the season, which is the ayurvedic way of following the law of nature. These days, so much produce is imported that buying "local" is difficult. But if you eat regionally grown fruits and vegetables, you pay attention to the influence of changing weather on the needs of your body. When it's cold, your body prefers hot meals that keep you warm. The local vegetables that are plentiful at this time of year tend to be gourds and tubers that need to be cooked. In warm weather, your body wants to cool down. During this time of the year, the market is usually filled with local produce that you can eat raw or that has a high water content, such as tomatoes, cucumbers, melons. By eating local produce, you avoid triggering the negative effect of the ayurvedic principle of like increases like, which can disturb your constitution.

The Spiritual Blueprint for Your Kitchen

Let's see how well the spiritual blueprint for your kitchen honors the assigned location of the five basic elements. In the Northern Hemisphere, the most favorable location for your kitchen is the southeast quadrant of the home. In the Southern Hemisphere, the best location is in the northeast quadrant of the home. In each hemisphere, this quadrant is governed by the element of fire, which is appropriate since cooking purifies your food.

If your kitchen is in another quadrant of your home, you should make an appeasement to the element of fire, which has trespassed into another quadrant, and a second appeasement to the element whose quadrant has been violated by the inappropriate placement of your kitchen. Both of these appeasements can use either calming colors or therapeutic objects that connect to the divine world of nature to restore the harmony in the offended quadrants and within your self. (See chapter 5, "Resolving Conflicts in Your Home and Workplace" for details.) If your kitchen is set into one wall in your home, please follow the advice in chapter 12, "Special Issues with Your Studio or Loft," which explains how to solve this particular problem.

☀ AVOID LIKE INCREASES LIKE

If you have a pitta or fiery constitution and you're a caterer or do other work that keeps you in the kitchen about six hours a day, the southeast quadrant can upset your constitution and put an end to harmony. You should place your kitchen in the calming northeast quadrant that belongs to the element of water. (In the Southern Hemisphere, the element of fire is in the northeast and the element of water is in the southeast.)

A caterer who created meals for people from her home had this problem with her kitchen. It was in the southeast and was even organized almost 80 percent vastu-compliant. Only the refrigerator and sink were improperly placed—problems that were acknowledged through appropriate appeasements. But her pitta constitution was severely aggravated. If it were possible, she would have shifted her kitchen into the northeast quadrant, where the element of water would cool down her fiery nature. But the entrance to her home was in the northeast, which ruled out this healthy solution.

The caterer decided to use colors, nature, and an image of someone she adored to restore balance to her constitution. She had her kitchen painted pale sage and introduced an array of green plants on the floor beneath a northern window and on the sill—creating a leafy tableau. She put a dark green coir rug in front of the sink and had her high-gloss redwood floor stripped and stained a dark, earthy tone.

Her finishing touch was her zone of tranquility in the northeast corner of her kitchen counter. She clustered tiny white seashells in front of a framed picture of the Dalai Lama, who was her spiritual leader. She said that his compassionate smile always inspired peaceful thoughts within her. She placed a thin, crystal vase with a single marigold, the flower that is typically offered to His Holiness, behind the photo. Her choices made a positive difference. The caterer overcame the negative effect of like increases like without shifting her kitchen to the northeast, the physically healthier quadrant for her and other people with a pitta constitution who spend many hours in this important space.

Your Placement of Furnishings and Appliances

As explained in chapter 12, "Special Issues with Your Studio or Loft," each of the major appliances relates to a specific element inside your kitchen. Since the sink, dishwasher, and washing machine require water, they are connected to the element of water and belong in the northeast quadrant. The stove, clothing dryer, and microwave create intense heat. They belong to the element of fire, which reigns in the southeast quadrant. The refrigerator, typically the heaviest and bulkiest appliance in your kitchen, is connected to earth and belongs in the southwest quadrant. Again, if any of your appliances are improperly placed, just make offerings to the two offended elements to eliminate the conflict.

Often your food preparation station is built in the center of a large kitchen. Its weight holds down the spiritual energy that originates here and prevents it from radiating throughout your room. If your kitchen has lots of good sunlight, you can make an attractive and useful appeasement to the element of space, which has been violated. Simply place a clay pot with a sacred basil plant on the absolute center of your workstation. This holy plant, which is connected to Lord Vishnu and frequently used in Hindu ceremonies, is believed to increase spiritual awareness and compassion. Basil also stimulates digestion and is a tasty addition to many foods.

Some apartment kitchens are so small that the eating area is in a separate dining room or adjoins the living room (see Figure 40). Other kitchens have only enough free space to place a small dining table in the northwest quadrant (see

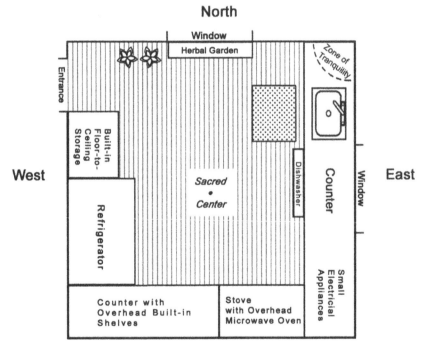

Figure 40: Spiritual Blueprint for the Food-Preparation-Only Kitchen

Figure 41). Since this quadrant is governed by the element of air with its property of quick movement, the ideal shape for the table is square-based, which has static energy. Its calming influence helps control your urge to race through your meal.

Flexibility governs the placement of your dining table and chairs in a spacious kitchen. Just avoid the direct center and the northeast, where furniture can block the healthy flow of the cosmic energy and spiritual power from the northeast quadrant to the southwest quadrant of your kitchen. If your kitchen has good lighting, try to place the table near the western wall to get the maximum benefit of the sun and minimum glare. But please remember that lightweight and low furniture belong in the north and the east, and heavy and bulky furniture belong in the south and the west.

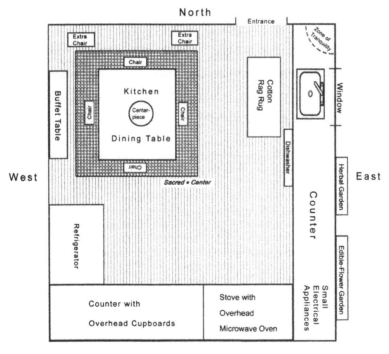

Figure 41: Spiritual Blueprint for the Eat-in Kitchen

⚜ Your Nourishing Décor

Draw Nature into Your Kitchen

Once you have done your best to honor the correct placement of the elements, introduce nature into your special room. Nature or natural products should be the main ingredient in your kitchen décor. After all, nature provides the food that nourishes your body. Nature also helps you reach the point of stillness that increases your inner peace and nourishes your mind and soul. Even when a kitchen is the most compromised area in your home, especially in cities known for small apartments, there is always room for nature.

Since your kitchen is about purity and nourishment, you can introduce nature by drawing on the qualities that connect to the sun. Nothing can survive without solar light and energy. So when you prepare food, you should even try to honor the sun by facing east in tribute to Lord Surya, the sun deity. If you must stare into a wall, add a touch of yellow, which connects to the sun, or put a decorative sun god on the wall.

COLORS THAT ENHANCE THE PLEASURE OF COOKING

Use contemplative, soft hues in your kitchen. Avoid bright colors that startle and overwhelm you and dark colors that are cold and unfriendly. Soft shades of yellow, green, white—along with their complementary nighttime colors—look lovely in this room. They connect to purity, serenity, and inspiration, which play important roles in this nurturing space.

Kitchen Gardens

Why not test your green thumb and become an indoor gardener if your kitchen is blessed with sunlight? Perhaps you can attach two shelves to a window molding and plant healthy herbs, such as holy basil, marjoram, sage, thyme, cress, chives, parsley, and mint (ginger mint, apple mint, spearmint, peppermint), and a few edible flowers, such as scented geraniums, marigolds, nasturtiums, and violets. As you nurture your kitchen-oriented garden, it nurtures you with delectable gifts that add pizzazz to your meals.

The Windowless Kitchen

If you have a windowless kitchen space, you can still display the bounty of nature. Hang a string of garlic bulbs, red chilies, or bouquets of dried roses and herbs from the ceiling. Even a one-wall kitchen can celebrate nature with a bamboo or jute soap dish, wooden dish rack and cutting board, earthenware and metal containers to hold spices and grains, cotton pot holders, cotton dhurrie on the floor in front of the sink. Let your focus on healthy meals guide your choices in the décor—buy real and organic, avoid chemicals and synthetics.

KITCHEN AIDS

WHEN THE BEE STINGS . . .
Grab the garlic. Mash up a clove and apply it to the irritated area.
Don't have garlic? Use a slice of onion.
No onion? Then crush some mint leaves and they'll bring relief.

WHEN YOU'RE BUGGED BY BAD BREATH . . .
To be up close and friendly again, chew raw parsley, fennel seeds, or any kind of mint leaf.

Your Zone of Tranquility

Your kitchen is one room that deserves a zone of tranquility that sincerely celebrates your special identity and your connection to nature. Your zone should be so rich with meaning that it beckons you into your kitchen and encourages you to take your time as you prepare your meals instead of rushing through with unhealthy shortcuts.

Your zone of tranquility can assume many forms in your kitchen, but it belongs in the gateway to the gods, which is the northeast quadrant governed by the soothing element of water. Your special display can hang from the ceiling and move gently like a mobile. It can be on the floor, on a windowsill, or on the wall. (In the Southern Hemisphere, your zone of tranquility belongs in the southeast quadrant.)

A young lawyer planted tulips, perennials that express their own rhythm of life, in a copper cooking vessel, which she placed on her counter near the northeast corner and close to her sink. She covered the soil with wood and metal buttons that were part of a collection started by her mother. She hung three blown-glass doves, which are the symbol of peace, on different lengths of blue ribbon from the ceiling directly above her tulips to complete her lovely zone (see Figure 42).

You don't need to be an artist to create your zone of tranquility. Your choices just need to come from your heart so that the display connects to you. As you focus on your display, try to let go of your worries. They keep you from relaxing and realizing a state of inner calm. These worries are also so mentally exhausting; they are one reason why cooking seems like one more chore. While cooking, you may need to reconnect with your zone when a wrong thought steals over you. Focus on the meanings attached to your display until the errant thought slides away and you are back in the now where you can unwind as you resume the rituals of cooking. Your preparation of a meal connects to creation and preservation. Creating healthy dishes maintains your body's well-being. The rhythms of cooking ease your tension, and this nour-ishes your mind and your soul. You feel good long before you sit down to enjoy the fruits of your creativity.

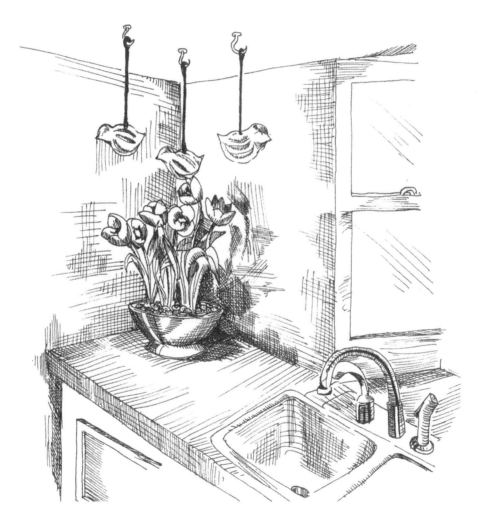

✳ Figure 42: Peaceful Zone of Tranquility

15

Nurture Your Dining Room

WELCOME TO THE VASTU LIVING DINING ROOM. PLEASE TAKE
OUT YOUR SPIRITUAL BLUEPRINT FOR THIS IMPORTANT SPACE
IF IT IS PART OF YOUR HOME AND REFER TO IT AS YOU READ
THIS CHAPTER.

Is your dining room practically kept under lock and key for use only on special occasions? Do you and your family avoid your dining room—only passing through to get to an adjoining living room or the kitchen? Does your dining room have such a formal ambience that you feel uncomfortable sitting inside this space? Does its oppressive décor suggest exclusion, not inclusion?

Many children know, and without being told, that the family's dining room is off-limits except during rare meals when they are forced to assume their best manners. And when family and guests do gather together, supposedly to share a meal and celebrate a happy event, the formality of the room affects everyone. Mealtimes in this room become so reserved that a nervous edge becomes an unwelcome side dish. Conversations are stilted. Thoughts are focused on eating quickly and getting out of this room into the warmth of a friendlier environment.

❊ THE VASTU LIVING AMBIENCE

Vastu living aims for an entirely different ambience in your dining room. This special room follows the same principles that influence the design of the vastu living kitchen—principles that are attached to the importance of food and the need to take good care of your body, mind, and soul. But while the vastu living kitchen puts an emphasis on the cook or the cooks and the meal preparation, the vastu living dining room emphasizes the pleasure that comes from sharing a delicious meal with family and friends.

Your vastu living environment eliminates that air of formality, which should never be confused with elegance. Your dining room becomes inviting—a place where you and your guests find pleasure in each other's company as you all break food together. Your surroundings should be calming and slow down eating, which is essential for good digestion and everyone's well-being.

A square or square-based table is a wise choice for your dining room. As I explained in an earlier chapter, the square represents static energy and conforms to the human form. You and your guests feel more comfortable at a square-based table and can savor the shared experience of a communal meal. If you play quiet music in the background, this also helps everyone sitting at your table unwind and relax.

The Importance of Warmth

When you walk into your dining room, you should delight in its warmth. The colors of your drapes and walls, as in the kitchen, should be soft, with hues that suggest the sunrise and the sunset. Your lighting should also promote warmth. Consider using candles on your dining room table or in sconces on the walls and dimmer switches that let you control the level of light and the room's ambience.

The Power of Connection

Try to establish a visual rhythm in your dining room that consciously binds this space to the rest of your home, especially your kitchen. Create rhythms through the reoccurring use of specific colors, aspects of nature, and special objects that connect to you—your love of art, gardening, animals, antiques, travel. Your styles of furnishings, from art deco, modern, or retro to family hand-me-downs, flea-market chic, or sidewalk rescues, can all honor vastu living. And please remember to avoid meaningless acquisitions and clutter. They create disorder, not order, and your special room ends up nurturing disharmony, not harmony—which doesn't lead to a healthy and relaxing eating experience.

THE SPIRITUAL BLUEPRINT FOR YOUR DINING ROOM

Let's check to see how well your dining room conforms to the vastu living guidelines. A nurturing dining room can be in either the east or the west of your home, but it should always be near your kitchen. A dining room in the east soaks up the inspiration and clarity that comes from the realm of the sun. A dining room in the west basks in the peacefulness associated with this direction, which brings on the hours of darkness.

YOUR PLACEMENT OF FURNISHINGS

Your dining room table is apt to cover this room's sacred center and violate the realm of Lord Brahma. But this conflict is easy to rectify. Create a dining room centerpiece that is a thoughtful appeasement to this offended deity and its element of space. One young wife placed an elegant red linen runner down the middle of her long rectangular table. On top of the runner, she placed a row of five violet-colored bowls, and inside each small bowl, she added a white candle. Violet is the complementary color of red, and these two striking colors dominated the rest of her table linen. She had red napkins and violet place mats. In Hinduism, red is auspicious and connects to spiritual power; white signifies purity. Her choice of colors contributed to a magnificent peace offering to Lord Brahma and his sacred realm (see Figure 43).

The vibrant colors were also a stylish contrast to her dining room décor. Its walls were antiqued in pale gold with a blue-stenciled border near the ceiling and the floor; her drapes were a pale blue raw silk with sheer cream panels. The double layers allowed the young wife to adjust the natural lighting and the visual play between the two complementary colors. She could either accentuate the pale blue or the translucent effect of the cream.

If you have a spacious dining room, place your table in the west or the south since this piece of furniture and its chairs are typically heavy. Your large

Figure 43: Appeasement to the Sacred Center

or bulky furniture, such as your china cabinet or buffet or serving table, also belongs near the south or the west wall where it can retain the cosmic energy and spiritual power that flows into the southwest quadrant.

Your delicate and lightweight furniture, such as a wine rack or side table or extra dining chairs, belong in the north or the east. But please try to keep this part of the room uncluttered so that the gifts that enter through the northeast quadrant can move freely in a wide arc to the southwest. Again, the center of your room should be uncovered. If this is unavoidable, please make an appropriate appeasement that is fitting for this room of nourishment. To increase the serenity in your dining room, incorporate a zone of tranquility into the northeast quadrant.

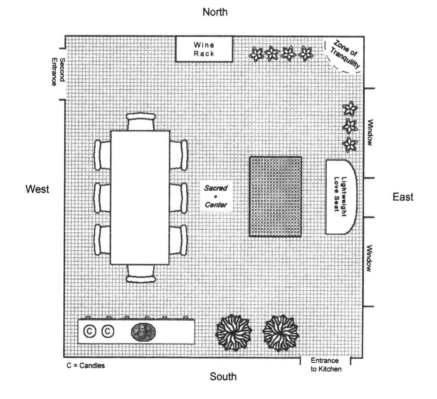

Figure 44: Spiritual Blueprint for the Dining Room

If Your Dining Area Is Part of a Larger Space . . .

A dining area that is part of a living room still has a specific purpose and function. The dining area needs its own spiritual blueprint, which demarcates its portion of the larger space. But if your dining area has a wall-less south or west, please don't block these open sides with tall or bulky furniture (see Figure 45).

Why? The answer ties back to the guidelines for maximizing the benefits of an open space. Your dining area is an extension of a larger room. You want the positive energy to travel freely throughout the entire space. The tall and bulky furniture in the wall-less south or the wall-less west holds this energy in place. So if your dining area is open in the south or the west, please place your heavy dining room furniture against the west or south walls of the larger room. If the area only has a wall-less boundary in the south, you can place the

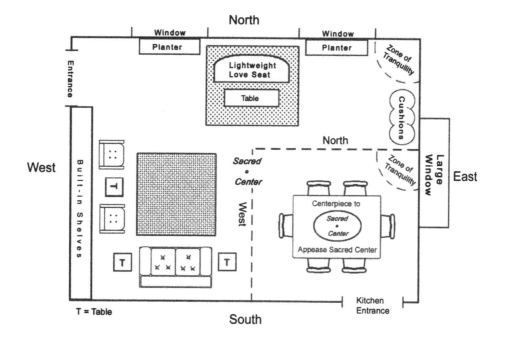

Figure 45: Spiritual Blueprint for the Dining Area Attached to a Room

heavy furniture against the west wall of the dining area. Similarly, if the wall-less boundary is in the west, the heavy furniture can be placed against the south wall of the dining area.

✳ Your Communal Décor

Joy of Nature

Have you neglected the presence of nature in your dining room? Perhaps, the same warning that discouraged the presence of your children in this room subconsciously extended to plants and organic products. Celebrate your interconnection with all existence and increase your well-being and the well-being of your guests. Invite nature into this room where you gather to enjoy nature's bounty.

If your dining room has ample sunlight, perhaps you can cluster plants together in an enchanting display. You can put healing plants on a shelf on the north wall or on a northern window if one exists in this direction and celebrate Lord Soma, the god of health. Or you can create a barrier in the southwest with a leafy palm tree and group smaller shade-loving plants around the palm's base.

If your dining room lacks windows or good sunlight, you can honor nature with a pure wool rug that uses vegetable-dye colors. Fresh fruit and flowers are a perfect centerpiece on a dining room table, but why not let your specific choices change with the seasons? Instead of hanging a glass chandelier above your dining room table, consider a simple chandelier with votive candles, where flickering flames cast shadows on the ceiling. Finally, when you decide to buy something new for your dining room, try to choose objects made from organic products, not synthetics. If you can't have the authentic thing—say, rose flowers—go for silk. Honor nature, which is your ally and deserves a prominent place in this nurturing room.

THE EDIBLE CENTERPIECE

Create a beautiful centerpiece that honors healthy foods and incorporates colors and textures, which become munchies anytime during the meal.

Put a layer of flavorful leaves from a bulb of fennel on the bottom of a wicker basket, then carefully arrange:

Red and green grapes removed from their stems.
Edamame (soybeans) gently cooked so they stay crunchy.
Bits of walnuts and almonds.
Baby carrots sliced the size of matchsticks.
Red and white raisins.

Garnish with blue pansies and yellow and orange nasturtiums.

YOUR ZONE OF TRANQUILITY

In your dining room, a successful zone of tranquility, which belongs in the northeast quadrant, should relate to the room's function. Your special display can celebrate the culinary gifts of nature, such as favorite fruits incorporated into candles or turned into fragile glass ornaments. Or your zone can include mementos that commemorate special times enjoyed in the world of nature or with dear ones who are close to your heart. (In the Southern Hemisphere, your zone of tranquility belongs in the southeast quadrant.)

A writer rescued a pine table from a junkyard and put it to excellent use. After he cleaned it up and added a light coat of wax, the recycled table, which was low and lightweight, became part of his zone of tranquility, set beneath a window in the north wall near the northeastern corner of his dining room. He draped a garland of aromatic dried herbs along the back edge of the table and let it trail down each side. The rest of the table held framed pictures of his close friends and family, who often shared meals in his dining room.

The writer loved cats, but he was allergic to them. So he showered his good feelings onto a weathered brass feline, in a pose of perfect contentment. He placed the cat on a small braided rug on the wood floor in front of the table. Near the northeast corner, he added a shallow marble birdbath where a trio of gardenia-shaped candles floated in the water.

His zone was so appealing that the writer added a wood bench with che-

North   East

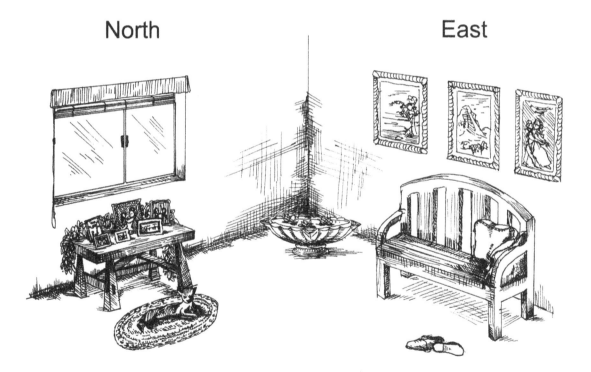

※ Figure 46: Purr-fect Zone of Tranquility

nille cushions by the east wall of his dining room. He relaxed here and focused on his display, which helped him let go of the tension that came with his deadlines. By gazing into the northeast, he also soaked up the cosmic energy and spiritual power that entered this part of the room. His dining room and his zone celebrated the rewards that come from giving and sharing. Through serving others, the light of love that shines within him filled his inner self with joy.

16

Honor Your Living Room

WELCOME TO THE VASTU LIVING ROOM. PLEASE TAKE OUT
YOUR SPIRITUAL BLUEPRINT FOR THIS IMPORTANT SPACE AND
REFER TO IT AS YOU READ THIS CHAPTER.

What is the first room that you typically see when you step inside a home or an apartment? Usually, it's the living room. And when you enter this room, your eyes typically sweep around to take in the environment, especially on your first visit. Your response is natural. As you look around, clues revealed in the décor help you form an impression of the individual or individuals who live here. You notice the colors, fabrics, decorative details—it all registers and adds up to an opinion. Sometimes these visual clues are positive, sometimes they are negative, and sometimes they are dead wrong.

Vastu living understands the significance attached to the living room—a significance that adds more meaning to its visual appearance. Once your guests step into your living room, they leave behind your transitional area (even if it is just the threshold of the door) and the outer world. They have entered the most public part of your sacred realm. It should reflect who you are, not superficially, but on a profound level that connects to your view of the world—your personal world within your home and the world that exists outside your home. Your living room is your welcoming space and should carefully observe the three vastu principles, which unmistakably express your belief in an all-encompassing holism that extends love and respect to all creation, including your own unique self.

Your vastu living décor in this space should focus on hospitality so that your visitors feel at ease and at home. Appealing rhythms, which establish continuity, help your guests relax. These same rhythms extend through your home. Repeating colors create rhythm and so do most of the objects on display. These decorative choices, which connect to you and anyone else who shares your home, often connect to strangers when they visit. They see pictures, books, a personal collection that matches their own interests, and they feel an unspoken bond that puts them at ease.

DIFFERENT PERSONALITIES — DIFFERENT NEEDS

The seating arrangement in your living room should satisfy different moods and different personality types. You know you yourself at times feel shy and at other times feel gregarious and outgoing. Or you may be a genuine extrovert and great communicator or a true introvert who is happy as a quiet observer.

All your guests deserve to feel comfortable in your living room. So your seating arrangements should accommodate individual needs. Be sure to dedicate a portion of your space to visitors who prefer to soak in the conversation rather than create it. Your entire living room still creates a cohesive whole, but it respects diversity. This approach satisfies everyone from the shyest person to the most social butterfly. Everyone feels at home.

In India, Hindus welcome each guest into their home with the word *namaste.* When they say this word, their palms, with fingers straight, are held together, and they bow slightly toward the recipient to acknowledge his or her divinity, which is the meaning of namaste. The guest is invited to sit and offered a cup of tea or a refreshing glass of cool lemon water, which, out of reciprocal kindness, is usually accepted. The welcoming nature of the vastu living room supports these customs, which represent a hospitality that exists in many Eastern religions, not just Hinduism.

Take a moment and think about your own living room. How does it measure up to this welcoming ambience? Think about your instinctive reaction to your visitors. Do you treat them as guests who are truly welcomed and accorded with deep respect? Do your eyes light up when you see them? Do you offer them something refreshing to drink when they step into this room—your sacred oasis?

THE SPIRITUAL BLUEPRINT FOR YOUR LIVING ROOM

Let's examine your spiritual blueprint and see how well your living room conforms to the recommended orientations. Your living room can be in any part of the north or the east or the west of your home as long as it is not in the absolute southeast or southwest.

Why the north? The guardian deities of this direction are Lord Kuber, who is the god of wealth and indulgence, and Lord Soma, who is the god of health. These two deities represent a healthy good time—the ideal atmosphere for a social gathering. When your living room is in the northwest quadrant, the element of air modifies this dynamic. The properties associated with air are apt to make your guests feel restless. They are unlikely to stay late. The living room in the northeast quadrant, which belongs to the element of water, is blessed with serenity. Beneficial cosmic energy and spiritual power shower social gatherings in this part of your home. And why the east or the west? A living room in the east of your home reflects the properties of the sun and showers warmth and enlightenment on your guests. A living room in the west reflects the properties of peace and quiet that come with the dark of night.

The southwest, however, is filled with strength and wisdom—properties that are better suited for your master bedroom. The southeast takes advantage of properties that work better in your kitchen. Finally, if your living room serves more than one function, please refer to the section "The Dual-Personality Room" in chapter 11, "Special Issues with Your Apartment." (If you live in the Southern Hemisphere, follow the spiritual blueprint on page 116, which shows the correct location of the elements below the equator.)

The Placement of Your Furnishings

Try to observe the rule of placing the heaviest and bulkiest items in the south and the west and the lightweight, delicate items in the north and the east. In this welcoming room, your furnishings should maximize the benefits of the cosmic energy and spiritual energy that come into the northeast. Lightweight furnishings encourage the flow of these gifts to the southwest, where they are retained by your heavy objects. You also want to try to honor your living room's sacred center—and keep it empty of weight so that its positive vibrations can circulate around the space.

Your living room often has a number of heavy objects—sofa, cabinets, lounge chair, piano, book collections in floor-to-ceiling shelves. To keep your space from resembling an overstocked furniture warehouse, please use all the space in the west and the south quadrants to satisfy this guideline. If you use your piano about an hour a day, consider placing it in the northwest, where the properties of the element of air may coincide with your playing habit. But since your piano is heavy, please make an appeasement to two offended elements: the element of earth, which rules in the southwest and connects to your piano, and the element of air, which has been violated by the presence of the piano (see chapter 5, "Resolving Conflicts in Your Home and Workplace," for details).

Also remember to accommodate the needs of all your guests so that your living room puts everyone at ease. Unfortunately, many people organize this room with seating areas in a square or a U-shape that draws everyone close

THE POWER OF THE RAGA

The soothing sounds of the classical Indian raga are therapy in the form of beautiful music. A raga, which is typically created for a specific time of day, releases positive vibrations that increase your inner harmony and appeal to the inner self. Here's a brief guide to help you match the ragas to the time of day along with a short list of some of India's great performers.

For the morning, choose Bhairav or Todi ragas.

For the afternoon, choose Sarang or Bhimpalasi ragas.

For the evening, choose Marwa or Kalyan or Poorvi ragas.

For nighttime ragas, choose Kedar or Bihag or Bageshwari ragas.

Consider listening to Ravi Shankar on the sitar, Hariprasad Chaurasia on the flute, Kumar Sharma on the santoor, or these vocalists—Bhimsen Joshi, Jasraj, or Kumar Gandharva.

together. This intimidating arrangement can make shy people feel exposed and self-conscious. They retreat inside their skin and count the minutes until they can leave (see Figure 47).

The vastu living room offers choices in seating arrangements. Consider creating a seating area with your sofa and heavier side chairs in the south or the west, but leave the north and the east open. Add a special tête-à-tête created with two chairs, or a love seat and a chair, or just a stack of comfy floor cushions if the space is small; place this grouping at a slight distance from your sofa and chairs. Your guests who sit in the tête-à-tête are still close enough to the sofa so that they do not feel ostracized. They can listen in and be part of the gathering, but they won't feel pressured into speaking (see Figure 48).

Your computer and TV can also create a problem in your living room. To discourage couch-potato behavior, try to place these two objects, which rightfully belong in the southeast quadrant of fire, in the northwest quadrant. Its element of air induces restlessness and boredom. Your couch potatoes abandon virtual reality for the reality of communal activities that are going on in your living room. Just remember to make appeasements to the two offended elements of fire and air (see chapter 5, "Resolving Conflicts in Your Home and Workplace," for details).

You can also conquer the couch-potato syndrome by putting your music system in the southeast quadrant, which belongs to the element of fire. Soft music, which doesn't overwhelm conversation, adds to your positive ambience. Studies show that classical music is healthy for plants; it is also healthy for us. Music calms our mind, transports us to faraway places, or reaches inside and stirs our soul.

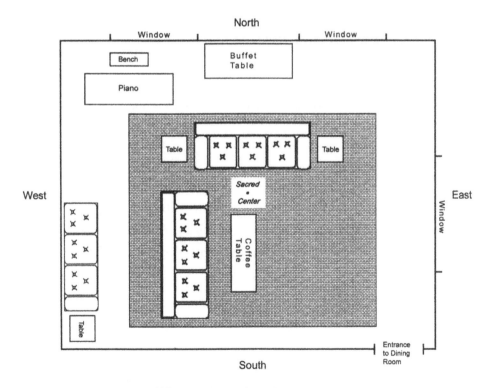

Figure 47: Speak-or-Else Living Room

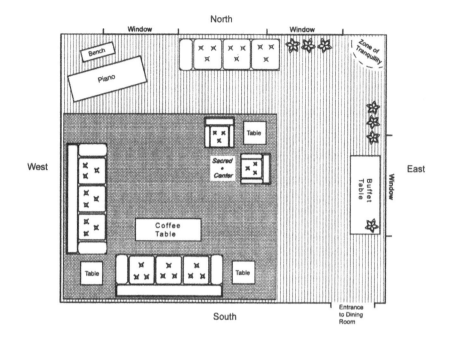

North
Window
Window
Bench
Piano
Zone of Tranquility
West
East
Table
Table
Sacred Center
Buffet Table
Window
Coffee Table
Table
Table
Entrance to Dining Room
South

✳ Figure 48: Spiritual Blueprint for the Thoughtful Living Room

Orientation Problems

The fireplace belongs in the southeast quadrant with its element of fire. But most fireplaces are built into the center of a wall. A violinist who lives in a lovely cottage on an old estate has a huge fireplace in the middle of the north wall of her living room. On either side of the fireplace, storage cupboards and built-in shelves stacked with books and old LPs extend up the wall to the exposed ceiling beams (see Figure 49B).

The violinist kept her expensive stringed instrument in the northeast, a perfect place for her valuable possession. But the violin was inside one of the cupboards that extended to the northeast corner and continued about two feet along the east wall. This heavy storage area, which belongs with the element of earth in the southwest, created an unwanted barrier in her sacred northeast quadrant. Luckily, she had two large windows on the east, one of them in the northeast quadrant. The violinist also had two large windows on the west wall.

The entire north wall was a source of conflict that ended up disturbing four elements. The element of fire, represented by the fireplace, was not in its proper place in the southeast. The heavy built-ins, which belonged in the southwest with the element of earth, violated the northeast and northwest quadrants, which were governed by the elements of water and air, respectively.

The violinist used her hobbies to create her offerings. On the windowsill

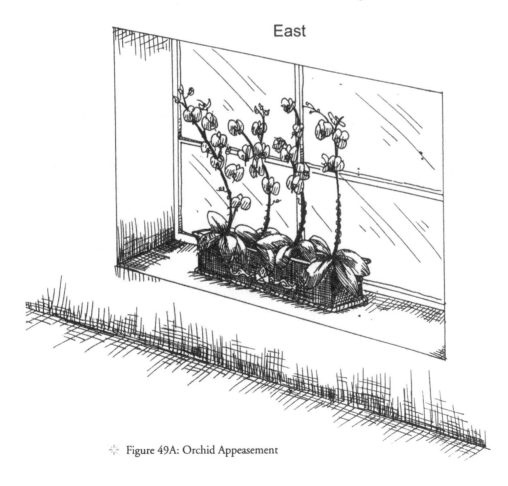

❊ Figure 49A: Orchid Appeasement

in the southeast quadrant, she appeased the element of fire with a planter that contained stunning orchids, which she worked hard to cultivate. She created two bouquets of dried flowers, preserved from her garden, and placed one bouquet on the northwest side of her fireplace mantel where it appeased the element of air and another bouquet on the floor in the southwest to appease the element of earth. On the northeast side of the fireplace, she placed a framed sheet of music and her silver metronome, which placated the element of water and helped her keep time when she practiced. These offerings, which honored the elements and nature, also celebrated her artistic nature.

North

Figure 49B: Overweight North Wall

✳ Your Welcoming Décor

Your living room décor should make meaningful statements. Objects in this room, which welcomes people into your personal environment, should never seem random or be perceived as fillers that take up space. Think about each living room object—photo, picture, trip memento, personal collection—and evaluate its significance in your life. If something on display draws a blank, then maybe it signifies clutter, nothing else. Consider removing it.

Also try to group related objects together so that they make a larger statement than a single object placed here or there. For example, celebrate the stages of life through the arrangement of your photos. Place pictures of your ancestors on the south wall or in the southwest quadrant so that you honor their wisdom and judgment. Place pictures of your children on the west wall so that they face the east, the direction that speaks of knowledge and enlightenment. Display pictures of adults who are still alive on the north wall so that you bless them with health and prosperity. Or take three objects—one that speaks of your past, another that represents your present, and a third that is ultramodern and suggests your future—and put them together to honor the unending cycle of life. In other words, turn objects into powerful symbols that add a deeper meaning to your décor. This approach, which creates an appealing

✳ The Palette

In general, the vastu living room can handle nearly any color or combination of colors as long as they don't create a somber mood. If your living room has dark paneling or lots of stone on the floor or walls, consider using autumnal tones that increase the room's warmth. If your living room is small, use pale hues on the walls and in the window treatments to create a spacious feeling, and restrict strong colors to accents in your décor—your cushions, upholstery, area rugs.

visual rhythm, reinforces a loving philosophy that makes your guests feel at home.

✳ YOUR ZONE OF TRANQUILITY

There are so many ways to create an effective zone of tranquility in your living room. If you have limited space, hang a photo of someone dear to you on the wall in your northeast quadrant. Add an object to your display that speaks of nature—a beautiful bird feather, antique silk scarf, sandalwood garland—and drape it on the photo. Position your most comfortable chair so that it faces your special display. When you sit here, concentrate on your loving symbols in this corner. (In the Southern Hemisphere, your zone of tranquility belongs in the southeast quadrant.)

If you have a large living room, let your imagination inspire you. Just remember that your zone always belongs in the quadrant governed by the element of water, and that your display needs to connect to your identity and nature. Then try to take an occasional five-minute break to look at your zone and cultivate the habit of focusing on your breathing. Learn to let go of your thoughts about the past and the future. Lose yourself in the "now" and go deep within to nurture your soul.

17

Treasure Your Study or Home Office

WELCOME TO THE VASTU LIVING STUDY OR HOME OFFICE.
PLEASE TAKE OUT YOUR SPIRITUAL BLUEPRINT IF YOUR HOME
INCLUDES THIS SPACE AND REFER TO IT AS YOU READ THIS
CHAPTER.

These days far too many of us have succumbed to the pressures that tell us
to hurry up and get things done. We rush through our work as if we're on
autopilot with the accelerator pressed to the floor. We are oblivious of each
step we take unless it becomes an obstacle that holds us back from the journey's end.

This preoccupation with the finish line interferes with our learning experience. Consider the audiobook, which lets us hear a best-seller in three hours
or less. We don't mind that it's an abridged version, and we readily surrender
the opportunity to savor individual words, underline a favorite passage, or
reread a paragraph to absorb the power of its message or to get to the heart of
its meaning. We've "read" the book and checked it off our list. We even like
doing two things at once—talking on the phone while we drive the car or
watching TV while we work out at the gym. We consider it a good use of limited time. But unfortunately, this good use of time robs us of the pleasure that

comes from fully concentrating on a single activity and getting absorbed in the "now." This is especially unfortunate when the single activity is connected to our work.

Your vastu living study or home office is purposely designed to honor the *process* that leads to learning and the completion of an assignment or work project. Your study or home office should be cozy and soothing so that you easily settle into this space. Its décor is subdued—easy on your eyes and free of clutter and room-related distractions. Its ambience helps you concentrate so that you experience the deep satisfaction that accompanies the process of discovery. Its focus on serenity reminds you to slow down and stay in the moment. It reminds you to let go of your preoccupation with the goal. Like the turtle that beats out the hare, you learn that you will finish in good time. Better yet, you savor each step of your journey.

The ambience of your study or home office expresses the three principles of vastu. The placement of your furnishings respects the proper orientation of the five basic elements so that you are surrounded by harmony and balance. Every object that you display connects to the world of nature and the special nature of your life. All this connects you to your soul. Your environment inspires you—a word that is related to "in spirit." When your environment puts you "in spirit" or in touch with your soul, inspiration flows into your work. You work with care, efficiency, and do your best to please your inner self, your spirit, your soul. You also pay attention to its needs and don't let your work consume you. Just as your study or office is in harmony and balance, you keep your life in harmony and balance.

This spiritual connection between the environment and the self supports the needs of the growing army of the self-employed who work at home, creating their own career and career path. Many of these solo workers often discover that stress over the bottom line and fear of failure is their unwanted partner. But in this positive environment, the self that is employed has the power to rise above these negative forces.

THE SPIRITUAL BLUEPRINT FOR YOUR STUDY
OR HOME OFFICE

A study or office in the northeast, which receives cosmic energy and spiritual power, is calming and serene. A study or office in the east is imbued with inspiration and creativity. The northeast and the east are ideal if you are a writer, artist, computer programmer, researcher, teacher—if you do any kind of cerebral work. A study or office in the west is peaceful and quiet—also good if your work requires contemplation. A study and office in the north leads to good health and wealth, including spiritual wealth that brings balance to your desire for material wealth.

But please beware of the northwest. If your office or study is in this quadrant, you may find it hard to concentrate. The properties associated with the element of air create indecision. You may spend hours leafing through books, flitting around the Internet, putting off important business decisions. You may end up more creative at finding reasons to avoid work and studying so that you rarely stay in your study or home office. (If you live in the Southern Hemisphere, follow the spiritual blueprint on page 116, which shows the correct location of the elements below the equator.)

Protect Your Constitution

If you work full-time in your home office, please remember to pay attention to the negative consequences attached to the principle of like increases like. If you have a pitta or fire constitution, you may aggravate your constitution by working in the southeast, which is the quadrant of fire. If you have a vata or air constitution, you may disturb your constitution by working in the northwest, which is the quadrant of air. If you have a kapha or water constitution, the northeast, which is the realm of water, may cause you trouble. If you have no choice but to work in the quadrant that matches your constitution, please follow the advice offered in chapter 5, "Resolving Conflicts in Your Home and Workplace." (In the Southern Hemisphere, fire is in the northeast quadrant, air is in the southwest quadrant, and water is in the southeast quadrant.)

✴ The Placement of Your Furnishings

Take advantage of the properties connected to each element and cardinal direction when you organize your study or home office. If your desk is heavy, put it in the southwest and sit so that you face the north, the northeast, or the east. By placing your back to the south, the properties of strength, wisdom, and judgment that are associated with this direction reinforce your leadership and decision-making skills. By facing the east, the northeast, or the north, you supplement the positive properties of the southwest quadrant with inspiration (the east), inner calm (the northeast), or health and wealth (the north).

Try to keep the north and the east relatively open or limited to lightweight and delicate furnishings so that the cosmic energy and spiritual power, which enter the northeast quadrant, can flow to the southwest quadrant. Conversely, place your heaviest and bulkiest furnishings, such as bookcases, sofa, desk, file cabinets, in the south and the west, where they become barriers that retain these gifts. Finally, do your best to keep the sacred center free of weight so that the energy from Lord Brahma's realm circulates harmonious vibrations that comfort your soul (see Figure 50).

If you have a music system in this room, try to keep it in the southeast, which is the realm of fire and connects to electricity. Also orient your computer so that it is on the southeast of your desk. But try to place your television in the northwest quadrant if you must have this potential diversion in your study or office. You will need to make an appeasement to the offended elements of air and fire (see chapter 5, "Resolving Conflicts in Your Home and Workspace"), but the properties associated with the element of air help you stay focused on your studies or work. You lose interest in the TV and turn it off.

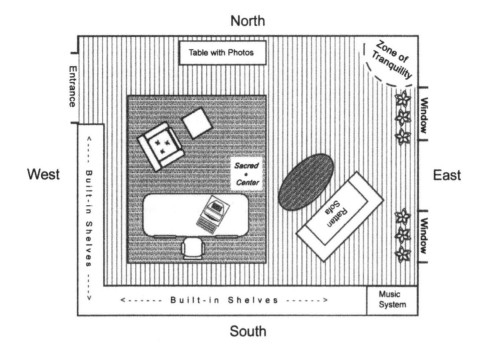

North

West

East

South

✴ Figure 50: Spiritual Blueprint for the Study or Home Office

Back against the Wrong Wall?

If your study or home office has an orientation that conflicts with vastu living, you can still make this space healthy and productive with a careful and considerate décor. Let's look at the solutions used by a graduate student who had no choice in the location of her study (see Figure 51).

This graduate student, who was studying for her doctorate in physics, had a small study in the northwest of her apartment, which was part of student housing in Philadelphia. Her study had lots of built-ins: a built-in workstation and built-in floor-to-ceiling bookshelves against the south wall and a built-in sliding-door closet in the northwest. The lightweight and heavyweight furnishings were in the appropriate quadrants, but the graduate student had to face the south when she studied.

I reminded her that when she faced this direction, Yama, the lord of judgment and death, would remind her to fulfill her duties and responsibilities. This would help her stay focused on her difficult studies and hold back the negative influence that came with a study in the northwest quadrant of her apartment. We also placed an eight-by-ten-inch mirror on the southwest corner of her workstation so that it reflected the northeast, the direction that she preferred to face. The mirror drew her attention to her zone of tranquility, which we established in the northeast corner of her study.

When she sat at her computer or read from a book, she could glance into the mirror and receive the benefits of the northeast—the serenity and quiet strength that come with the cosmic energy and spiritual power that

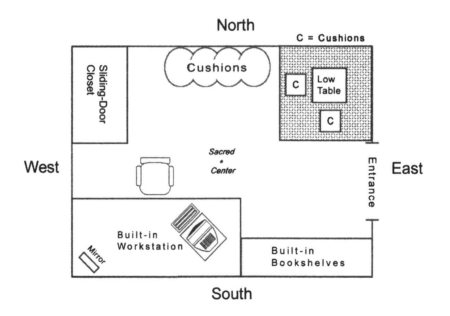

Figure 51: Remedy for the Desk Facing the South

enter this quadrant. These properties also help still the restless properties that are associated with the room's element of air. When she needed to take a study break, she could leave her workstation and absorb the power of her beautiful zone of tranquility up close. She could sit here alone or with a friend on side-by-side cushions placed before a low wood table and drink calming herbal tea from her tea set, which she had brought back from Japan, where she had been a foreign student. Her year studying there represented the most influential period in her young life. On the northeast corner of the low table, she placed a cluster of small votive candles. On the north wall near the northeast corner, she hung two old parasols—another special gift that she had carried back from Japan. Round cushions lined the north wall.

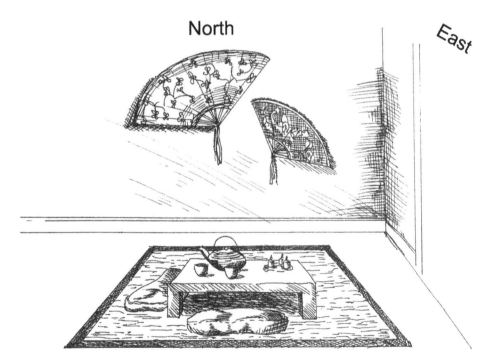

✻ Figure 52: Simple Zone of Serenity

Your Contemplative Décor

Let nature have a healthy presence in your study or office. Nature does so much good in this room. If you have sufficient lighting, cluster plants together in attractive displays. The sun acts like a spotlight that draws your attention to the details of the foliage and blooms—their changing colors throughout the day. Their loveliness reaches into your soul and fills you with inspiration.

Even products created out of nature exert a calming influence that helps you focus on the now of your work or studies, not issues that are unrelated to the activity at hand. Earth tones in natural grasses, wood, terra-cotta, even metals, such as brass and copper, and fabrics with vegetable-dye colors warm up the room and increase your comfort. Try to keep plastic, which is cold and severe, out of this room.

Increase the soulfulness of your study or office with carefully chosen objects that speak to your heart. Again, don't let these important items get lost inside the room. Organize groupings that make them stand out so that you notice them. Remember that pictures of loved ones who are deceased belong in the south, which is the realm of Yama, the lord of judgment and death. A

Colors That Enhance Serenity

Greens and blues promote serenity. Yellow encourages inspiration and clarity. These three colors work well in a study or home office. But it's best to stick to soft hues; bright colors can interfere with your concentration. Also, if this room is your home office—a place where you spend lots of time—remember to let your constitution be your "color" guide (see chapter 5 "Resolving Conflicts in Your House and Workplace"). You don't want to create a negative work environment where the principle of like increases like interferes with your harmony.

photomontage of your ancestors placed above your desk or favorite reading chair, if it's in the southwest, empowers you with their collective wisdom and helps you make wise decisions. Also celebrate the power of love inside this room—artwork created by your kids or memorabilia connected to shared experiences with good friends or family. These objects remind you that life is not just about work. It's about love and giving both to others and to your intimate self.

YOUR ZONE OF TRANQUILITY

Just a glance at your zone of tranquility in your study or office should remind you of your inner essence and your interconnection with all that exists. So often when we are reading, writing, or simply thinking about our studies or a project at work, our mind takes a break of its own volition. The eyes stare into the room or out a window—on a quiet search for inspiration. During this moment, your zone of tranquility, which belongs in the northeast quadrant, should seize your attention and connect powerfully to your inner self so that this break serves a positive purpose. (In the Southern Hemisphere, your zone of tranquility belongs in the southeast quadrant.)

If possible, let your zone of tranquility be a special environment all its own—a shrine to nature and your special identity. Do you have a window in the north or the east near the northeast corner? Consider adding a set of three shelves in this quadrant on the wall opposite the window. The passage of light can showcase three rows of special objects. Perhaps one row can hold candles and cherished objects that connect to your life. Another row can hold photos of loved ones. The third row can hold a few bud vases that each contain a single fresh flower (see Figure 53). All these objects celebrate the remarkable diversity that fills your world and your life with abundance and special meaning. The candles speak of the sacred and the divine. The fresh

Figure 53: Life-Affirming Zone of Tranquility

flowers, which need to be changed every few days, introduce a ritual that speaks of the cycle of life. You can even dry the blooms and recycle them as potpourri in your home.

Ultimately your zone of tranquility helps you stay balanced and centered in this particular room in which you cultivate your mind and possibly your career. These objects clearly yet quietly remind you that the greatest wealth in life comes with your time spent with family, friends, and the self. A life overtaken by work does not add up to a rich life. It ultimately leaves you impoverished and even robs you of your physical, mental, and spiritual well-being. Your zone of tranquility here will fill you with positive thoughts that are reenergizing and reinvigorating so that you are able to return to your work or studies with renewed focus and give your best effort to whatever you are doing.

SPICE UP THE ROOM

Create your own spicy potpourri to add fragrance to your study. Remove peels from two lemons and two oranges and break the peels into small pieces. Dry the pieces in a warm place until they turn brittle. Mix in four ounces of whole cloves, four ounces of allspice, five broken cinnamon sticks, and five crumbled bay leaves. Put the mixture into a recycled, wide-mouthed glass jar. Store the tightly sealed jar in a dark, cool place for six weeks so that the aromas blend together. Then put the opened jar in your study or office. Draw in the yummy fragrance.

18

Love Your Bedroom

WELCOME TO THE VASTU LIVING BEDROOM. PLEASE TAKE OUT YOUR SPIRITUAL BLUEPRINT OR BLUEPRINTS FOR THIS IMPORTANT SPACE AND REFER TO THEM AS YOU READ THIS CHAPTER.

Your bedroom, which is intimately connected to you, is the most personal room in your home. In vastu living, you want this space to feel so safe and secure that you let down your guard and always stay true to your self when you step across its threshold. And once you succumb to the pull of sleep, your vastu living bedroom should be your protective shelter—a security blanket wrapped around your soul.

For many of us, our attitude about the private nature of our bedroom makes it off-bounds to many visitors, and its closed door exposes the limits to our hospitality. Many of us only allow close family members, dear friends, and lovers inside this room—even in our absence. And often when we, as strangers, enter someone else's bedroom to use an adjoining bathroom or to put our coat on a bed during a party, we feel like a trespasser encroaching on someone's personal space. We often become so uncomfortable that we leave the unfamiliar room as quickly as we can.

Our reaction is appropriate. Your bedroom is much more than a private and personal space; it is your sacred zone within your home. Your bedroom is connected to the intimate act of creation, which sets in motion the cycle of life—a cycle that is played out on a smaller scale during your daily sleep. The hours that you spend seemingly inactive in your bed represent an important time of renewal and regeneration for the physical body. These critical hours are essential to the maintenance of good health. This act of renewal sanctifies every bedroom in your home, whether it belongs to your child or your room-mate who shares your home. Even your temporary bedroom, which may be nothing more than a convertible sofa opened up in the living room or study, is a sacred offering to your guest.

Ultimately, your vastu living bedroom is your haven inside your home. When you close its door, you become one with this room. It's no stretch to say that your bedroom should fit you like a second skin. You need to feel safe enough to reveal the most private thoughts in your heart to a dear friend or loved one whom you let into your special space. You need to feel safe enough to share and enjoy the physical expression of love that unites two bodies. This sense of oneness should also be at the core of every child's bedroom. Your youngsters deserve a special retreat where they can lose themselves in their most fragile thoughts or creative endeavors from singing, writing, and paint-ing to playing a musical instrument. They must feel secure in the knowledge that in this one place no one will disturb them or judge them while they are on their personal road to discovery.

GENERAL GUIDELINES FOR ALL BEDROOMS

Your Spiritual Blueprints

Take out your spiritual blueprint for your bedroom or bedrooms and examine their location in your home. In general, the vastu living bedroom can be in any part of your home except the southeast quadrant, which is related to the element of fire. The properties associated with this element—extreme heat and excitability—can make it difficult to calm down and fall asleep, unless you have a strong kapha (water) constitution, which douses the properties of fire. If you have a pitta or fire constitution, this warning is particularly relevant. The negative consequences of like increases like can turn your bedroom in the southeast into an emotional cauldron that is too hot for your body to handle (see chapter 2, "Personalizing Vastu Living").

You should also consider the properties associated with the governing element in each quadrant when you determine the location of your master bedroom, your children's bedroom, or your guest bedroom. A couple who lived in a three-bedroom home with their twin daughters shows the consequences when the wrong elements lord over the wrong family member. This couple struggled to get a good night's rest in their bedroom in the northwest quadrant of their home. They tossed and turned and kept each other awake. Meanwhile, their twin daughters slept soundly in their bedroom in the southwest quadrant. Their houseguests stayed in a third bedroom positioned in between the two other bedrooms and straddling the northwest and southwest quadrants.

These sleeping arrangements made poor use of the properties of the five basic elements—a fact also borne out in the behavior of the children. They were bossy. The two girls were receiving too much strength and wisdom—the properties of the element of earth, which governed the southwest. The master bedroom belonged in this quadrant to restore order inside the home. The little girls belonged in the guest bedroom in the west—the direction that provides the peace and calm that comes at night. The houseguests should be sleeping in the northwest, where the element of air and its property of movement would inspire them to leave and not overstay their welcome. (For more vastu guidelines for the master bedroom, children's bedroom, and guest bedroom, see below.)

Honor Your Special Constitution and Its Needs

Since you spend about a third of your time sleeping, it is wise to place your bedroom in the quadrant that *does not* correspond to the element that dominates your constitution. If you have a vata (air) constitution, for example, and sleep in the home's northwest quadrant, which is governed by the element of air, you may suffer from the negative consequences of like increases like. Sleep time can turn into disaster time, neither recuperative nor renewing. So please take care of your particular needs and try to follow this simple chart when you decide where to sleep in your home.

UNHEALTHY QUADRANTS FOR YOUR CONSTITUTION IN VASTU LIVING

CONSTITUTION OR DOSHA	NORTHERN HEMISPHERE UNHEALTHY QUADRANT	SOUTHERN HEMISPHERE UNHEALTHY QUADRANT
Vata / Air	Northwest (Air)	Southwest (Air)
Pitta / Fire	Southeast (Fire)	Northeast (Fire)
Kapha / Water	Northeast (Water)	Southeast (Water)

If it is impossible to control the location of your bedroom and you must sleep in an unhealthy quadrant, see *first* if the bedroom is upsetting your constitution (see chapter 2, "Personalizing Vastu Living"). If you are dominated by pitta (fire), are you irritable and overjudgmental—an emotional tinderbox? If you are dominated by vata (air), has indecision turned into radical flip-flopping? Can you even decide how to answer this question? If you are dominated by kapha (water), has your customarily slow-moving self become nearly inert? If you see that your constitution has slid out of balance, don't despair. Examine this second chart and try to place your bed in a quadrant inside your bedroom that can help restore your body's imbalance.

Healthy Quadrants for Your Constitution in Vastu Living

Constitution or Dosha	Northern Hemisphere Healthy Quadrants	Southern Hemisphere Healthy Quadrants
Vata / Air	Northeast and Southwest	Northwest and Southeast
Pitta / Fire	Northeast and Southwest	Northwest and Southeast
Kapha / Water	Southwest, Southeast, and Northwest	Northwest, Northeast, and Southwest

---

If you can't put your bed in a healthy quadrant inside your room, you can still give a boost to your particular needs with the therapeutic power of color and objects (again, see chapter 5, "Resolving Conflicts in Your Home and Workplace"). If your pitta or vata is agitated, incorporate calming influences into your bedroom décor to calm yourself down. Use soothing colors, introduce plants or organic products that introduce nature's serenity, and display meaningful objects that connect to your inner essence. If your kapha is disturbed and you struggle to get out of bed, use stimulating colors—fiery red, orange, yellow—in your décor. Review the use of this solution in a bedroom in the section "The Dual-Personality Room," in chapter 11, "Special Issues with Your Apartment." Remember, when your soul feels at home in your bedroom, positive vibrations flow through your body and increase your harmony. Call it soul, instead of mind, over matter.

The Placement of Your Furnishings

Place lightweight and low furnishings in the north and the east of your bedroom. Put heavy and tall furnishings in the south and the west. By following this vastu guideline, your bedroom radiates positive energy and encourages you to spend time in your sacred space.

Your bed, which is typically the heaviest and bulkiest item in your bedroom, can often interfere with this guideline. If you have an uncooperative bedroom and can't place your bed where it belongs—in the southwest quadrant—please remember to make an appeasement in the southwest to the element of earth, which has been slighted, and a second appeasement to the element whose space has been violated by the inappropriate presence of your bed (see chapter 5, "Resolving Conflicts in Your Home and Workplace").

Your bed can also cause trouble with the element of space by violating its realm in the center of your bedroom. If your bed must cover the sacred center, please make an appeasement to Lord Brahma and the element of space to restore their harmony and your own inner harmony (see chapter 5).

Finally, two people who sleep in the same bed often have different constitutions and this can create a problem. Someone with a vata (air) constitution may share a bed with someone who has a kapha (water) constitution. In this example, the best location for the bed is the southwest quadrant, which is healthy for any constitution. But if this quadrant isn't an option, place your bed so that it straddles two quadrants. Perhaps you can put the bed so that it straddles the southwest and southeast quadrants or the northwest and southwest quadrants. In each situation, the person with the vata constitution should sleep on the southwest side of the bed, and the person with the kapha constitution should sleep on the southeast and northwest side of the bed, respectively (see Figure 54 A & B). Someone with a kapha constitution can often tolerate the heat of fire, which reigns in the southeast. The kapha cools

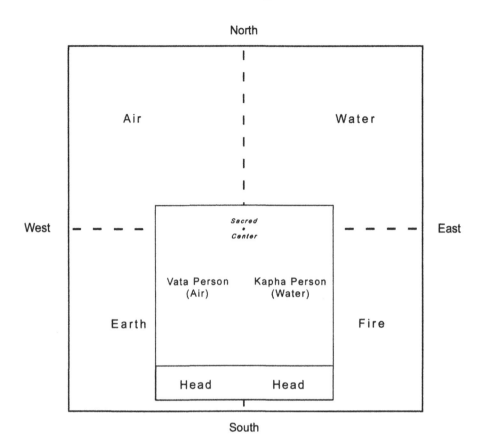

North

Air

Water

West

Sacred
•
Center

East

Vata Person
(Air)

Kapha Person
(Water)

Earth

Fire

Head

Head

South

Figure 54A: Keeping Calm in the Bedroom

down the emotional heat. But when each person sleeps on the *side* of the bed that is healthy for the constitution, this can restore the harmony.

Guidelines for a Healthy Sleep

Sleep with your head in a positive direction. When your head is to the south, this direction offers a deep, satisfying sleep. When your head is in the east, this direction, which connects to inspiration and enlightenment, enriches your subconscious as you sleep. Sleeping with your head to the west is a neutral direc-

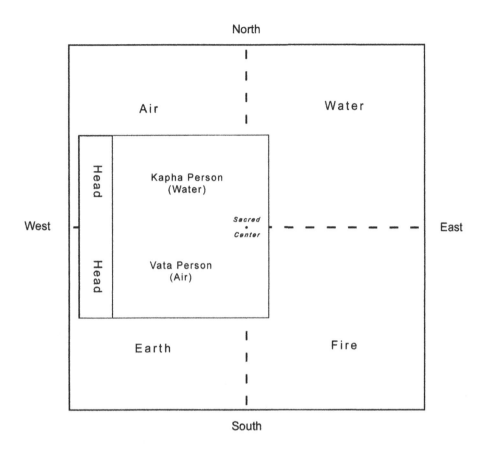

North

Air   Water

Head | Kapha Person
     | (Water)

                    Sacred
                    •
                    Center

West — — — — — — — — — — — East

Head | Vata Person
     | (Air)

Earth   Fire

South

　 Figure 54B: Keeping Calm in the Bedroom

tion. It does no harm. But sleeping with your head in the north spells trouble. Your head is considered the north pole of your body. When you sleep in the same direction as the earth's magnetic north pole, the two poles behave like magnets. They repel each other and interfere with your sleep. Many people have asked me what they can do when they must sleep with their head to the north. I simply say that they don't have to sleep with their head to the north. Their headboard can be in the north, but they can turn their body around and put their head in the south. This may seem like a strange thing to do, but it works.

HELP YOURSELF
FALL ASLEEP

You probably know that a warm bath can help you relax before you slide into bed, but here's a bath with a restful twist. Take a small muslin bag or cheesecloth, fill it with some dried lavender and chamomile, and hang the bag from the hot water tap as you draw in the water for your bath. Sit back and relax. You will grow sleepy.

Also remember to place your bed and any chair or sofa in the bedroom four inches from the wall. The wall emits energy that can disturb the energy that is released by your own body. This interaction can easily disturb your inner harmony and peace.

Your Nurturing Décor
Peace through Comfort

Your vastu living bedroom décor supports the act of renewal that is associated with this part of your home. Select window treatments that you can draw shut to block out the sunlight when you need to take a nap in the afternoon or sleep late in the morning. You want to be able to control the lighting in your bedroom so that you can get enough sleep to keep your body healthy.

Guard your inner peace and carefully choose the images that you display inside your bedroom. Photos and pictures in your room need to be a source of positive inspiration, especially the image that you are mostly likely to see when you first open your eyes. Subject matter that is upsetting and negative can poison your mood. It doesn't belong in this room that serves as your personal oasis.

Finally, do you remember the Western flirtation with the circular bed? The popularity of this bed was short-lived. The body didn't like the shape and kept moving around. Many people woke up feeling anything but rested. The circular bed is a good example of the dynamic energy that comes with this shape. Furnishings that are circle-based may be appropriate in environments where you want animation and a fast pace, but they do you little good in the bedroom. Small circular objects will not cause problems, but let square-based furniture and mirrors reign supreme in your boudoir so that your mind calms down and your body relaxes.

Peace through Nature

Bring nature into your bedroom—lots of it! What better way to honor the cycle of life than through objects from the natural

PAIN IN THE NECK OR BACK?

If you wake up with a sore back or stiff neck, don't ignore these body signals. Treat your self with care. Please replace an unhealthy mattress or futon or pillow that punishes your body. The negative consequences seep through your body into your mind and soul.

world? All of nature respects harmony and order, and when it surrounds you in your bedroom, its presence has a soothing impact on you. It reminds you of your interconnection to all that exists. You feel the harmony and order that governs your world and every form of creation.

Use organic products—lots of them, too! A bedroom filled with products that connect to the earth amplifies the comfort that should define this space. Picture a wastepaper basket made of plastic; picture one made of grass fiber. Which would you prefer in your bedroom? And don't overlook the bed linens (and even your bedclothes). Sheets and coverings that are made of natural fibers breathe. They help keep your body cool in the heat of the summer and warm in the cold of the winter.

Finally, let fresh air into your room for at least five minutes every day. Try to remember to open a window in your room every morning and leave it open while you make your bed—even in the winter. Fresh air is healthy and invigorating. Breathe it in deep at the start of your day.

COLORS OF PEACE AND HARMONY

Bedroom colors need to be gentle on your eyes and relaxing to the spirit so that you can settle down and fall asleep. Use bright colors sparingly. Their vibrancy and intensity go a long way—like a splash of perfume. You can use cheerful, warm colors from coral to yellow, but keep their hues soft—a hint that can be accentuated in the window treatments or rugs or other décor touches. Warm tones can improve the ambience of your bedroom if it lacks natural light. Cooler tones, such as pale blues and greens, can make your bedroom feel more spacious. But please stay away from brash colors that shout at you in this special room where you want to relax and sleep.

Honor the Self

Every bedroom is about the self—so let your bedroom speak of you—quietly, yet clearly. The self and the world of nature are of equal importance in your room's décor. But display these objects prominently so that you notice them. Objects, photos, or mementos that are placed haphazardly on a bookshelf or surface are lost to the eye. You want to show them off and create a visual statement that expresses the special interests that define your essence—and also help you feel connected to this sacred space. Organize photos in meaningful displays on your bureau, nightstand, or wall. Group together mementos and other collectables so that you are aware of their presence and importance. Just remember that pictures of the deceased belong on the south wall, which is reserved for ancestors and the departed.

Your Zone of Tranquility

Your zone of tranquility serves many important functions in your bedroom. Your special display, which connects to your inner self, strengthens the per-

SAY NO TO CLUTTER AND BEDROOM DISORDER

Please don't let clutter take over your bedroom—like dust balls that multiply under the bed. Clutter keeps us from seeing what matters. Also choose order, not disorder. Don't let your clothes collect in a heap on your bedroom floor or chair, or let a mess go unchecked on the shelves of your bureau, bookcase, or closet. If you can't keep your most private room in order, what does this say about the rest of your life?

sonal nature of this room and enriches its sanctity. Your zone of tranquility also helps calm your constitution if it is disturbed by a less than perfectly located bedroom or bed. It can help soothe your mind and reduce irritations that may interfere with your ability to relax or sleep. Every bedroom, even your temporary guest bedroom, deserves its special zone of tranquility, which should be placed in the northeast quadrant of the room. (In the Southern Hemisphere, your zone of tranquility belongs in the southeast quadrant.)

YOUR MASTER BEDROOM

The Orientation of Your Master Bedroom

A master bedroom in the southwest quadrant brings wisdom and strength; this is definitely the ideal location for parents. The balance of power remains in their hands—not the hands of their children. If you live alone or with a partner or a roommate, any location is acceptable for your bedroom, except the southeast. Just be mindful of your constitution and try to sleep in a part of your home that is healthy for you and anyone else with whom you share your bedroom. (In the Southern Hemisphere, the master bedroom belongs in the northwest quadrant.)

The Placement of Your Furnishings

Your bed should also be located in the southwest quadrant to reinforce the strength and wisdom that comes with this part of the room. If you must place your bed somewhere else, then pay attention to the principle of like increases like and choose a healthy quadrant (see "The Placement of Your Furnishings," page 223). Also remember to appease any elements that have been violated by the inappropriate placement of your heavy bed. If you disturb the harmony of the five basic elements, you are probably disturbing your own inner harmony.

If you have a spacious bedroom, consider creating an intimate area inside your personal space. Put a love seat or divan or an Indian swing that hangs from the ceiling in the northwest quadrant and orient the furniture so that you can face the northeast, which is serene and calming and holds your zone of tranquility (see Figure 55). Use this area for private tête-à-têtes or as your special place to sit with your lover to get in the mood for romance, or as your place to relax for a while and absorb the power of the northeast. The northwest, which belongs to the element of air, will not let you stay too long in this quadrant. You will get up and leave after you have experienced some quality time. You can also place this private area in the southeast. This quadrant, which belongs to the element of fire, can fuel passionate desires that are played out in your bedroom. Or you can place this area in the west where you can look into the east for inspiration or the northeast for spiritual enrichment.

Your Décor

If you live alone, let your bedroom reflect that love that flows from your heart. Surround yourself with mementos and images that connect to the special people who have enriched your life—a significant other, members of your family, dear friends, even favorite books and paintings that have touched your soul. If you are married or share your bedroom with someone special, celebrate the love that brought the two of you together. If possible, create a wonderful display on the northern wall that celebrates your relationship—pictures that commemorate the courtship, the wedding day, and special times thereafter. The north, which is governed by Lord Kuber and Lord Soma, showers your relationship with wealth (including spiritual wealth) and health. Consider grouping photos of your child or children on the west wall where they face into the east, which is connected to inspiration and enlightenment. But do remember to keep pictures of loved ones who are deceased in the south where you can draw their wisdom into your personal life, your relationship, or your role as a parent.

Think of a wedding or any romantic event—even the prom that you attended when you were sixteen. Nature was there in abundance, wasn't it?

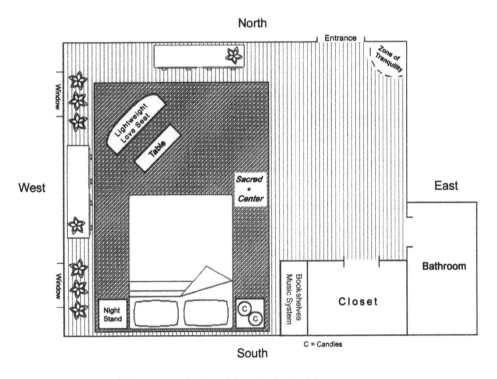

Figure 55: Spiritual Blueprint for the Master Bedroom

Flower centerpieces graced the tables; garlands may have draped the doorways. There were corsages, bouquets, boutonnieres. Can you imagine these events without the presence of nature?

Nature belongs in your bedroom; synthetics don't. Plastics are impersonal; they work against the ambience that you want in this room. Try to keep arrangements of fresh flowers or dried flowers, potpourri, or candles on surfaces where they spark thoughts of love and romance. And keep an entertainment system in this room. Music, sensual or contemplative, helps create a positive and healthy mood. Just try to keep the speakers small and discreet and try to conceal the synthetic components in a cabinet.

Your Zone of Tranquility

Your perfect zone of tranquility in the master bedroom is an expression of love—a love that is boundless and life-affirming. You can honor your partner, your child or children, a noble soul who has inspired you with his or her selflessness and unlimited compassion, even a beloved pet whose dedication to you is unconditional and constant. Let this source of love become the focus of your zone so that you acknowledge the importance of this meaningful relationship in your life.

If you have a partner, you can commemorate an important occasion involving both of you—your honeymoon or a special trip that cemented your relationship. Honor this moment in your display. See if you can find pieces of old luggage in a flea market or secondhand store where their age and battered edges speak of travel and journeys. Let this luggage symbolize the journey that commenced between you and your partner, and stack two pieces near the corner of the northeast quadrant. Display three pictures of you and your partner or the entire family that has come from this union on the top suitcase. Put a couple candles on the southeast corner, which belongs to the element of fire and symbolizes purity (see Figure 56).

Open the third suitcase and put it in front of the other two pieces. Place three ceramic planters inside and fill each with a plant or flowers that reminds you of your special moment. If your trip was in the desert, create three environments with cacti or other desert plants. If your trip was in the mountains, choose ferns that thrive in the forest. If your trip took place in the tropics, choose blooms with hot, sensual colors.

When you or you and your partner focus on your zone of tranquility, imagine that the three ceramic pots with plants or flowers, the three suitcases, and the three photos represent the past, the present, and the future or the cycle of life that begins with creation. Let your entire display celebrate love, interconnectedness, eternity. As you sit here together, think of the memories attached to your special moment commemorated in your display,

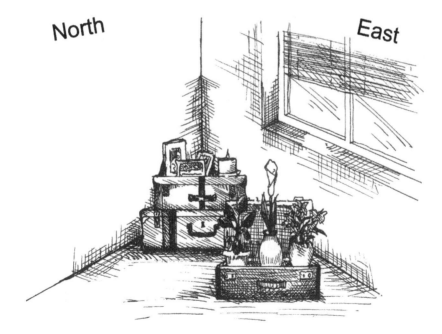

Figure 56: Zone of Love

and let the love shine from your souls and flow unimpeded into your special bedroom.

Your Child's Bedroom

The Orientation of Your Child's Bedroom

Try not to place your child's bedroom in the southeast or southwest quadrant of your home. Unless your child has a strong kapha or water constitution, the properties associated with the element of fire can create rambunctious behavior. A child's bedroom in the southwest, as you have seen, upsets the balance in your home. The property of earth gives the child too much power. A child's bedroom in the east fills children with inspiration and enlightenment. A child's bedroom in the west increases the peace and calm that comes with the night. A child's bedroom in the south, but not in the southwest or southeast corner, fills children with responsibility and judgment.

If your child has graduated from college and you would like him or her to flee the nest, give this son or daughter a little assistance. Place the bedroom of your reluctant adult in the northwest quadrant of your home or at least place the bed in the northwest quadrant of the bedroom. The properties of air generate thoughts to move out of the home and enter the next stage of life. (In the Southern Hemisphere, this bedroom would be in the southwest quadrant.)

The Placement of Your Child's Furnishings

Children, who are in the formative years, should receive the healthy benefits that come from the cosmic energy and spiritual power that enter the northeast quadrant of their bedroom. Since these gifts need to flow in a wide arc to the southwest quadrant, please keep low and lightweight furniture in the north and the east. Also place the heavy and bulky furniture in the south and the west so that they create a barrier that help retains these gifts in their room. Also try not to cover the sacred center with its creative power so that your children receive the positive vibrations that circulate from this realm.

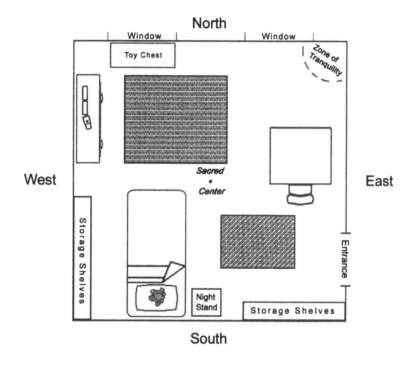

Figure 57: Spiritual Blueprint for a Child's Bedroom

If two children share a bunk bed and they each have a different constitution, try to place the bunk bed in the southwest, which is healthy for any constitution. If one child ends up sleeping in a part of the room that is not good for his or her constitution, then introduce therapeutic influences inside the room that will help restore the balance in an agitated constitution (see chapter 5, "Resolving Conflicts in Your Home and Workplace").

Try to place desks, reading chairs, or reading areas so that your children face the east or the northeast. These directions fill them with inspiration and creativity. But if your children hate to study, consider placing their desks or study area so that they face the south, the direction that reinforces duty and responsibility. This direction reminds them to work hard. Children who study in the northwest lose their focus. The distracting properties that come with the element of air inspire your children to do anything but their homework. They create inventive excuses to pop up and down from their desk.

If your children must have a television in their bedroom, place it in the northwest quadrant, where the properties of air do some good. Your children will lose interest in TV, which is all too often a distraction from doing homework. Watching TV is also a passive activity that robs your children of the benefits that come with positive interaction and engagement. Children who become absorbed in video games may develop fast reflexes, but is this asset a reasonable trade-off?

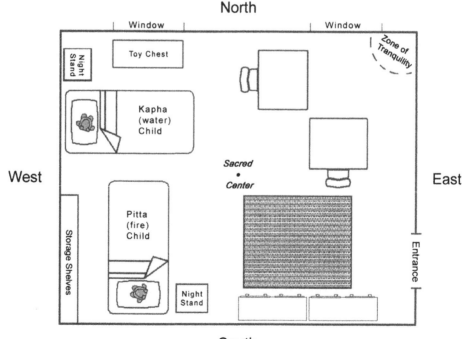

Figure 58: Spiritual Blueprint for the Children's Bedroom for Two

Your Child's Bedroom Décor

Encourage your children to participate in the decoration of their own bedroom. Their bedroom is all about them—including their process of discovery and enlightenment; it is not about your intentions or dreams for them. You can guide them along their path and give them the tools that they need; but they should make the choices that fill in the blanks. For example, you can provide them with a bulletin board, preferably placed in the healthy direction of the north or the east. But you should let them choose what to display. The bulletin board should celebrate what they love. Or you can suggest that they devote a shelf in a bookcase to objects that are important to them. And yes, many objects that belong to your young child may very well be plastic—but again you need to let them choose what belongs on this special shelf.

All these efforts pay off. In time, your children will have fully claimed their bedroom as their own space—their oasis that they love because it speaks of them and to them. When children love their bedroom, it is so much easier to teach them the importance of keeping it neat, clean, and organized. Each time they go through the traditional ritual of "spring cleaning," they become aware of their own changes and growth. They rethink their relationship with objects and let go of things as they move on. Their room changes as they change, but there is one constant: the bedroom stays connected to them. They never lose sight of the importance of claiming their space and making it their own. They find comfort inside their sacred space.

Help your children incorporate nature into their bedroom. Encourage them to choose objects from the world of nature to display inside their room. This is such an easy and winning way to teach them to respect their world with all its beauty and diversity. Nature also "warms up" the ambience inside their bedroom and makes it friendlier and more welcoming.

Consider initiating interactive experiences. If your children's bedroom has good lighting, show them how to start a special garden that they can grow from seeds or from cuttings that they collect on their own. Or let them have an aquarium if they are able to commit to the care of aquatic life. Or let them create their own imaginative underwater scene in a big bowl of water that they fill with objects from the sea, except for marine life.

Your objective when it comes to incorporating vastu living into your children's bedroom is to convey the message of the three vastu principles to these special young souls. You want your children to understand that they are special, unique, and specially loved. They, in turn, need to learn to love their own uniqueness, all humankind, and all creation. They need to see that all existence is sacred and worthy of respect.

Your Child's Zone of Tranquility

Don't overlook the zone of tranquility in the organization of your child's bedroom. And children, even a child as young as four, should be given the opportunity to decide what goes into their personal display. You may need to guide or assist your younger children, but this turns the creation of their zone of tranquility into a special shared moment. You hear your children describe what matters to them in their young life. And when it comes time for them to add something from nature, you can initiate a thoughtful discussion about holism, without even using this word. You can help your children understand that everything in the world has value and deserves their love, respect, and protection. You can help your children understand that this love and respect extends to themselves, everyone whom they know, and all the people unknown to them who share this world.

Children, with all their exuberance and energy, benefit from having an area in their bedroom that celebrates serenity and reflection. Once their zone of tranquility is set up in their room, they may get interested in the practice of simple yoga postures. Or at bedtime, when you sit with your children for a few minutes, you can talk with them about their zone of tranquility and listen to them express important thoughts about the objects that they have incorporated into their display.

North   East

※ Figure 59: Child's Zone of Tranquility

※ YOUR GUEST BEDROOM

Often a guest bedroom is impersonal—the second function in a room that is primarily a den or a living room—a "makeshift" converted space that is dismantled once a guest leaves. Yes, your guest bedroom can be a temporary bedroom, but it should still welcome your guest who has been invited to spend the night. Your guest bedroom should never feel like a hotel bedroom—

impersonal and painfully transitory—even if it is an inflated mattress blown up into shape and placed on your living room floor.

The Orientation of Your Guest Bedroom

Your guest bedroom belongs in the northwest quadrant, where the properties of air ensure that your visitors leave before they overstay their welcome. When you arrange the room's furniture, follow "The Placement of Your Furnishings," page 223. (In the Southern Hemisphere, the guest bedroom belongs in the southwest quadrant.)

Your Guest Bedroom Décor

Your overnight guests need to feel welcomed inside your home. If your guest bedroom does double duty and serves as a study or living room, then the décor of this space already conforms to vastu living. It reflects your personal identity and reveals your respect and love for nature. When you have a separate guest bedroom, please let the rhythms of your home flow into this room. Your guest bedroom should not be alienated from the rest of your home. Its colors and the objects on display should reflect the special interests connected to your unique identity and nature.

Don't ignore the importance of your guest bedroom décor. Too often, this bedroom gets the leftovers, hand-me-downs, and room discards. If this describes your guest bedroom, please give these furnishings new life. Recycle them with love and make them inviting and friendly to every soul.

Your Guest Bedroom Zone of Tranquility

Surprise your houseguests with the wonderful welcoming gift of a sweet zone of tranquility that you have created just for them. Even if your guest bedroom is a convertible sofa opened into a bed or an inflatable mattress on the floor, you can create a tiny display right on the bed. Lay a single flower across the northeast corner of the pillow; add a wrapped piece of chocolate along with a few words of welcome written on a note by you or someone else in your family. Nature. A piece of chocolate. A note expressing sweet sentiments. This large-hearted display offers warmth to your guests and helps inspire good dreams.

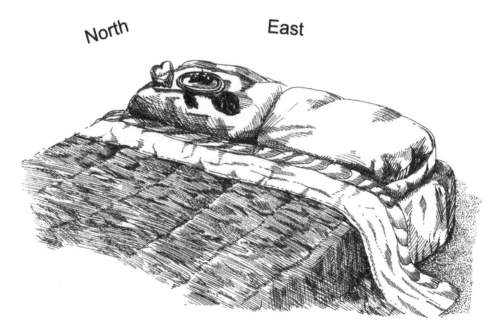

North   East

Figure 60: Sweet Something

19

Venerate Your
Zone-of-Tranquility Room

WELCOME TO THE VASTU LIVING ZONE-OF-TRANQUILITY
ROOM. IF YOU HAVE A ROOM THAT YOU CAN DEDICATE TO
YOUR SOUL, THIS CHAPTER SHOWS YOU HOW TO CREATE THE
NURTURING ENVIRONMENT THAT IT DESERVES.

How fortunate if you have a spare or underused room in your home. You can turn this space into a dedicated zone of tranquility—a room of harmony that offers love and respect to your special self. Your zone-of-tranquility room becomes your refuge—a place that you enter every day to surround yourself in serenity. You can learn to meditate, where you cultivate and savor a rewarding ritual in which you learn to turn inward and focus on your soul. You completely empty your mind of all thoughts and concentrate exclusively on the quiet voice of your inner being. A wrong equation is corrected: your mind stops controlling you; your soul points the way.

When you sit in this room and focus on your display, which is the heart of this special space, you let yourself begin a profound journey of self-discovery. You come to see your connection to all creation, which brings you great com-

TRY TO QUIET YOUR MIND

Lie down on your back on a mat or a towel in the evening with your arms stretched along the sides of your body. Point your toes, and as you slowly inhale, slowly lift your arms, keeping them straight as you raise them over your head and place them down on the floor. Hold this pose for a few seconds. Then slowly exhale while you bring your arms over your head and back down to the sides of your body.

Repeat this exercise three times. It is a wonderful way to still your mind and stretch your body.

fort. You find great joy in your realization of the divinity that defines the essence of all existence, including your own precious soul. Your soul is liberated and sets in motion a process that helps you discover inner peace and inner harmony as you re-establish your natural state of equilibrium that improves the well-being of your body, mind, and soul.

By taking time from your busy day to still your body and your mind, you also discover the inner strength that comes from stillness. Steady breathing for as little as five minutes rejuvenates you and helps relieve the tension that builds into stress over a day, a week, or a month. By focusing on your inner self, you realize an important truth: when you take good care of your soul, it takes good care of you.

THE SPIRITUAL BLUEPRINT FOR YOUR ZONE-OF-TRANQUILITY ROOM

You are deeply blessed if the room dedicated exclusively to your zone of tranquility is in the northeast quadrant of your home. This realm, governed by the element of water, is the gateway to the gods. It is a repository of the cosmic energy and spiritual power that enter your home. (In the Southern Hemisphere, your zone-of-tranquility room belongs in the southeast quadrant.)

✴ THE PLACEMENT OF YOUR FURNISHINGS

Your zone of tranquility, which is your oasis of peace and serenity, should have few furnishings—the fewer the better. You need your special display, which is your point of focus, and a comfortable sitting area. Your seating area should be simple—mattresses or mats or just a group of cushions. If you find it difficult to sit on the floor, then consider a low divan or even an Indian swing that

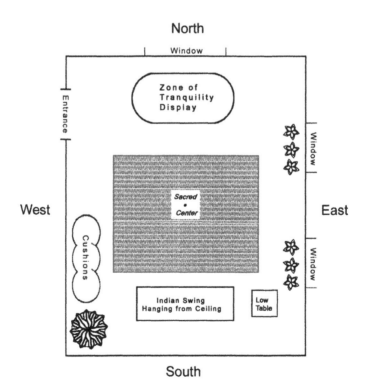

✴ Figure 61: Spiritual Blueprint for the Zone of Tranquility in the Northeast of the Home

hangs from the ceiling. Minimum furniture allows the positive vibrations to circulate freely in this room. Minimum furniture also gives you enough space to practice healthy yogic postures and breathing exercises that are good for your particular constitution.

If your zone-of-tranquility room is in the northeast quadrant of your home, then place your special display in the north, the northeast, or the east (see Figure 61). Place your mat, mattress, cushions, or low divan in the southwest quadrant so that your back is to the south or the west so that you can focus on your display. The wisdom of the ancients connected to the south and the peace and quiet connected to the west are extremely beneficial to you in this powerful space.

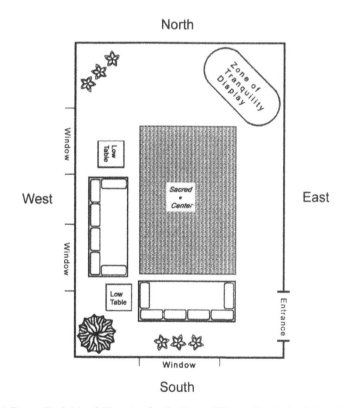

Figure 62: Spiritual Blueprint for the Zone of Tranquility in the Other Quadrants

If your zone of tranquility is in another quadrant of your home, then place the display in the northeast quadrant, and again, sit in the southwest (see Figure 62). This arrangement makes it easy for you to focus on your display. You also receive the positive benefits that flow to this part of the room from the northeastern gateway to the gods.

☀ Your Becalming Décor

Please keep the décor of your zone of tranquility simple so that you don't inadvertently create distractions. This is a nurturing space. It requires a calming ambience. Restrict your use of stimulating colors, such as red, orange, or yellow, to your special display. Even here, use them sparingly so that you don't defeat your quest for inner harmony. Stay with shades of white, which speak of purity, or pale hues of the colors in the visible spectrum along with their complementary nighttime color for your walls, seating area, and area rugs (see the color chart in chapter 4, "The Power of Color"). Also create muted lighting with a dimmer switch or a table lamp that uses a low-watt bulb or an arrangement of candles, with their flickering, hypnotic flames. But incorporate these candles into your special display so that they don't pull you away from your point of focus.

Your zone of tranquility, while simple and purposely understated, is beautiful, but on a personal level that connects to your display. A painter had a small room adjoining his bedroom. It was designed as a dressing area, but he meditated daily and realized immediately that this space would serve a greater value as his zone of tranquility. His bedroom was in the northwest of the home, but the dressing room was built off the northeast of the bedroom and perfectly located. It even had two windows: one in the north and one in the east.

This painter has a great eye for textiles and colors. He took a long silk scarf from India, with gold threadwork and a palette that reflected the colors of the sunrise, and hung it on the eastern wall near the northeast corner. The scarf shimmered so in the early-morning light that it was easy to see why the light that comes in from the north is called the painter's light.

On the floor, the painter placed a simple coir mat, and directly below the scarf, he used eight bricks to form a perfect square. This became his altar. He took a small square piece of white linen and set it on the center of his altar where just the edges were visible under a beautiful wood carving of the Buddha that was the focal point of his display. He placed three white votive candles on the southeast corner. His meditation bench in front of his lovely altar was the final touch.

The earthy red of the bricks and the flames from the candles spoke of the purity of fire. The white linen also symbolized purity. The bricks, silk scarf with its gold threads, coir mat, Buddha carving—every element of the display—spoke of nature and its diversity. The painter's zone of tranquility was spiritually powerful, and the room's simplicity, absent of all distraction, helped

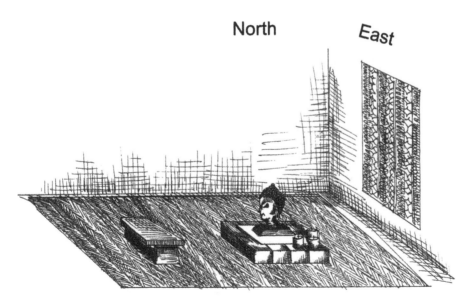

❖ Figure 63: Painter's Delight

him focus on his perfect display that celebrated his faith and his love of the arts—which was so beautifully expressed through the hand woven textile and its remarkable interplay of color that captured the sunrise.

I have seen other effective zones of tranquility where a display is woven around the positive vibrations associated with music and objects that express nature. The focal point is an instrument, such as the *tabla* (Indian drum) or just a couple of small brass bells. Quiet music plays in the background. A candle burns nearby. The music induces calm, and the instrument and flickering flame become a source of reflection that rids the mind of negative distractions. All the energy is channeled inside and focuses on the inner essence.

Another successful motif for your dedicated zone of tranquility accentuates the element of water, which governs the northeast quadrant, and honors it in your display. You can take a shallow bowl of water and float leaves and petals inside. Add a low-burning candle to the southeast of the water, which speaks of purity and enlightenment. On the wall, you can hang a picture of your family or someone in your life who makes you feel good to be alive.

Whatever you choose to acknowledge in your personal display, please remember that it must always represent your personal identity and speak to your heart, honor an aspect of nature, and add up to a celebration of the divinity that exists in all creation. Whatever minimal furniture or decorative touches that you put into your room should also pay careful attention to the proper placement of the elements and the vastu guidelines that are related to heavyweight items in the south and the west and lightweight items in the north and the east. This is one space where you don't want too many conflicts that require appeasements. And a minimal décor usually makes this an easy goal.

20

Purify Your Bathroom

WELCOME TO THE VASTU LIVING BATHROOM. PLEASE TAKE
OUT YOUR SPIRITUAL BLUEPRINT FOR THIS IMPORTANT SPACE
AND REFER TO IT AS YOU READ THIS CHAPTER.

✴ THE ROOM FOR YOUR TEMPLE

Our bathroom is frequently the most mistreated room in our home. Yet, this room, which is inextricably connected to purification, is extremely important in vastu living. Your bathroom is where you take care of your physical body—where you keep it clean, keep it healthy, and pamper it. The statement that I made about the vastu living kitchen bears repeating here: how well you take care of your physical body indicates how well you take care of your soul.

Is there a coating of grime in your bathtub or shower stall? Does your sink have a web of human hair as its drain catch? Do your towels smell . . . well, anything but sweet? If you don't keep your bathroom clean, you cannot keep your body clean. One follows the other, especially in vastu living.

Your vastu living bathroom is also orderly—free of the clutter that comes with too much stuff or too much color in the décor. A jumble of patterns and colors in this usually small space and an assortment of messy shelves distract you from the important daily rituals that occur here. When you are caring for your body, your mind needs to stay centered on your body's needs. It shouldn't suddenly be thinking about *finding* that new blade for your shaver or a box of Band-Aids. Everything in your bathroom deserves a special place. You want to be able to find whatever you need without wracking your brain and leaving the here and now of your rituals to rummage in shelves under your sink through who knows what.

Your zone of tranquility also deserves its special place inside your bathroom—a place of honor. It should capture your attention so that you willingly linger and pamper your body—as if you were spending time in a spa. But the spa in your bathroom caters to your soul. It's a spiritual spa that feels good to you or anyone who shares your home. When you settle into the tub or take a shower, your eyes should be able to zero in on your special display, which helps you wash away your stress. Your soul is cared for along with its temple.

Honor the Elements of Fire and Water

Your vastu bathroom also celebrates fire and water. These two basic elements are essential to your daily rituals of purification. For example, you need hot water, which combines fire and water, to remove the impurities from your skin. Water and fire are so good to your body that you don't want to harm them in return.

Respect these elements and try to stay away from personal-care products with polluting chemicals that flow out of your tub and sink and harm our ecosystem. Instead, go organic and use chemical-free bath salts, soaps, lotions. Use recycled-paper goods that save our forests and reduce land erosion. Offer thanks to the healing properties of the sun and enhance the effect of natural light if it flows into your bathroom. If you don't have a window in your bathroom, add a candle to your décor to honor this element. By the way, the candle is a great way to remove bathroom odors. When you strike a match, the sulfur, like magic, cleanses the air.

❋ THE SPIRITUAL BLUEPRINT FOR YOUR BATHROOM

If your bathroom is in the northeast quadrant of the home, it is important to make an appeasement to the element of water (see chapter 5, "Resolving Conflicts in Your Home and Workplace"). The impure water that flows out of the toilet and sink pollutes the purity of the northeast quadrant, which is the gateway to the gods. The water of the northeast element is sacred and should be kept as clean as possible. In the Southern Hemisphere, you need to make an appeasement if your bathroom is in the southeast quadrant, which belongs to the element of water and is the sacred gateway to the gods.

A bathroom in any other part of your home is fine with vastu. But it's best when your bathroom is in the east and also has an eastern window, as the morning rays streaming onto your body make your soul feel radiant and warm (see Figure 64). In India, Hindus often face the east when they bathe to accentuate the spiritual dimension of this daily ritual.

In vastu, medicines are traditionally kept in the north, which belongs to Lord Soma, who guards over your health. Each time you face your medicine-cabinet mirror when it's on the north wall, you receive healthy blessings from this deity. The north is also a good location for a garden of healing herbs. You also benefit from a toilet that lets you face the north (health) or the south (duty and responsibility). Why? Regularity adds up to good health. If the toilet is in the northeast of your bathroom, do remember to make an appeasement to the element of water (see chapter 5, "Resolving Conflicts in Your Home and Workplace"). Your bodily wastes pollute the sacred quadrant.

North

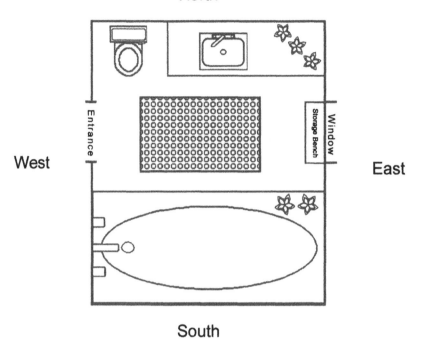

West

East

South

✳ Figure 64: Spiritual Blueprint for the Bathroom

✳ YOUR PURIFYING DÉCOR

It's easy to give even the shabbiest apartment bathroom a face-lift or makeover, and it doesn't have to cost much either. Just make a thoughtful trip to a secondhand store and recycle a few objects from the world of nature rather than the world of synthetics: a small wicker basket that you can fill up with bars of glycerin, a couple metal candlestick holders so that you can place candles close to the tub, an old silk scarf to drape across the top of the toilet tank. If you like to read in your bathroom, find an old bushel basket. Clean it up and fill it with books and magazines for your bathroom library. Or take a stroll along the beach and find a small piece of driftwood that can cradle a natural sponge, look for sea glass, polished stones, and seashells. Maybe you'll even find a shell that is large enough to hold a bar of natural soap.

If you have a window with good light inside your bathroom, use the ledge for plants that like a warm and steamy environment. If your window is built into a wall of the tub or shower, create a mini-rain forest with beautiful green plants that delight in the mix of water and light. Just use your imagination and bring lots of nature or natural objects into your bathroom.

Don't overlook the quality of your towels and washcloths. Use cottons, which breathe, and stay away from synthetics, which do a lousy job of absorbing the water that collects on your body. Keep your towels and washcloths clean and soft so that they feel good against your skin.

COLORS FOR INTROSPECTION

A bathroom that is dominated by white—the essence of light, which contains all the colors in the sun's visual spectrum—and a contemplative shade of green creates an ideal ambience. Let a third color along with its nighttime complement serve as accents. But remember, a splash of each color goes a long way, just like perfume.

YOUR ZONE OF TRANQUILITY

Try to place your zone of tranquility in the northeast quadrant of your bathroom on a ledge or a windowsill or hang it from the ceiling. Angle it so your eyes easily settle on your display while you bathe. In the Southern Hemisphere, you should place your zone in the southeast quadrant. As you stand in the shower

North   East

Figure 65: Spiritual Spa

stall or sit in the tub, the stillness expressed through the beauty of nature that is
exhibited in your display should help you relax and quiet your mind. Your special objects give you the positive power that comes when you connect with your
soul. As your body soaks in sudsy, warm water, your spiritual self revels in the
deep pleasure of your calming zone.

SWEET GIFTS FROM THE BEES

Treat your body to the wonders of honey:

Bath Sweetener: Add one-quarter cup of honey to your bath and luxuriate in fragrant, silky water.

Skin Cleanser: Mix one tablespoon of honey, two tablespoons of finely ground almonds, and one-half teaspoon of lemon juice. Gently rub it onto your face. Then rinse it off with water. Smile at your squeaky-clean face.

Moisturizing Mask: Add together two tablespoons of honey and two teaspoons of milk. Apply this milk and honey mask to your face and throat. Let it sit for ten minutes. Then rinse it off. Your glistening skin will thank you.

The Welcoming Workplace

✳

So many of us don't like whom we become when we are doing our job or our work. As soon as we step into our workspace, we feel diminished, disconnected from our real self, and rattled by a world in which machines and megafast computers outsmart and outperform us. Even workplace terminology feels impersonal and demeaning. Just think for a moment about these two words—*downsizing* and *headhunter*.

Downsizing is a terrible euphemism for wholesale cutbacks that cost many of us our livelihood. *Headhunter* conjures up the image of a slaughter; the word *should* make us shudder. Loyalty has vanished—or been banished—and from all sides of the work-world equation. We see entire companies gobbled up in mergers and acquisitions—more emotionless terms for events that can turn so many lives upside down.

These are just a few reasons why vastu living has so much value and relevance in your workplace. Vastu's underlying philosophy helps you move beyond many of these traps that have redefined our work world. Vastu's three principles help you shed the negativity that you can easily attach to your job. Vastu helps you make life-affirming and lifesaving mind shifts as you transform your workspace so that it celebrates love and respect for the self. This is so necessary in your personal environment where you often spend such a great deal of time.

21

Vastu Living in Our New Work World

✳

Have you brushed aside your soul in your workplace? Has it been vacuumed up with the dust, swept under your papers, checked at your threshold? This is a major reason why work has become a chore that fails to bring many of us great pleasure. Our soul is disassociated from whatever it is that we do.

Many of us don't even say "my work"; we say "work." Most of us even say "housework," not "my housework." This is the start of our problem. If we are unable to claim our work and call it ours, then we are on a slippery slide to job-related negativity.

This is why the first step in your practice of vastu living in your workspace may require a shift in the way that you think about your career, your job, your work. You need to cultivate healthy attitudes that express worthiness, not worthlessness. When you honor your worthiness, you honor your soul. You create a space that celebrates this most important part of you. You acknowledge your undeniable divinity.

✳ THE VALUE OF NOW

So many of us need to remember, really remember, the value of now and the benefits that come with staying connected to the present moment. We feel better when we are focused on where we are—here and now. And we lose out when we dwell on what happened yesterday at work or what may happen tomorrow. By failing to remain in the present, it is impossible to become absorbed in what we are doing. We rob ourselves of the satisfactions that come with each personal discovery that unfolds during our work.

Think of a child who is finger-painting—or better, think back to when you were a child and you were finger-painting. Try to recall the cool (as in temperature) sensation of the gloppy paint and how it felt to your fingers as it flowed onto the wet surface of the smooth, glossy paper. Remember the fun of watching the colors mix together—how the red and the yellow created orange or the blue and the red turned into purple. Didn't you love the process that went into making your paintings? Many times you may have crumbled up your art and thrown it out or maybe you hung it on the wall. That part of the process was inconsequential—the good part was the doing, the creating.

As a child back then, with your fingers swirling around the thick paint, you stayed in the now of that moment. Children are usually always in the now. Just watch them when they play. They don't get caught up in the clock and the movement of its hands. This is how you want to feel when you are working. You want to get into your work and experience it—no matter what you do for a living.

When you get absorbed in your work, something wonderful happens. You instinctively do your best job because you have no other option. All your senses are trained on the present moment. Your mind is cooperating and you are having a positive experience. You can view each obstacle like a missing piece in a jigsaw puzzle—a challenge to outwit and overcome.

When you learn to let go of future results or distant goals and stay in the now, you enjoy yourself as you work. You discover the rhythm in your work—because all work has rhythm if you let yourself experience it. Best of all, when you become centered in the present, you often eliminate silly mistakes that occur when you rush blindly toward a goal. The quality of your work improves. You are even apt to finish way ahead of time. You surely savor each step along the way.

THE CELEBRATION OF YOUR DIVINITY

Could you possibly be a complicit partner contributing to your own soulless work environment? For example, the minute you get to work, do you disconnect from your authentic self? If this describes you, then you need to make another life-affirming mind shift. You need to realize that the work that brings you to this workspace is done for your self. It is not done for someone else. A boss may sign your paycheck; others may work with you and contribute to the process. But you must accept that you are working to please the self and learn to claim your work as your work. This does not mean that you become bossy or covetous or demanding. These emotions connect to the ego, and as we all know, the ego—towering egos, in particular—are the source of much trouble at work.

When you learn to work from this inner place that promotes love, respect, and selflessness, you always try to do your best work. Your self accepts nothing less. This deep awareness helps hold back the stress that is so often part of everyone's job description. When your boss or associates are displeased with the results of your work, you want to be able to hear their comments. You don't want to turn criticism into an emotional event that magnifies all out of proportion. By knowing that you have done your best work, you can remain calm and turn a critique into a moment of positive discovery.

This second mind shift is a hard one, but when you try to follow this advice, you see that your inner essence is there to boost you with positive feelings that are connected to self-esteem, self-respect, and forgiveness. The self is not fickle. If you stay in touch with your inner voice, it guides you through moments that might otherwise fill you with stress. So try hard to work to please your self or your soul. Detach yourself from the need for praise or rewards that come from others. Stay in the moment and stay in touch with your own inner essence.

☀ THE QUIET POWER OF NATURE

In our alienating work world, nature is your true salvation. Nature's presence in your office, cubicle, or boutique is soothing and calming and makes the most formal and impersonal space feel warm and welcoming. Nature puts you at ease, and when you are doing your work, your surroundings nourish you. It is hard to give your best to your work if you feel ill at ease, guarded, or uptight. You need tranquility and calm to hear your inner voice, which is there to support you.

The world of nature also keeps you mindful of the governing principle of holism—the symbiotic relationship, based on interconnection and interdependence, that binds together all existence. This underlying principle, which is an essential message to carry with you when you work, represents the third life-affirming mind shift that improves how you feel about your self and your job.

Everyone whom you encounter in your workday has a role to play, just as every form of creation has its role to play in the functioning of the universe. Your co-workers, your boss, your customers or clients—everyone who contributes to your company or your business is worthy of your respect (and this, of course, includes your self). You need the maintenance person who keeps your building in good shape, the postal worker who brings your mail, the delivery person who delivers your packages. You also need to extend the love that you feel for your self to everyone around you. You need to show them your respect so that they are continually aware of their own worthiness and your gratitude.

You do all this without expecting anything in return. You do this because it reflects the love that exists in your soul. In the end, nature in your workplace brings more than warmth and beauty. Nature makes you aware of the great Truth: everything that exists is divine.

If you can embrace these three life-affirming and lifesaving mind shifts, then you can approach your practice of vastu living from a place within you that is positive and reinforcing. You create a healthy home-away-from-home for your soul when you work. Your work environment feels better and looks better. It celebrates your special self and the perfect universe. When your space reflects the three important principles of vastu living, your soul expresses itself in your work and you feel fulfilled.

22

General Guidelines for the Company

WELCOME TO THE VASTU LIVING COMPANY. IF YOU ARE A
PRIMARY OFFICER IN A COMPANY, PLEASE TAKE OUT YOUR
SPIRITUAL BLUEPRINT FOR THIS IMPORTANT WORK ENVIRON-
MENT AND REFER TO IT AS YOU READ THIS CHAPTER.

Many business owners spend a fortune on the décor of their company so
that it makes the right statement. But unfortunately, this right statement is rarely about the soul. Many companies are housed in modern buildings that aren't very soulful either. They're designed with little regard for the
well-being of the human body. Banks of windows are sealed shut so that everyone breathes recycled air. Artificial lighting has become a second-rate substi-
tute for natural lighting. Central air-conditioning and heating disregard the
unique needs of each individual.

These buildings are designed for artificial intelligence—machinery that
needs an unchanging environment; but we humans need the rhythms that
come with our universe and keep our bodies, minds, and souls in good working order. The ambience inside these fake environments, however posh they
may be, makes everyone feel disconnected from the real world, which reinforces our feelings of disconnection from one another and even our self.

If you rent your company space, you're probably unlikely or unable to make serious structural changes. But through the practice of vastu living, you can still work around built-in disadvantages and give a boost to the well-being of every individual who works for you. Vastu living can't unseal the sealed windows so that your employees can breathe fresh air; but this holistic science can make a positive change in your corporate climate.

PLEASE REMEMBER . . .

1. If your company observes 51 percent of the vastu guidelines, it is on the winning side of vastu living.

2. Make appeasements through the use of color or therapeutic objects when you are unable to observe the assigned location of the five basic elements (see chapter 5, "Resolving Conflicts in Your Home and Workplace").

3. Encourage the presence of the zone of tranquility in your company. It helps everyone stay centered, focused, and grounded.

4. Readers who live in the Southern Hemisphere should review chapter 7, "The Southern Hemisphere," and follow the spiritual blueprint on page 116, which shows the correct location of the elements below the equator.

THE SPIRITUAL BLUEPRINT FOR YOUR COMPANY

See individual chapters that follow for the healthy location of offices and other areas commonly found in companies.

Your Company Entrance

Many company officials have expressed concern over the location of their company entrance. They have heard that it can determine their company's destiny. But every cardinal direction has its merits in vastu living, so any entrance is acceptable. Just be mindful of the symbols and properties that are associated with each cardinal direction so that you can be guided by their wisdom (see "Significance of Each Direction," below).

The northeast quadrant also brings an extra benefit worth noting. An entrance in the northeast quadrant of the building or space receives positive cosmic energy and spiritual power—valuable gifts that increase the well-being of everyone in the company.

SIGNIFICANCE OF EACH DIRECTION

An entrance in the east faces the realm of Surya, who is the lord of the sun and the provider of inspiration and enlightenment. The east encourages curiosity and the pursuit of knowledge.

An entrance in the west opens into the realm of Varuna, who is the lord of the oceans, the night, and the rains. The west brings peace and quiet and reminds us to dispel the darkness that comes from ignorance.

An entrance that faces the north looks into the domain of Kuber, the lord of wealth, and Soma, the lord of health and the moon. Lord Kuber also symbolizes indulgence, so this direction with its dual set of symbols and properties speaks of wealth that encompasses spiritual wealth, which keeps us healthy and enriches us.

An entrance in the south looks into the domain of Yama, who is the lord of death and judgment. Lord Yama is not a frightening force. He reminds us of the virtues that define a noble life—compassion, respect, and selflessness. These principles are worth cherishing in our work world, where motivations connected to the ego often undermine worthy actions.

Company doors should be off center, clearly inside one of the four quadrants. In vastu, only temples, which are homes for the deities, have their doors in the direct center of a wall. We mortals are imperfect. We feel more comfortable in the asymmetry that defines the world in which we live.

Interior Doors

Once again, please don't worry about the location of doors in your company. But do remember that a door in the northeast quadrant receives the cosmic energy and spiritual power that soothe the soul and increase inner calm, which are crucial in your workplace, so appreciate it if you have one.

Windows and Outdoor Areas

Vastu acknowledges the sun's duality. It helps us enjoy the sun's healthy properties and avoid its harmful properties. Your company should try to let the sun flow in from all the windows in the north and the east. Northeastern windows also bring the therapeutic cosmic energy and spiritual power. North light is called the painter's light: it is gentle and pure. The morning light of the east, which is the farmer's choice location for vegetable gardens, is healthy and nourishing.

But once the sun reaches the southeast corner and begins its journey to the southwest, its rays turn unhealthy and drain us of energy. Windows in the southwest quadrant should have drapes that block out the harmful sun and retain the positive cosmic energy and spiritual power, which flow into this quadrant from the northeast. If you choose layered window treatments for your company, you can use the sun to your advantage.

If there are balconies, verandas, or terraces attached to your company environment, be mindful of the symbolism attached to their location (see "Significance of Each Direction"). Create attractive spaces by displaying plants that honor nature, and use chairs and tables that are created of organic materials, such as wood or metal. Avoid impersonal plastic and other synthetics, which harm the environment and are so unappealing. Your employees should be drawn to sit in these soothing transitional areas where they can take a contemplative break from the world outside and from their own work world.

Inventory Exit

Try to keep your inventory in the northwest quadrant of the premises. Properties associated with the element of air, which governs this midpoint direction, are good for your bottom line. Movement and quick action, which reflect the air and the wind, lead to quick sales—and quick delivery, which delights your customers who appreciate prompt service. In the Southern Hemisphere, your inventory exit should be in the southwest quadrant.

Corridors

Vastu guidelines suggest openness in the north and in the east of your company and inside each individual area. The north and the east are ideal for corridors and passageways since they encourage the flow of cosmic energy and spiritual power that enters your company's northeast quadrant.

Drinking Fountains and Coolers

Drinking water is clean and pure. If possible, place your drinking fountains and coolers in the northeast quadrant, which is governed by the element of water. (In the Southern Hemisphere place your fountains in the southeast quadrant.)

Bathrooms

If you can control the placement of the bathrooms, avoid the northeast quadrant of your company space. Bathrooms are fine in any other location. If your bathroom is in the northeast, just remember to make an offering to appease this quadrant's element of water and its deity. (In the Southern Hemisphere, the element of water is in the southeast quadrant.)

While the activities that occur inside the bathroom help purify the body, these activities create wastes, which should not pollute the sacred realm of the northeast. Ideally, toilets should face the north, which is the direction of health, or the south, which is the direction of duty and responsibility. Far too often, we wait forever to go use these facilities when we are on the job, which is an unhealthy habit that we should try to break.

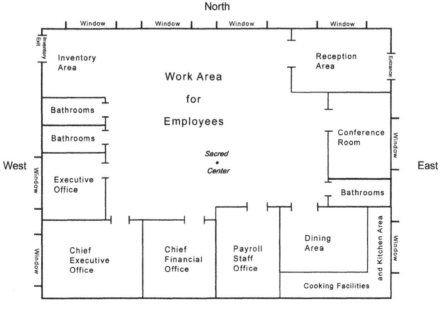

Figure 66: Spiritual Blueprint for the Company with Financial Office in the South

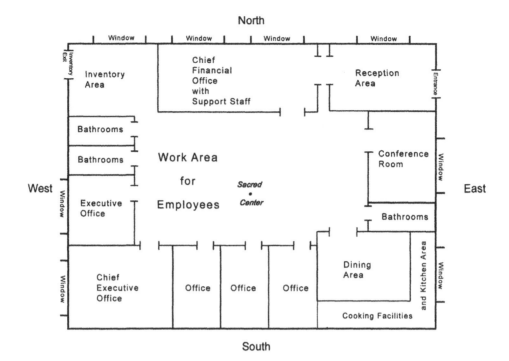

Figure 67: Spiritual Blueprint for the Company with Financial Office in the North

☀ The Placement of Your Furnishings and Equipment

Try to follow these general guidelines in the organization of the furnishings throughout your company. Specific environments may have special needs, which are addressed in the appropriate subsequent chapter.

Desk or Workstation

When a desk or workstation is the heaviest item in an individual workspace, try to place this furniture in the southwest quadrant; if the desk or workstation is lightweight, you can place it in the northeast or the southeast as long as these

MAXIMIZE THE HARMONY IN YOUR COMPANY

1. Place lightweight and low furnishings in the north and the east of the workspace so that the cosmic energy and spiritual power can easily flow in a wide arc from the northeast quadrant to the southwest quadrant.

2. Place heavy and tall furnishings, such as bulky desks or cabinets and floor-to-ceiling, built-in storage areas, in the south and the west where they help retain these beneficial gifts.

3. Heavy-duty electrical equipment, such as circuit breakers and furnaces, belong to the element of fire, which reigns in the southeast quadrant.

4. Protect the fragile center of the company and each workspace by keeping it unburdened by any weight. You want the sacred power of Lord Brahma, who reigns over this area, to radiate positive vibrations in every direction.

5. If you work in the Southern Hemisphere, remember to refer to the diagram and information in chapter 7, so that you make the proper adjustments in your practice of vastu living.

6. When you are unable to adhere to the appropriate location of an element, make an appropriate appeasement to restore the harmony of the affected space (see chapter 5, "Resolving Conflicts in Your Home and Workplace"). These appeasements, which are visually appealing, use healthy colors or symbolically powerful objects.

7. Guard everyone's energy, which creates an aura around his or her body: keep the back of chairs and sofas at least four inches from any wall. The energies that vibrate off walls can interfere with everyone's well-being.

quadrants don't aggravate the individual's constitution. Think carefully about placing any desk or workstation in the northwest: the properties of the element of air, which govern this quadrant, may disturb one's ability to concentrate. Also avoid placing any desk on the sacred center of the company premises or on the sacred center inside an individual work area. The center should be uncovered so that its gift of positive vibrations can circulate with ease.

Healthy Seating Arrangements

When You Work . . .

Try to orient workstations and desks so that employees, including yourself, can have their back to the south, which provides strength and wisdom, or to the west so that they symbolically reject the darkness and ignorance associated with this direction by facing the east, which speaks of inspiration. Do you or any of your employees tend to shirk responsibilities? This problem can be resolved by facing the south, where the realm of Yama, the lord of death and responsibility, reminds everyone of his or her obligations.

When You Relax . . .

When it's time to relax for a moment, everyone should try to turn to face the north to soak in its properties of health and wealth (including spiritual wealth), or the east with its enlightening properties, or the tranquil northeast. This calming quadrant, which belongs to the element of water, receives the beneficial cosmic energy and spiritual power that help everyone maintain inner peace during a hectic or difficult day.

Computers

The computer, which is connected to the element of fire, should normally be in the southeast quadrant of fire. But your company can satisfy this guideline by simply placing the computer, which uses so little electricity, on the southeast quadrant of each work area. An individual who faces east to see the computer monitor is blessed with inspiration and creativity. An individual who faces northeast is blessed with serenity and calm. An individual who faces north is blessed with wealth (including spiritual wealth) and health.

Televisions

Many businesses require televisions for presentations, but TVs can become a distraction. Although TVs are connected to the element of fire and belong in the southeast quadrant, play safe. Keep them in the northwest quadrant, where the properties of the element of air make people come and go. A would-be TV addict loses interest and moves on. But please make appeasements to the elements of air and fire, which have been violated in this arrangement. The element of air has been violated by the trespassing element of fire; the element of fire has been moved from its rightful location in the southeast (see chapter 5, "Resolving Conflicts in Your Home and Workplace," for details).

YOUR SUCCESSFUL DÉCOR

Honor Nature and the Self

Too often companies treat the presence of nature at the workplace as an afterthought. Yet nature and organic products are indispensable in the business environment. Our connection to nature is so visceral that nature has the power to elevate our mood and attitude, which, in turn, improves our work performance. And when nature is absent, the workplace feels sterile and impersonal—an environment in which machinery holds sway.

In your practice of vastu living, let nature greet everyone the second he or she enters the reception area of your company, and encourage the presence of nature inside each individual workspace. If there are windows with adequate sunlight or decent overhead lighting, display plants in every common area. Help them flourish with adequate care. They will bless your company with their beauty.

If your company lacks natural sunlight, add bouquets of fresh or dried flowers, wood or rattan wastebaskets and glass containers, any products from the world of nature. Celebrate natural floor coverings, such as tiles, wood, bricks, rugs of cotton, wool, silk, or inexpensive grasses. Everyone from your employees to your clients and customers feels more comfortable in a space that acknowledges our universal interdependence and interconnection to nature.

It is just as important to encourage everyone to honor the self at work—its unique identity. Let your office serve as the example and celebrate the connection that exists between you and your loved ones by displaying pictures or mementos that are visible reminders of the other people in your life. Their presence swirling around your workspace reminds you of your good fortune. Or reveals a favorite hobby or passion. If you love vintage cars, park a few miniature replicas on a prominent shelf. If you love antiques, incorporate this interest into your décor.

SPECIAL TIPS FOR THE BUSINESS TRAVELER

When you go on a business trip, take vastu living with you and turn a temporary hotel room into a healthy sleeping space or off-site work area. Just bring along a compass and sleep and work in a healthy direction. If the bed has its head to the north, put the pillow at the other end. If the bed straddles two quadrants, sleep on the side that is healthy for your constitution. To soak in the benefits of the northeast, shift the reading chair so that it faces this direction. Small adjustments have a major impact on your well-being when your work takes you on the road.

Let your visitors get a sense of your inner self even when they are perfect strangers. They feel more at ease when they are with you, and this is often the foundation to a successful work relationship.

Pay Attention to Your Special Needs

Always remember the important ayurvedic principle of like increases like. Unless your job keeps you on the move, you probably spend at least eight hours daily inside your workspace, so you don't want its location to aggravate your particular nature or constitution. For example, if pitta (fire) dominates your constitution, you want to avoid working in the southeast quadrant of the building or the southeast quadrant inside a space, which belongs to the element of fire. The southeast could trigger the negative consequences of like increases like. You may find that you are too harsh on yourself and others. You may never be satisfied with anyone's best effort, not even your own. So please treat yourself with care and try to follow this simple chart when you work.

UNHEALTHY QUADRANTS FOR YOUR CONSTITUTION IN THE WORKPLACE

CONSTITUTION OR DOSHA	NORTHERN HEMISPHERE UNHEALTHY QUADRANT	SOUTHERN HEMISPHERE UNHEALTHY QUADRANT
Vata / Air	Northwest (Air)	Southwest (Air)
Pitta / Fire	Southeast (Fire)	Northeast (Fire)
Kapha / Water	Northeast (Water)	Southeast (Water)

If you must work in an unhealthy quadrant, *first* see if your workspace is upsetting your constitution (see chapter 2, "Personalizing Vastu Living"). Perhaps you are dominated by vata and you work in the northwest quadrant, which is governed by the element of air. You find that you are unable to sit still long enough to write a five-word E-mail. Or you are dominated by pitta and work in the southeast. You realize that you are quibbling with everyone, even your own voice-mail message. Or you are dominated by kapha and work in the northeast, which is ruled by water. You are moving so slowly that moss could grow over your shoes.

If your constitution is out of balance, don't despair. Use the healing properties of colors or objects to restore the balance to your constitution (see chapter 5, "Resolving Conflicts in Your Home and Workplace"). Surround yourself with calming colors or objects that speak of peace and help you stay focused or deter your combative edge. Or if you see that you need more energy and fire, choose colors that perk you up. Healthy choices in your décor can restore the body's balance when you can't adjust the location of your workspace or its furnishings to suit your constitution. These resolutions can even eliminate the problems that may occur when you share a workspace with a co-worker who has conflicting needs and requirements.

Your Zone of Tranquility

It is impossible to overstate the benefits of the zone of tranquility in your workplace. When you set up a special display that celebrates nature and your own special identity, you make an investment in your well-being. Your zone of tranquility nurtures your soul and reinforces an important point that we all need to remember. When we take care of our soul, our soul takes care of us.

The location of your zone—always in the northeast quadrant, which is governed by the element of water—fills you with calm and serenity. Your zone can be small and unobtrusive: it can sit in the northeast corner of your desk or hang from the northeast corner of the ceiling in your individual workspace. (In the Southern Hemisphere, your zone should be in the southeast quadrant.)

The power of your zone comes from the meaning attached to your display, not from its physical size. The objects that connect to nature and your special self, which form the essence of your display, draw you to that place deep inside where your indistinguishable light of love resides.

Once you learn to focus on your zone of tranquility and turn inward when you feel tired or feel the need for a break from your work, you realize the artificiality of the boost that comes from a caffeine break. You return to your work with renewed vigor, improved focus, and a sense of purpose that comes with your connection to your true self.

Finally, your personal zone of tranquility inside your workspace can be a positive first step that leads to group meditation or group yoga in your company. At the very least, you should encourage every employee to set up his or her own zone inside his or her own space, and you should provide zones of tranquility in common areas, such as the dining room, conference room, or reception area. These special zones provide therapeutic benefits to everyone and enhance the well-being of your company.

23

Respect Your Office

WELCOME TO THE VASTU LIVING OFFICE. PLEASE TAKE OUT YOUR SPIRITUAL BLUEPRINT IF YOU WORK IN THIS PARTICULAR ENVIRONMENT AND REFER TO IT AS YOU READ THIS CHAPTER.

There is something terribly defeating and woefully illogical when company offices reinforce individual egos rather than the soul and, by extension, an unyielding adherence to hierarchy where non-office-bearing employees (in every context of this phrase) feel undervalued and devalued. Often these employees are even reluctant to enter company offices. They hang back at the doorway, and when they are asked inside, they feel so uncomfortable that any chance for a productive exchange of ideas and strategies is left on the far side of the threshold. Employees clam up and feel no connection to the person sitting behind the desk.

Such an environment is the antithesis of a vastu living office, which is founded on interconnection, not a lack of connection, and interdependence, not supremacy. Your vastu living office should honor the three principles of vastu. It should consciously convey the selflessness of your soul and the magnanimity of your spirit. A healthy ambience, with its accent on nature and the celebration of the self and its divinity, creates an environment that puts your clients and co-workers at ease. Your environment reveals your commitment to respect, not elitism; inclusion, not exclusion—noble attitudes that make everyone feel worthy when they visit you—and your company benefits as a result.

✳ THE SPIRITUAL BLUEPRINT FOR YOUR OFFICE

Are you the **head of the company** or **CEO?** Your office belongs in the southwest quadrant of your company. This quadrant, which is in the realm of the element of earth and ancestors, endows you with the strength and wisdom that helps you keep your company on a healthy course (see chapter 22, Figures 66 and 67).

Are you the **financial officer?** Your office belongs in the south just right of the CEO's when you both work closely together and make joint decisions. If you have considerable autonomy, your office should be in the north, which is the realm of Kuber, the lord of wealth, and Soma, the lord of health. These two deities embody qualities that assure financial health and wealth, including the spiritual wealth that reminds your company of its social responsibilities (see Figures 66 and 67).

Are you the **managing director** or **chief operating officer?** Your office belongs in the west directly north of the CEO's office. Other **senior executives** should also occupy offices in the west and the south of the company so that they can draw on the wisdom that flows into this area (see Figures 66 and 67).

If you work in an office that is not in the southwest quadrant, just remember to pay attention to your constitution and watch for any negative effect that comes with the principle of like increases like (see chapter 2, "Personalizing Vastu Living"). In general, if you have a vata (air) constitution, you should be careful with an office in the northwest quadrant, which is governed by the element of air. If you have a kapha (water) constitution, you may have trouble in the northeast quadrant, which belongs to water. If you have a pitta (fire) constitution, you may suffer in the southeast quadrant, which is the realm of fire.

UNHEALTHY QUADRANTS FOR YOUR CONSTITUTION IN THE WORKPLACE

CONSTITUTION OR DOSHA	NORTHERN HEMISPHERE UNHEALTHY QUADRANT	SOUTHERN HEMISPHERE UNHEALTHY QUADRANT
Vata / Air	Northwest (Air)	Southwest (Air)
Pitta / Fire	Southeast (Fire)	Northeast (Fire)
Kapha / Water	Northeast (Water)	Southeast (Water)

THE PLACEMENT OF YOUR FURNISHINGS

Try to observe the guidelines under "The Placement of Your Furnishings and Equipment" in chapter 22, "General Guidelines for the Company." Place your desk or workstation, providing it's a heavy object in your office, in the southwest quadrant, where the properties of earth give a boost to your strength, including the inner strength that comes with knowledge. Irrespective of the location of your desk, please sit with your back to the south so that the collected wisdom and experiences of those who led before you serve as positive reinforcement. As a second choice, sit with your back to the west, which shuts out the unknown and darkness (see Figure 68).

And what direction should you face when you work? Evaluate your job and your needs. The north keeps you mindful of the company's health and wealth, including the spiritual wealth that leads to good works. Just imagine if companies changed the business term *goods and services* to *good service* and observed this principle. Are you an innovator or idea-generator? Face the east and let the creative energy of the sun and the enlightenment associated with this direction inspire you. The northeast, which is quietly powerful and reflective, suits everyone at work. This quadrant helps your mind stay in the now instead of wandering off into the future, where worries about demands and deadlines only interfere with the work that you are doing in the present.

If you want a lightweight reading chair or divan in your office as an alternative seating area, it belongs in the north or the east of the room. A heavy sofa, however, belongs in the west or the south, where its weight acts as a barrier to hold in the cosmic energy and spiritual power that flow here from the northeast. Always try to place the sofa or chair so that you can focus on your zone of tranquility, which is in the northeast quadrant. It captures your attention and you take time to turn inward and connect with the self. Finally, try hard to keep the absolute center of your office free of any furnishings that can trap the positive energies that radiate outward from this sacred area and enhance your well-being.

When You Have Visitors . . .

Always provide a gracious welcome to your clients, co-workers, and any other guests who visit your office. But let them sit facing the south. They

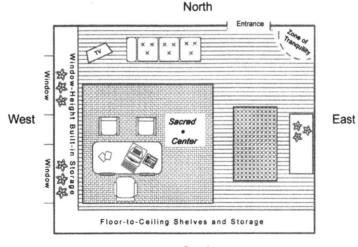

Figure 68: Spiritual Blueprint for the Executive Office

remain mindful of their responsibilities, while your back is reinforced by the strength and wisdom that lets you conduct productive business meetings.

☀ Your Inclusive Décor

A healthy office décor acknowledges the interconnection and interdependence of all creation—a powerful statement for any company, where teams create success, not the single efforts of one high-powered individual. Remember the Vedic phrase "Thou Art That" in which *That* refers to the Supreme Creative Force. Let the truth of our shared divinity shine through your office ambience so that it radiates love and an all-encompassing respect.

Introduce Nature

Most people with offices have a degree of power within the company, and with that power comes responsibility. So surround yourself with nature and natural products that sooth your inner self and keep you steady in the face of pressures and demands. Create attractive displays of plants or dried flowers or any pleasurable objects that come from the earth and display them where they are easily noticed by you and your visitors. Their beauty, their diversity, and their expression of universal rhythms are mirrored in the external world beyond the company and within each private life that is connected to the company.

Reveal Your Self

Make room for your personality and your special interests inside your office. Put pictures of friends and loved ones on your desk or on a wall. Show off part

SOOTHING OFFICE COLORS

Many offices use neutral shades that are unobtrusive and inoffensive. They also contribute nothing to the character of a space. Add a dash of color, but let your constitution guide your choice. If you have a fiery personality or if you are extremely active, you can control excess energy with cool and calming colors, such as green or blue along with its complementary nighttime color of yellow. If you feel chronically sluggish, you can get an energy boost from stimulating colors, such as red and orange along with their complementary nighttime colors of violet and indigo, respectively (see chapter 5, "Resolving Conflicts in Your Home and Workplace"). When you introduce bright colors, use them judiciously. They can make a room feel small, whereas pale hues make a room feel larger.

of an eclectic art collection or trip mementos. Make choices that work for you, and let the office reflect who you are—not just the trappings of your title or position.

When your office connects to your special identity, you feel comfortable and so do your guests. They see the hidden facets that define your character and your personality. They also have an opportunity to find a shared link that lets them lower their reserve inside your office. How beneficial if this ambience could be replicated throughout the company, where formality and distance serve no good and often show up in negative work performance and the company's bottom line.

YOUR ZONE OF TRANQUILITY

Every company environment benefits from a zone of tranquility. Your special display, which can be subtle and make a quiet statement, belongs in the northeast quadrant of your office and connects to the heart of your self. Choose an object from the world of nature that fills you with joy and a personal object that fills you with love so your display has the power to draw your attention during the most chaotic day. (In the Southern Hemisphere, your zone of tranquility belongs in the southeast quadrant.)

You gain so much when you turn inward daily. This is your opportunity to do a reality check—and to hear the inner voice that is there to keep you

North   East

Figure 69: Office Zone of Tranquility

true to your self instead of your ego. When you let the display lead you to a point of inner stillness where you concentrate on your breathing, your tension slides out with each exhalation and is replaced by positive energy that comes in with each new breath. You return to your work feeling renewed and reinvigorated.

EASE AWAY YOUR HEADACHE

Keep a tiny bottle of vegetable oil mixed with an equal amount of lavender oil or peppermint oil in your desk. If you get a headache, dab a couple drops onto your temples and at the point of pain on your forehead or under your eyes. Massage the drops into your skin. Relief should come your way.

24

Acknowledge Your Cubicle

WELCOME TO THE VASTU LIVING CUBICLE. PLEASE TAKE OUT
YOUR SPIRITUAL BLUEPRINT IF YOU WORK IN THIS ENVIRON-
MENT AND REFER TO IT AS YOU READ THIS CHAPTER.

The cubicle is usually small, usually white, and as you know if you work in one, usually identical to the cubicles on the left and the right, one row over and one row back. You may also agree with other cubicle dwellers who insist that the isolation, sameness, and inconsequential size of this sterile environment also define their job. When you work here, you feel dehumanized, dispensable—your identity seems reduced to the digits on your social security number. You feel stuck doing a meaningless job.

The practice of vastu living and the acceptance of its underlying philosophy can redeem this work area. Your cubicle can become a workable space—in every sense of this word. But the first step toward success occurs in your mind. You change your attitude about your physical space.

When you work in a cubicle, you stop thinking small and think cozy. You embrace the symbolism of its color white—its positive connection to purity, peace, and knowledge. Finally, you eliminate all your cubicle's associations with dehumanization by claiming this space as your own, just as you need to claim the work that you do as *your* own work done for the self—no one else. These changes in attitude, so seemingly subtle, add up to a positive, life-transforming first step. From this "self"-supportive mind-set, you approach your cubicle from a positive point of view.

Once you accept your cubicle as your space, you can introduce the practice of vastu living so that it reflects your self and makes you feel comfortable whenever you are sitting there. You do your best to honor the five basic elements, if only through appeasements, and you mindfully celebrate your individual identity and nature in your cubicle's limited décor.

Just remember that it is next to impossible to create a vastu living environment that is 100 percent correct—even when you build a personal environment from scratch. This perfect number is also not ideal for us mortals. We are imperfect and feel more comfortable with a bit of imperfection around us. One hundred percent vastu-correct befits a home for the gods. So if you can reach 51 percent in your practice of vastu living inside your cubicle, you are on the winning side. And this number is easy to reach. No matter where you are, you can create an environment that beckons you inside.

☀ THE SPIRITUAL BLUEPRINT FOR YOUR CUBICLE

The one location that is definitely unhealthy for your cubicle is the direct center of the company premises. This area, which belongs to the element of space or ether and the Hindu Lord Brahma, the god of creation, is sacred. The absolute center of the floor needs to be uncovered so that this realm's creative energy can radiate positive vibrations throughout the company. If you discover that your cubicle is violating this space, make an appeasement to Lord Brahma and protect your harmony and his domain (see chapter 5, "Resolving Conflicts in Your Home and Workspace"). Also, be aware of potential distractions that can accompany a workspace in the northwest quadrant, which belongs to the element of air. The properties associated with this element may make your mind wander. You may struggle to complete your work.

All other locations are acceptable, but do take advantage of the properties that come with each quadrant. The northeast, which belongs to the element of water, is soothing and reflective; it also gives you the boost that comes from the cosmic energy and spiritual power that enter this quadrant. The southeast, which belongs to the element of fire, can provide you with stimulation and energy. The southwest, which belongs to the element of earth, gives you strength, and its association with ancestors fills you with wisdom. (If you live in the Southern Hemisphere, follow the spiritual blueprint on page 116, which shows the correct location of the elements below the equator.)

Honor Your Constitution

You spend a lot of time at work—probably no less than one-third of your day at least five days a week. Please remember that if you work in the quadrant governed by the same element that dominates your constitution, the scales of good health can tip against you. The negative principle of like increases like may aggravate your constitution and cause problems with your emotional, physical, or mental well-being (see chapter 2, "Personalizing Vastu Living"). Perhaps someone in the company can swap work areas with you. If this is not feasible, and it probably isn't, then introduce therapeutic objects from nature or a touch of healing colors to restore the balance to your constitution (see chapter 5, "Resolving Conflicts in Your Home and Workplace").

Unhealthy Quadrants for Your Constitution in the Workplace

Constitution or Dosha	Northern Hemisphere Unhealthy Quadrant	Southern Hemisphere Unhealthy Quadrant
Vata / Air	Northwest (Air)	Southwest (Air)
Pitta / Fire	Southeast (Fire)	Northeast (Fire)
Kapha / Water	Northeast (Water)	Southeast (Water)

The Placement of Your Furnishings

You are probably stuck with most of the furnishing arrangements inside your cubicle. Don't fret. You can succeed with vastu living by making sincere appeasements that draw upon therapeutic colors and the world of nature. They can bring you to your goal of 51 percent (see chapter 5, "Resolving Conflicts in Your Home and Workplace"). In addition, your appeasements add inspiring touches to your décor. You just need to be careful with your choices: you don't want to overwhelm your cubicle with a mess of objects and a mélange of color. Vastu living is about cohesion and interconnection, rhythm and harmony—not chaos and an abandonment of proportion.

And what are the preferred locations for furnishings? Your desk or work-station and file cabinet are usually the heaviest objects in your cubicle. They rightfully belong in the southwest quadrant, where they trap the beneficial cosmic energy and spiritual power that flow into this quadrant from the northeast. Nothing, not even your chair, should cover the sacred center of your cubicle. You want to receive the additional benefits of the positive vibra-tions that flow from this realm of Lord Brahma and his element of space or ether. Your computer, which belongs to the element of fire, should normally be in the southeast. But in the vastu living hierarchy of guidelines for the cubicle, pay greater attention to the direction in which you face when you work. Sacrifice the computer in the southeast, if you must. You can resolve the conflict between the element of fire and the trespassed element through the use of appeasements.

What direction should you face when you sit in your cubicle? Try to face the north, the northeast, or the east. The north blesses you with health and wealth—especially spiritual health and spiritual wealth, which are so good for you and so sorely lacking in the workplace. The northeast fills you with calm and tranquility, and the east showers you with clarity and enlightenment. By facing one of these three directions, your back is to the west, the direction of darkness and the unknown, or the southwest, which gives you strength, or the south, which provides you with the wisdom of the departed.

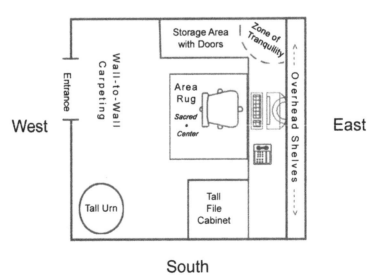

Figure 70: Spiritual Blueprint for an Acceptable Cubicle

❋ Your Cozy Décor

You may question the notion that your cubicle has a décor, but it does. Take a look around your workspace. Is it neat? Is it messy? Does it contain lots of personal stuff, such as pictures, gym bag, food stashed on a shelf, CDs, extra shoes, half-empty water bottles, knickknacks? All this stuff and the presence or absence of organization define your present décor. And this décor says something about you—either positive or negative.

Ultimately, there is no escaping this truth: every physical space, from a telephone booth or an elevator to a forest glen, makes a positive or negative statement that registers instantly in the eyes of the beholder. There is no such thing as a neutral space; and in man-made environments, the décor, intentionally created or not, determines this statement—positive or negative. A mess can define a décor, if you think about it. And a mess says something significant about the person who created it.

So if you don't like the present look of your cubicle defining your décor, then take this housecleaning test inside your space. Examine your accumulation of personal possessions. Is anything coated with dust? If so, you haven't picked up the object, touched it, or used it in days. Most likely you don't need it at work.

Do stacks of papers cover every surface of your cubicle, including the floor? Go through each pile and file away every paper, even if it means tossing some into your circular file by your desk. When you are about to create a new stack, remind yourself that clutter in a cubicle doesn't just define your décor, it clutters your mind and interferes with your work.

Now, let's eliminate the blahs that come with the blandness and the sameness that run, like a computer virus, through each cubicle inside the company. As always, your vastu living décor should focus on your identity—who you are, what you like, what you love, what matters to you—and the intrinsic power of nature.

If anything in your space doesn't fit into either of these two categories, then consider removing it. On a metaphysical level, every object in your vastu living cubicle should be cohesive and interconnected. Every aspect of your décor should add to the rhythm that flows inside your space. Every object should enhance your harmony. If any aspect of your décor fails to contribute to the whole, then try to resolve the problem.

Since your cubicle is cozy, you don't want to upset its balance and proportion either. Incorporate just a few personal objects, with deep meaning, into your décor. If you love art, introduce a single piece of sculpture created by your child or significant other or a single painting done by a good friend or a copy of a famous work by some well-known artist. Or place a small photomontage of important people in your life under a piece of glass on your desk or on a small tackboard on a partition. Create a zone of tranquility that absolutely expresses the heart of your self so that it connects to you and everyone else who comes to visit.

If your cubicle has too little lighting for plants, use organic products with earthy colors to draw in the world of nature. In this physical space, which can make you feel isolated and alone, nature not only creates warmth, it reminds you of the oneness that binds together all creation.

Start by replacing all the nonbiodegradable and impersonal receptacles in your cubicle, from the wastepaper basket to the paper-clip dispenser. Find substitutes that are made of wood, clay, jute, brass, glass, even papier-mâché. If you have a cold metal file cabinet, drape a lovely piece of fabric across the top and down one side. At the start of each week, treat your self to a fresh bouquet of flowers and turn Monday blues into Monday hues.

Just keep in mind that vastu living asks you to be mindful in your choice of the objects that ultimately define your décor. By keeping your focus on nature and your identity, you create a cohesive statement. Your décor blends into a meaningful visual expression of holism, which is so important to vastu living and the world in which we live.

FOCUS ON YOUR BREATH

Try to do this simple exercise three times a day while you sit in your chair in your cubicle. Just keep your spine straight and put all your attention into your breathing as you consciously inhale and consciously exhale. Say "so-o-o-o" as you slowly breathe in and "hum-m-m-m" as you slowly breathe out. By concentrating on these two words, your mind doesn't wander. Do this simple exercise for three minutes. You will find that you can empty your mind of stray thoughts. Your focus is improved when you return to your work.

YOUR ZONE OF TRANQUILITY

Your zone of tranquility, which always sits in the northeast quadrant and celebrates nature and the self, creates an invaluable point of focus that lets you empty your mind and turn inward when you work inside your cubicle. You can even focus on your zone of tranquility while you do the exercise described above. Your zones's personalized display should capture your attention during each workday and let you connect with your interior self—rejuvenating you, refueling you, filling you up with positive energy. (In the Southern Hemisphere, your zone belongs in the southeast quadrant.)

In your cubicle, you always have a definable northeast quadrant—just as you have a sacred center that you can easily demarcate. Even if the entrance into the cubicle is in the northeast, and this is an extra benefit since it lets in the beneficial energies, you can allocate a small portion of this quadrant to your zone of tranquility.

A young publicist was a member of a creative arts organization that worked every Saturday with disadvantaged children in a big city. Monday through Friday she worked in her windowless cubicle for a public relations firm. The publicist took a photo of the children and placed it in a burnt-wood frame on the northeast of her work surface. She had helped make the frame with some of the children. A plaster-of-paris mouse in colorful patchwork colors sat near the photo—another communal art project that was created on one of her important Saturdays.

These three objects—mouse, frame, photo—represented hope, love, creative inspiration. On a deeper level, her display connected to that essential part of her that spoke of selflessness and interconnection. When she worked in her cozy cubicle, her display nurtured that vital part of her—the spirit hidden within.

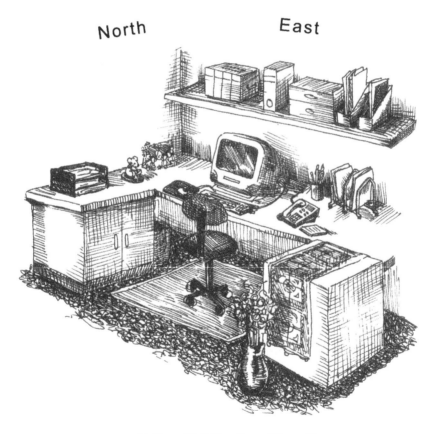

Figure 71: Selfless Zone of Tranquility

25

Appreciate Your Part of the Pod

WELCOME TO THE VASTU LIVING "POD." PLEASE TAKE OUT YOUR SPIRITUAL BLUEPRINT IF YOU WORK INSIDE A PART OF A POD AND REFER TO IT AS YOU READ THIS CHAPTER.

In the past few years, many companies have done away with the cubicle and replaced it with a new design arrangement called the pod—a group-oriented work environment that really does bring to mind the phrase *peas in a pod*. Typically, two rows of "peas" are arranged side by side and back-to-back in each pod or group work setting. Each "pea" has reasonably low side-partitions that extend a few feet into the room. The pod, as a whole, creates a unified environment in which employees who share tasks or project responsibilities can easily interact and work together.

The size of an individual portion of a pod is generally smaller than a cubicle and rarely exceeds the size of the work surface. Built-ins are normally limited to one or two overhead shelves, a tackboard, and a couple of file cabinets, which are often tucked under the desk. There is usually little room for anything else inside the space. There is certainly not much room for privacy. Workers usually have their back to one another, but a back is not a wall or a door. The voice travels.

The pod also maintains the formulaic sameness of the cubicle and the fixed nature of its furnishings. There's no way to shift much of anything around without calling in the maintenance crew and construction workers. Dream on . . . right?

So how do you introduce the practice of vastu living into this crowded and inflexible workspace? Your physical space may be unyielding, but through vastu living, you can draw upon the Truth expressed through nature and celebrate your individuality and let it shine inside your piece of the pod.

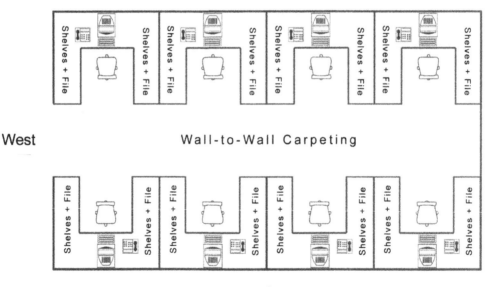

Figure 72: Diagram of the Pod

✳ THE SPIRITUAL BLUEPRINT FOR YOUR POD

What do you take into account when you determine the orientation of your workspace? Your part of the pod, nothing more. Just demarcate a square around your portion of the group environment to create your spiritual blueprint. Then determine its physical location within the entire company space.

Since you probably can't control the location of your pod or the location of your part of the pod, just be mindful of the orientation of your own work area. Then draw on the strengths connected to its location and compensate for its weaknesses. (If you live in the Southern Hemisphere, follow the spiritual blueprint on page 116, which shows the correct location of the elements below the equator.)

If your actual work area defies the law of probability and is right on top of the center of the company floor, appease this sacred spot, which belongs to the element of space and Lord Brahma (see chapter 5, "Resolving Conflicts in Your Home and Workplace").

Have you discovered that you are working in the northwest quadrant of the company? Do you find yourself easily distracted? The element of air, which governs this realm, could be part of your problem. Try adding a calming color (with its complementary nighttime color), such as blue or green, into your work area or a soothing object from nature to make you feel more settled. Either of these remedies can offset the flighty property of air so that you focus on your work (see chapter 5, "Resolving Conflicts in the Home and Workspace").

Honor Your Constitution

Have you discovered that your part of the pod is in the quadrant that belongs to the element that governs your own constitution (see chapter 2, "Personalizing Vastu Living")? For example, are you a pitta, governed by fire, and working in the southeast, which is the realm of fire? If so, observe how you feel at work. If you find that the negative principle of like increases like is aggravating your constitution, then introduce pacifying colors or calming organic objects that can restore your harmony on the job.

UNHEALTHY QUADRANTS FOR YOUR CONSTITUTION IN THE WORKPLACE

CONSTITUTION OR DOSHA	NORTHERN HEMISPHERE UNHEALTHY QUADRANT	SOUTHERN HEMISPHERE UNHEALTHY QUADRANT
Vata / Air	Northwest (Air)	Southwest (Air)
Pitta / Fire	Southeast (Fire)	Northeast (Fire)
Kapha / Water	Northeast (Water)	Southeast (Water)

THE PLACEMENT OF YOUR FURNISHINGS

The north speaks of health and wealth—including ample spiritual health and wealth that provide nourishment to the inner self. The northeast, which receives the beneficial cosmic energy and spiritual power, is calm and soothing. The east is rich with inspiration and creativity. How perfect if you face one of these healthy directions when you work in your part of the pod. But unfortunately, most of the furnishings inside this environment are stuck in place. It's difficult to shift anything around. And while some pods have individual L-shaped or U-shaped work surfaces that allow some flexibility, many of these work environments only let you face one direction.

The placement of the furnishings in your workspace may be wrong. The lightweight objects may be in the south or the west; the tall and heavy objects may be in the north or the east. Your chair may sit on top of the center of your space—violating this sacred realm. All five basic elements may be unbalanced and disharmonious—meaning the elements in your part of the pod aggravate the natural configuration of the elements inside you. But don't feel defeated and don't underestimate the power of appeasements.

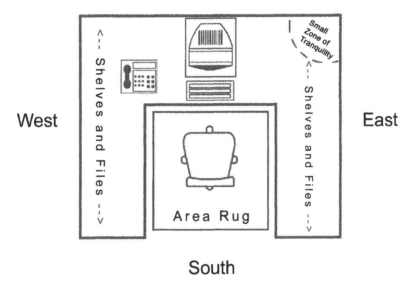

Figure 73: Spiritual Blueprint for an Acceptable Personal Space in the Pod

✳ YOUR PERSONALIZED DÉCOR

Appeasements are the key to your successful practice of vastu living in this environment—thoughtful appeasements, which let you reach the winning number of 51 percent and also enhance your décor. Your part of the pod should connect to the world of nature, which is interdependent and indivisible, and to the interior world of your self, which is unique and divine.

You can express the quiet of nature, which is so beneficial at work, through a few discrete choices that blend together inside your small space. Let

SOOTHE YOUR EYES

Your eyes get exhausted from staring into a computer monitor. Give them a health break a couple times a day. Drench two sterile cotton balls in cold water or cold skim milk, or take two cucumber slices, or dip two slices of raw potato into cold water until they are good and moist. Lean back in your chair, close your eyes, and place one of these remedies on each lid for three minutes. The cool moisture refreshes your eyes.

discretion also govern the celebration of your personality. Don't go whole hog and devote every square inch of your space to yourself. You end up sacrificing proportion; worse, you end up offending your neighbors. You want to honor the self, not the ego. When you observe this distinction, the objects in your part of the pod speak quietly and pointedly to your soul. They are similar to words spoken from the heart that express the truth. No one can fault that.

Your physical environment may have so many restrictions that it is inspiring and useful to see how I worked with a proofreader for a newspaper who was struggling to make her part of a pod a pleasant place to work. She had been a stay-at-home mom for over six years. But when her daughter entered the second grade, she decided to return to work.

Narrow side-walls, which were about six feet high and about five feet deep, and the wall that she faced when she sat at her computer on the workstation, were unpainted, rough wood. Two pine shelves wrapped around a good portion of the upper part of her three walls, and a metal file cabinet extended into the space from each side wall. The proofreader thought that her work environment was makeshift and unfinished. She called it cheap and believed that the unpainted wood spoke volumes about the management's attitude toward its employees who turned out the weekly newspaper. The young mother also missed her daughter; and although she wanted to work, she struggled with the guilt that accompanied her decision. Her unfinished workspace came to symbolize her concern that she had not properly completed her term as a stay-at-home mom (see Figure 74).

Once the proofreader clarified her feelings, she saw how they had conspired with the environment to disturb her well-being. She needed to embrace her work and her space: claim them both as her own. Then she could make conscious changes in the décor so that it created a positive and supportive environment.

She needed to celebrate her unique self, which included celebrating her love for her young daughter. She needed to honor the oneness that came through the presence of nature. If she created an environment that made her feel good about herself, she would feel good about her work. She would see that the joy of doing work came from within and not from without. She would work to please her self, not her employers or anyone else.

First, the proofreader reclaimed her work territory. She sorted through piles of papers and newspapers that she had let usurp much of her work surface, shelf space, and even a large part of the floor. Once she removed the clutter and organized her space, it seemed larger, and it was. She had more usable space.

Next she rubbed beeswax on the pine shelves, which created a soft sheen that added warmth to the natural planks. She affixed a thin blue ribbon on the edge of each shelf. This subtle change helped complete the bare wood, while the choice of colors was emotionally calming. Blue exuded tranquility and its complementary nighttime color of yellow was suggested in the yellowy hue of the pine wood.

She oriented her computer monitor so that she faced the north wall in her workstation—the direction that offered health and wealth. She did not want to orient herself so that she worked facing the northwest, which is governed by the element of air. Its negative property of movement and indecision could accentuate her lack of focus and ambivalence about her work.

The proofreader's work area was so small that her chair covered the direct center and held down the creative energies that should have circulated through her space. So she appeased the sacred element of space, which is governed by Lord Brahma, by placing a small square area rug, woven from natural fibers, under her chair. The square, with its static energy, introduced more calm inside her work area, and its location honored the element of space and Lord Brahma. Soft blues, her color of choice for her workspace, dominated the fabric border on the rug.

On the back of her chair, she hung a small blue-and-white quilt that she bought at a flea market. It blended nicely with the rug and the blue ribbon on the shelves. She put a deep blue vase on the northwest corner of her workstation, where she let the coming and going associated with the element of air reflect the changing seasons. She decided that she would always display a small bouquet of seasonal flowers or foliage that was consistently yellow, green, or white—yellow was the nighttime complement of blue, green created harmony and peace, white expressed purity. In October, she brought in a cluster of yellow maple leaves; at the start of December, she used a fragrant sprig of pine to remind her of the upcoming holiday season.

Her final touch of nature was incorporated in her special zone of tranquility—a clay sculpture that connected to her daughter. She also had a picture of her daughter from her days as an infant copied onto a mug that she kept on a shelf above her computer where she could see the baby's grin.

All these changes were judicious and spoke clearly and quietly to the young mother. They neither overwhelmed her part of the pod nor disturbed her neighbors. She worked well inside her environment. Its décor spoke of nature and her self—in particular, it expressed her connection to her daughter. She felt at ease and could focus on her work and get into her proofreading—finding satisfaction through staying in the moment and not thinking about the past when she was a stay-at-home mom or leaping into the future when she could be with her husband and daughter after work was done. She had claimed her space and was learning to embrace her work.

✳ YOUR ZONE OF TRANQUILITY

In this environment, your zone of tranquility, which is always in the northeast quadrant, can occupy a small area on your desk or on the wall or even on the floor, as long as you don't trip over it. (In the Southern Hemisphere, your zone of tranquility belongs in the southeast quadrant.) Your display needs to be proportionate with the space, and it should be so appealing that you want to stare at it frequently during your day. When you sit in an environment that lacks fresh air or natural lighting, your body tires quickly. This often leads to a quick cup of coffee or a sugar infusion—artificial stimulants that are unhealthy and quickly wear off. A meditation break brings about a healthy rejuvenation, and your zone of tranquility gets you into the mood to be still and turn inward.

Your display, which highlights an aspect of nature and a deeply personal object, acts like a mental magnet. It periodically draws your attention, usually when you are tired and your mind begins to wander. Its special objects remind you to take good care of that most important part of you—your inner essence, spirit, or self. You silence your meandering thoughts and learn to turn inward to enjoy the quiet voice of the soul that is life-affirming and positive.

During this time, you help beat back the stress that takes its toll on you. Stress is so pervasive at work that your zone of tranquility is as important as anything else in your workspace, especially in the pod where the majority of the elements are apt to be out of alignment.

The proofreader used her daughter's clay sculpture in her special display. It incorporated both nature and that part of her self that was so important to her—her child. The clay sculpture was actually a bust of her daughter's young face, and its expression showed delight. Her daughter had immortalized herself with a huge red smile. A blue bow was plunked onto her short hair, which was the yellow of summer sunshine. Her two big eyes were vivid, bright blue. She did not look like an unhappy child sitting at school and missing her mommy (see Figure 74).

The proofreader placed this small clay sculpture on the northeast corner of her workstation. She put a picture of her husband in a silver, heart-shaped frame next to the sculpture. His eyes were the same vivid blue as his daughter's. The proofreader hung a preserved yellow rose from a nail on the shelf above this part of her workstation. The rose, a Peace rose, symbolized true love and hung directly above her two special objects. Her thoughtful display was alluring; it did the trick.

Whenever the young mother stared into her zone of tranquility, she knew that she was tired and that it was time for a meditation break. She focused for a few minutes on her display to draw in the energy that comes with deep stillness.

North East

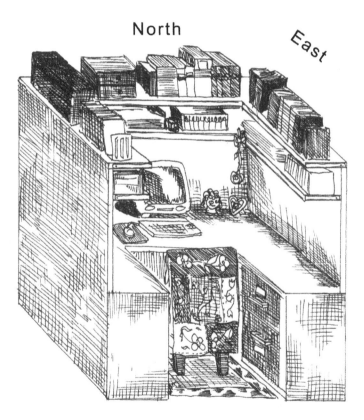

Figure 74: Intimate Zone of Tranquility

26

Cherish Your Reception Area

WELCOME TO THE VASTU LIVING RECEPTION AREA. PLEASE
TAKE OUT YOUR SPIRITUAL BLUEPRINT FOR THIS IMPORTANT
SPACE AND REFER TO IT AS YOU READ THIS CHAPTER.

The reception area in your company serves the same function as the living room at home. It is your welcoming room in the work world—the place where strangers form their first impression of your company. When visitors step into your reception area, they instinctively look around and soak in the details and the ambience as they wait to meet with you or anyone else in your company. Vastu living is mindful of this room's significance and consciously creates a positive and welcoming statement in its design and décor. After all, first impressions count; they are hard to change and harder to erase.

Before you learn how to organize your reception area, remember that this space is also about receiving—receiving your guests with unqualified respect. This is how you do justice to the word *reception*, which means the *act* of receiving. Even if your receptionist temporarily steps away from her desk, the room's décor should extend a welcome that puts every visitor at ease when he or she sits here.

❋ The Spiritual Blueprint for Your Reception Area

The only area that is poorly suited for your reception area is the southwest quadrant, which belongs to the element of earth with its property of strength. The power, which is built into this quadrant, is better suited for your company officials. The southwest is wasted when it is used as a space for people who essentially come to wait, temporarily, before they move on. (In the Southern Hemisphere, the element of earth is in the northwest quadrant.)

❋ The Placement of Your Furnishings

Observe the general guidelines under "The Placement of Your Furnishings and Equipment" in chapter 22, "General Guidelines for the Company." In particular, try to place your receptionist's desk or counter in the south or the west so that he or she faces the north, the northeast, or the east. These directions bless the receptionist with good mental, physical, and spiritual health. Your receptionist will then be in good spirits and graciously receive every visitor who comes into the room.

Please make an effort to keep the center of the reception area uncovered—free of any furnishings, except a rug. You want the beneficial energies that come from this sacred realm, which is governed by Brahma, the lord of creation, to circulate freely around the room.

Seating areas for visitors belong in the northwest if the furniture is lightweight (see Figure 75). This quadrant, which is connected to the element of air, is an ideal location for people who come and go. If the chairs and sofas are heavy, place the seating area in the south or the west so that it helps retain the cosmic energy and spiritual power that flow to this quadrant from the northeast (see Figure 76).

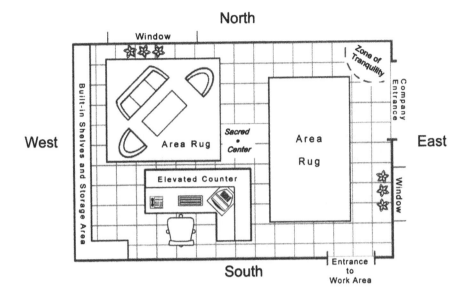

Figure 75: Spiritual Blueprint for the Reception Area with Lightweight Furniture

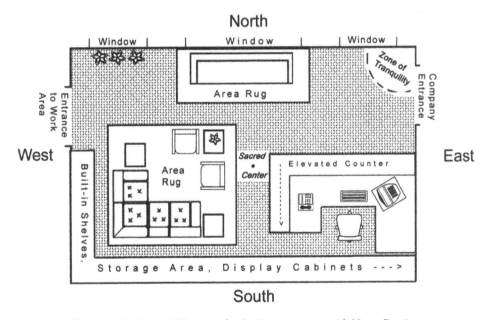

Figure 76: Spiritual Blueprint for the Reception Area with Heavy Furniture

❊ Your Inviting Décor

Friendly. This word describes the perfect décor for your reception area. Provide comfortable chairs and sofas so that your visitors can relax and feel comfortable. Unleash the healthy powers of nature and use them liberally in your décor. Plants help purify the air, which is especially beneficial to any environment where the air is recycled. If your reception area has windows, use natural window treatments, and organize a lovely display of greens or seasonal blooms that draws the attention of your visitors. Your display will help steady the nerves of those waiting to make a pitch for a job or a deal.

If your reception area lacks windows, incorporate natural products and stay away from unfriendly synthetics. Use natural-fiber area rugs or natural flooring, such as bricks or tiles. Dress up the reception area with objects made of stone or terra-cotta or highlight a handsome collection of vintage glass. Please the eyes with a bouquet of dried flowers or a basket filled with gourds, pinecones, seashells, small stones.

INVITING COLORS

Use warm colors, not cool colors, in your reception area. Warm colors cheer up the space and the mood of anyone who is sitting there. Use quiet hues on the walls, with brighter accents in the cushions, carpeting, or window treatments. Strong, dark colors on a wall can be psychologically overwhelming, even intimidating.

Celebrate your company and reveal its identity. Leave materials and brochures on the tables in your waiting area, so that visitors can read about your company and brush up on their facts if they have come for a meeting. If there are stacks of magazines or newspapers on any tables, keep them current and remove shabby, coverless issues. A messy and dingy reception area is more than an eyesore—it speaks poorly of your company. Your welcoming room should be organized and tidy.

Cramped for Space

Does your reception area have all the charm of a walk-in closet? Does it lack windows? Is it so small that your receptionist sits on the far side of a closed glass partition—a situation that creates a physical and psychological distance

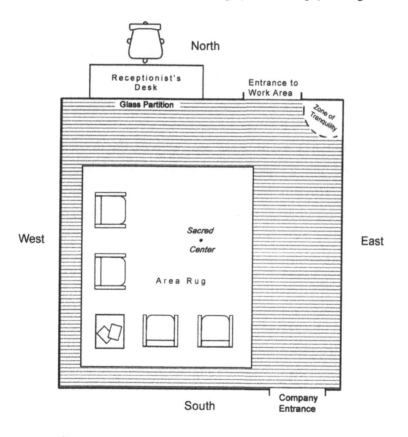

Figure 77: Spiritual Blueprint for the Small Reception Area

from your visitors? Despite these limitations, you can still get to the acceptable 51 percent correct with your practice of vastu living. You *can* turn a cramped space into a welcoming reception area.

Let's examine how I helped the owner of a small start-up turn his foyer, which had every one of these handicaps, into a positive environment that reflected well on him and his young company. The entrance to his foyer, which could only comfortably accommodate four chairs, was in the southeast quadrant. The glass partition that separated his visitors from his receptionist was cut into the north wall next to a door that connected to his company offices (see Figure 77, above).

We started the positive transformation of this cramped space by removing its wall-to-wall carpeting to expose an old, dark wood floor, which he then had buffed to a sheen. The owner added a beautiful kilim, with its rich, dark colors that came from vegetable dyes. This kilim, which he had brought back from a trip to Morocco, showcased the lovely dark wood border and floor molding (see Figure 78, below).

His reception area was so small that we kept the décor and furnishings simple to avoid any feeling of clutter that would make the room seem smaller. We put four sturdy, canvas-backed chairs near the south and west walls and placed a glass-covered rattan table in the southwest corner. For reading material, he put out a few issues of *National Geographic* magazine that dated back to the early 1900s and reflected his interest in foreign places and foreign cultures.

The organization of the furnishings created the illusion of a larger space. It also honored the sacred center, which was left uncovered. Finally, it observed the principle of a light and airy north and east, which allowed the cosmic energy and spiritual power to move from the northeast to the southwest.

Since the owner had a special affection for Morocco, we used his interest as the focal point in his zone of tranquility in the northeast quadrant. We hung a beautiful Moroccan tapestry on the east wall not far from the north-east corner. To the east of the tapestry, we placed a tall, glazed urn on the floor, which contained tall and stately snake grass.

This reception area became a comfortable, welcoming space. Its décor had character and expressed the interests of the owner of the start-up. The presence of nature established warmth. The careful placement of the furnishings created a feeling of spaciousness. His receptionist still sat on the far side of the glass partition, but the waiting area was inviting and reflected the owner's concerns for the well-being of his visitors.

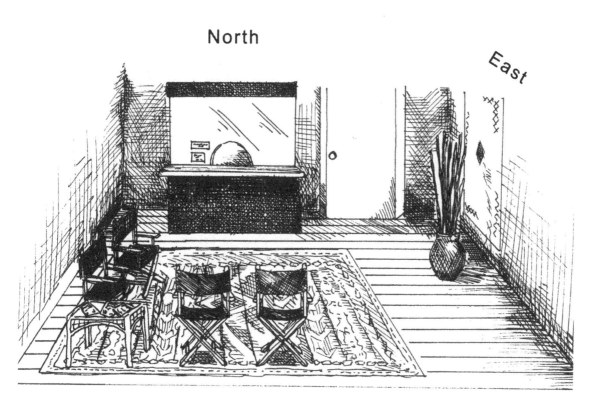

Figure 78: Comfy Waiting Area

Your Zone of Tranquility

Your zone of tranquility in your reception area is not solely for the benefit of the receptionist. Your display, which speaks of nature and celebrates the soul, should have a powerful effect on everyone. We have all experienced waits in reception areas that try our patience. Your zone of tranquility, which is always in the northeast quadrant, becomes a positive distraction. Your visitors can focus on the display and center their mind. Their wait can be used as an opportunity to turn inward. (In the Southern Hemisphere, your zone of tranquility belongs in the southeast quadrant.)

An effective display in your reception area is universal in nature. It can be a vase of fresh flowers, sprigs, or cuttings that consciously reflect the current season and, therefore, the cycle of life—lilacs for spring, daisies for summer, zinnias for autumn, holly for winter. Complete your display with a powerful statement that is beautifully inscribed by hand—a pearl of wisdom that inspires healthy reflection, such as this statement by Swami Chinmayananda: "Our work is love made visible."

Take a Journey toward Stillness

The reception room can be a perfect place to practice how to move toward stillness. You are waiting for someone and you are alone for the moment. Sit perfectly erect in the chair or sofa and cross your ankles. Place your hands, palms down, on your knees. Close your eyes, if you can, or at least close out the vision around you. Repeat to yourself, "I am still as a rock," and try to visualize this stillness in yourself as you keep your body from moving, except for the slow, rhythmic breathing in and out. You will move toward that quiet place within you and feel peace flow over you.

27

Recognize Your Conference Room

WELCOME TO THE VASTU LIVING CONFERENCE ROOM. PLEASE TAKE OUT YOUR SPIRITUAL BLUEPRINT FOR THIS SPACE IF IT EXISTS IN YOUR WORK ENVIRONMENT AND REFER TO IT AS YOU READ THIS CHAPTER.

Inspiration, innovative solutions, creative thinking outside the box—these are just a few words that describe a successful brainstorming session in a conference room. But creative thinking and inspiration only occur in an environment that encourages mutual respect, where every person who sits in the room feels valued irrespective of his or her title or position within your company.

This is the objective of the vastu living conference room. It radiates good-will and telegraphs the principle that we are our thoughts, or we should be—meaning that the self should be the guiding force behind our words. When we embrace this principle, we always speak from a place of love and mutual respect, and we always speak the truth. When we speak to please someone else or score points, we are speaking from the ego—and there is a big difference between the ego and the self. The ego has an agenda that can succumb to ulterior motives. So when the self inspires all the thoughts that are spoken in your conference room, your company gains—so does everyone who sits at the table.

To create this environment of giving rather than taking, your vastu living conference room celebrates interconnection and interdependence. Its entire décor blends together to create a cohesive statement. It speaks of the old and the new—the continuum that goes on and on. It draws upon nature to remind everyone of the value in diversity—a diversity that is most likely reflected within your company and in the faces of the people who sit around your conference table.

The moment people walk into this space, everyone, from your company employees to visitors, connects to its positive and uplifting ambience. When they sit around the table, they feel that they're in a supportive environment that is caring and just. And the only time your conference room expresses any somberness is when the lights are turned low for video presentations.

Even your zone of tranquility, which acts as a positive source of inspiration and well-being, connects to your décor and everyone who is present at the meeting. When visual harmony flows through this room in which important issues make up the agenda, this ambience brings out the best in everyone who sits here. It helps ensure a productive outcome.

THE SPIRITUAL BLUEPRINT FOR YOUR CONFERENCE ROOM

The three particularly good locations for your conference room are the east, which is associated with inspiration and creativity; the northeast, which is calm and reflective; and the north, which connects to wealth and health. The west is a neutral location; it does no harm. When your conference room is in the southwest, meetings can be inspired and filled with the wisdom that accompanies this quadrant. But since your conference room often sits idle, let this wisdom and strength flow through the offices that belong to your executives. They make better use of the southwest quadrant. Your conference room in the northwest quadrant can suffer from unproductive meetings. The properties related to the element of air can interfere with concentration. Your conference room in the southeast quadrant, which is governed by fire, may experience volatility. Dialogues may easily turn into arguments. (If you live in the Southern Hemisphere, follow the spiritual blueprint on page 116, which shows the correct location of the elements below the equator.)

THE PLACEMENT OF YOUR FURNISHINGS

This is one room where it may not be possible to observe some of the vastu guidelines that govern the proper placement of furnishings (see "The Placement of Your Furnishings and Equipment" in chapter 22, "General Guidelines for the Company"). Your conference table, usually the heaviest object, often monopolizes this room, which may be small and unable to accommodate openness in the north and the east. So play safe and insure harmony by making appeasements to the five basic elements when they are not properly oriented (see chapter 5, "Resolving Conflicts in Your Home and Workplace"). You want positive energy and healthy objectives to inspire each meeting.

Typically, conference tables tend to cover the room's sacred center, which belongs to Brahma, the lord of creation. To permit the circulation of the creative energies that originate from this realm, consider using a U-shaped table, which won't cover the center of the room (see Figure 79). This shape, which is circle-based and creates dynamic energy, also stimulates an active exchange of ideas and keeps discussions in motion. If your conference table covers the sacred center and company meetings fall short of the mark, please make an appeasement to Lord Brahma and his element of space (see Figure 80).

Your presentation screens or monitors belong in the north, which is connected to health and wealth, or the east, which inspires enlightenment and

North

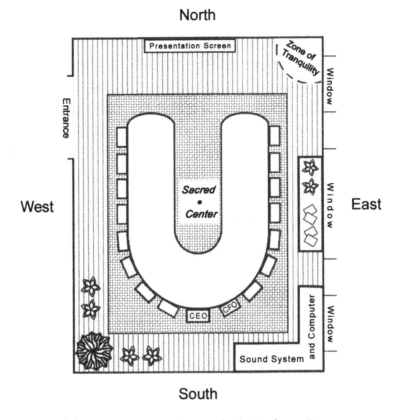

West

East

South

Figure 79: Spiritual Blueprint for the Conference Room

creative thinking. Try to keep computers in the southeast quadrant, which belongs to the element of fire. If you introduce fire into another quadrant, make appropriate appeasements to restore the balance.

Your Seating Arrangements

The individual who chairs a meeting in your conference room should sit in the south and face the north. When numerous executives attend a meeting, the financial officer should also face this direction, which connects to wealth

Figure 80: Appeasing the Sacred Center

and health, and sit to the right of the CEO. The other officers should try to sit in the south or the southwest. Remaining company employees should sit in the west. Visitors who attend a meeting should sit on the east side of your conference table, where they face the west—the realm of the unknown—or they should sit in the north, where they face the south—the realm of responsibility and duty. The objective: Your company is the host. Your company employees should sit so that they control the flow of the meeting and face the directions that lead to a productive outcome that benefits everyone—the north, the east, and the northeast.

Your Inspiring Décor

Nature, our great source of inspiration and positive thoughts, is often overlooked in the conference room. Perhaps this is because the room is often empty and isn't under the constant care of any one person. But your conference room is important to your company, and the quiet presence of nature turns this space into a welcoming retreat that encourages contemplation and well-reasoned thoughts. Nature promotes harmony and speaks of order and the value of all creation—good associations for a room where people gather to come up with winning solutions and innovations.

Everything inside your conference room should reinforce the contemplative effect of nature. Your chairs should be comfortable so that everyone focuses on the mind, not on the lack of good ergonomics. Your décor should be understated so that it doesn't divert attention from the subject matter of the meeting. Try to weave nature into many aspects of this room. If it has a wooden floor, expose part of it—at least a healthy border. Choose natural-fiber window treatments, and use an underlayer that lets you increase or decrease the flow of sunlight. Place a square or rectangular silk, wool, cotton, or handsome grass rug under a circle-based conference table. The square-based area rug is connected to static energy and acts as an excellent counter-force to the dynamic energy created by your round table. Harmony prevails.

Use quiet colors on the walls to inspire creative thoughts—creamy hues of whites, yellows, blues, and greens. Introduce brighter shades of these colors as accents in your upholstery, products from nature, and artwork. And be mind-

TEAS FOR THE MOMENT

Feeling sluggish at a conference meeting? Peppermint tea is a good pick-me-up. Feeling anxious? Calm your nerves with chamomile. Feeling cold or chilly in the room? Ginger tea warms you right up. When you prepare tea, put the tea bag or fresh herbs in a strainer into the pot or cup, then add the boiling water. Put the lid back on the pot or a saucer over the cup, so that the healthy properties of the herbs don't escape. Let the tea brew for about three minutes. If you like a sweetener, add honey. Enjoy.

ful of the themes of the paintings that are hung on your walls. Keep the themes positive. You don't want negative thoughts to sneak, unwittingly, into your room.

YOUR ZONE OF TRANQUILITY

Your zone of tranquility in your conference room should reinforce the principle that the self should guide the thoughts expressed around your table, not the ego with its ego-driven needs. Your display, which belongs in the northeast quadrant of water, should be deeply calming. As always, it includes an aspect of nature and celebrates the self—in this case, the self of every employee in your company. (In the Southern Hemisphere, your zone belongs in the southeast quadrant.)

If possible, your conference room is an excellent location for a reflective pool of water, either a small indoor pond or fountain with floating blossoms surrounded by an attractive display of plants. Water is a source of deep contemplation. When participants in a meeting are searching for the right solution or the brilliant innovation, their eyes find comfort in this display. As they stare at the soothing water, it is renewing, rejuvenating, and helps focus their mind. Let your display also include something that connects to all your employees—such as a group photo—or let it feature a different employee every month. Your company surrenders more than it can afford when it lets go of its human face. When your company disconnects from its employees, your employees disconnect from your company.

28

Give Thanks to Your Dining Area

WELCOME TO THE VASTU LIVING COMPANY CANTEEN OR
DINING AREA. PLEASE TAKE OUT YOUR SPIRITUAL BLUEPRINT
IF THIS SPACE EXISTS IN YOUR WORK ENVIRONMENT AND
REFER TO IT AS YOU READ THIS CHAPTER.

Some companies have a kitchen canteen with a table and a few chairs, refrigerator, microwave oven, coffee machine, dispensers filled with Snickers, Doritos, and Mountain Dew. The canteen may have a cheery decor, but the dispensers set the tone: fast food and fast departure—in other words, this room offers convenience. An employee can grab a quick snack or store a meal brought in from home and reheat it for lunch in the microwave. Other companies provide the equivalent of an in-house restaurant with a menu or a buffet. Employees can sit down and stay awhile.

At work, it is so easy for us to rush through our lunch and hardly be aware of what we eat. We don't savor the taste of anything, and we are only nominally connected to the act of eating. On some days, we even skip lunch. Gulping down food may seem an improvement over imbibing nothing more than air, but neither of these scenarios does us any good.

You may find this hard to admit, but when you deny your body its nourishment and punish it by disrupting the natural rhythm of the digestive process, you are abusing yourself, and this abuse catches up with you. By midafternoon you're tired, you can't think properly, you're cranky. And this is just the noticeable top layer of the damage. When you don't eat properly, every part of you suffers. So in your practice of vastu living, you want to accord the same level of respect to your dining area at work that you accord to your kitchen at home. Your company dining area should be considered a room of ritual where everyone comes to nourish the body, which is the temple of the soul. We must always remember that how we treat our body is an indication of how well we treat that most valuable part of the self—the soul.

THE SPIRITUAL BLUEPRINT FOR YOUR DINING AREA

Please note: The company canteen has a spiritual blueprint with one set of quadrants (see Figure 81). But the company dining room with separate cooking facilities requires a blueprint divided into two sets of quadrants: one for the dining area and one for the food preparation area (see Figure 82).

Your company dining area belongs in the southeast quadrant, the realm of fire. Fire cleanses and purifies, and these two processes go into the preparation of most of your food. Fruits and vegetables are carefully washed before you enjoy them. Many meals are cooked, and this purifies the ingredients so that they are safe to eat. Your southeast quadrant honors these actions.

Take extra care with your company dining area if it is located in the northwest quadrant. The northwest, which is governed by the element of air, can reinforce bad eating habits. The properties of air, which are associated with quick movement, can intensify the urge to bolt down a meal and rush back to work or outside to do some quick errands. To encourage everyone to eat slowly, introduce calming influences into your dining area if it is placed in this quadrant (see "Your Healthy Décor," below). (If you live in the Southern Hemisphere, follow the spiritual blueprint on page 116, which shows the correct location of the elements below the equator.)

THE PLACEMENT OF YOUR FURNISHINGS AND APPLIANCES

In the canteen and the dining area with separate cooking facilities, try to keep the heavy objects in the south and the west and the lightweight objects in the north and the east. This arrangement encourages the beneficial flow of the cosmic energy and spiritual power from the northeast quadrant to the southwest quadrant and traps them inside the space (see Figures 81 and 82).

If your company refrigerator is the heaviest object in this area, try to place it in the southwest, preferably against the west wall. When the door is opened, the stored perishables receive the blessings of the east and the sun. Just as food supplies us with our fire or energy, the sun provides everything on earth with its energy. Without its presence, nothing could exist.

Your appliances that generate heat, including the microwave oven and coffee machine, belong to the element of fire. Try to keep them in the southeast quadrant of your kitchen or dining area. Your dishwasher, sinks, water fountains, or watercoolers belong in the northeast quadrant, which is governed by the element of water. Dining-room bathrooms, however, belong in the west, the northwest, or the east. The water, which flows out of the bathroom, contains human wastes. Their impurity defiles the northeast quadrant.

If possible, your food preparation counters should enable your employees to face east when they prepare meals. The preparation of a meal, which is another action in the ritual connected to the nourishment of the body, should acknowledge the greatest source of purification, the sun.

Your company canteen or dining area should try to keep the center space uncovered. An open center allows the creative energies that emanate from this sacred realm of Lord Brahma to circulate freely throughout the space. This benefits everyone. The flow of positive energy helps your employees create healthy meals that provide nourishment for their body and soul. They return to their job filled with caloric energy that helps them work better and positive energy that helps them work from a healthy point of view.

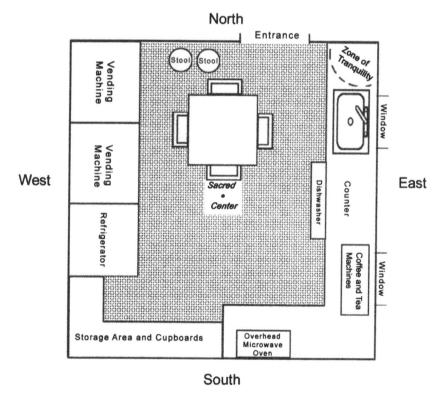

Figure 81: Spiritual Blueprint for the Company Canteen

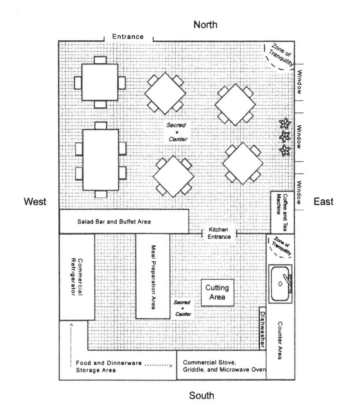

Figure 82: Spiritual Blueprint for the Company Dining Room and Cooking Facilities

❋ YOUR HEALTHY DÉCOR

Your company dining area, whether a canteen or a restaurant, should have a calming ambience so that everyone slows down to give the body and the mind a health break. Try to create a décor that is as pleasing as the aroma and taste of the food that is slowly consumed during a meal. To start, place nature here in abundance—plants or fresh flowers or any organic products that come from the earth. Nature is healing, inspiring, reinvigorating. Use colors of the harvest—soft yellows and oranges that also relate to the sun—and pay homage to the bounty that comes with summer.

REMEMBER THE DIFFERENCE BETWEEN THE CIRCLE AND THE SQUARE

The circle creates dynamic energy, which is unsettled, active, on the move. The square creates static energy, which is fixed and unchanging. The square represents the heavenly realm of the deities. As I explained earlier, our body, which creates a perfect square, finds greater comfort with this shape.

You don't really want your employees to rush through their meals, so use square-based tables in your company dining area. They slow people down when they eat and help them relax. Circle-based tables motivate your employees to eat fast and talk fast. They turn your dining area into a "pit stop" where your employees rush through their meal and get on with their day. The body suffers from this unhealthy eating behavior and so does work performance.

Show your company's concern for the environment and shun the use of nonbiodegradable products, such as styrofoam cups, plastic utensils, plastic plates. Recyclable dinnerware not only saves money over time; it sends out a positive signal to everyone who eats in this room. In a quiet way, this cost-saving measure celebrates the value of the self. As colleagues and coworkers share a meal together, each time their spoon or fork enters their mouth, they don't taste plastic. When they move a knife across their plate, they don't cut into plastic. They are interacting with natural products that do no harm to them or the larger environment.

Let music—but please, never artificial Muzak—play quietly in the background in this special room. Soft melodies, with their underlying rhythms, encourage people to slow down. Thoughtful music can even inspire listeners to turn inward to *discover* and *enjoy* the self as well as one another. Even if your

HONOR YOUR CONSTITUTION WHEN YOU EAT

Before you decide what to eat for lunch at work, take stock of your well-being. Are you struggling to stay focused or do you feel indecisive? Your vata may be aggravated. Steer away from a salad or lots of fiber, which stimulate vata. Are you so judgmental and critical that you get into arguments with everyone, including your self? Skip pitta food, such as spicy, hot dishes, so that you can rein in the fire that may be overstimulated inside you. Are you feeling tired and sluggish? Choose a light salad or a meal with lots of fiber to rev up the movement inside you.

employees come into the dining room to brainstorm over a company issue or to talk out the next step in a project, the nurturing décor should still foster a healthy approach to eating—the ritual that is celebrated in this company space.

Ultimately, your dining room should replicate some of the attributes of a sanctuary. People should automatically lower their voice when they enter so that the soft music is heard at even the most remote table. The décor, with its emphasis on nature, should accentuate the calm that is experienced inside a sacred space. Every aspect of the dining area should be a continuum of harmony, cohesion, and an expression of honor for all creation. Within such an environment, everyone connects to the self and to the self of each other. This is how a health break nourishes the body and the soul.

YOUR ZONE OF TRANQUILITY

Even your company's small canteen has room for a contemplative zone of tranquility in its northeast quadrant. Your zone can be a mobile hanging from the ceiling—created out of gourds and flowers. It can be a tiny display in the northeast corner—a single flower in a bud vase, with a positive quote on the wall as food for thought. Before your employees begin their meal, these wise words may translate into a silent form of grace that blesses the self. (In the Southern Hemisphere, the zone of tranquility belongs in the southeast quadrant.)

In your company dining room, let your zone of tranquility in the northeast quadrant celebrate the members of your company team and the glory of nature. A CEO of a software company who decided to practice vastu living invited his employees to bring in photos of people who were their source of inspiration—family member, best friend, spiritual leader, competitor in the same field. He promoted the spirit of inclusion so that everyone participated. Every month, he placed a different group of photos from this collection inside an old wood wheelbarrow, which was missing all the slats on one side. Its antiquity and defect became a handsome setting for his company's display, which was enhanced with a few plants.

Then, he asked his employees to add other objects from nature around the base of this wheelbarrow. These objects were also personal statements.

Figure 83: Food for Thought

Someone added a salvaged birdhouse, which, in turn, inspired a bird, a duck, a turtle, and then a pair of pink flamingos. A metal mouse showed up, then a cat and a small stuffed dog. This company zone of tranquility had humor. But the humor inspired deeper meanings that spoke of mutual respect and love for all creation—and this message went straight to the soul.

29

Value Your "Silicon" Workspace

WELCOME TO THE VASTU LIVING "SILICON" WORKSPACE.
PLEASE TAKE OUT YOUR SPIRITUAL BLUEPRINT IF YOU WORK
IN A ROOM FILLED WITH COMPUTERS AND REFER TO IT AS YOU
READ THIS CHAPTER.

The computer revolution has spawned new theories about the workplace, and the testing ground for many of these theories has been right inside the high-tech world. Silicon start-ups, with their zest for freedom, have stretched the work envelope so that their employees can literally think outside the box as they shoot pool at the company pool table or take aim at the company dartboard. The pooch is no longer canine non grata and snoozes away under a desk or workstation. Parrots have their right to chatter overhead.

Silicon companies have flattened their business structure, reduced their hierarchy, and try to promote a collegial spirit. They encourage open communication, spontaneous meetings, and collaborative teams. But, despite all these changes, the Silicon shop is still loaded with stress. Survival is often on the line—the company's survival and consequently, each employee's survival. Innovation doesn't always translate into financial success. Dotcom and

Internet companies quickly contract and collapse. Or work hours expand, with employees staring into computer monitors way into the night. The mind burns out and frazzles. The body, especially aching hands and blurry eyes, grows weary.

A large number of Silicon companies keep their servers, hard disks, routers, hubs, and switches in an enclosed area where they can monitor the temperature to prevent excessive heat buildup and control unauthorized access. Serious damage to this equipment does serious damage to the financial health of a company. Isolating this equipment may also help protect the physical health of the company employees. Magnetic fields and radiation connected to computer paraphernalia may be hazardous to a worker's health—the final verdict is yet to come in.

But Silicon companies are still likely to organize many of their high-tech staffers into teams who sit inside rooms or defined areas in close proximity to numerous computers and banks of display monitors. This environment within the dotcom and Internet world needs to promote the well-being of the body, mind, and soul. In this environment the practice of vastu living can be a godsend and a salvation.

THE SPIRITUAL BLUEPRINT FOR YOUR SILICON WORKSPACE

The southeast quadrant, which is the realm of fire and modern electricity, is the preferred location for this workspace. If you have a pitta or fiery constitution, this quadrant may pose a problem. Assess your body's reaction. If you sense that the negative principle of like increases like is interfering with your well-being, then introduce objects from nature or pacifying colors that can calm down your overstimulated constitution (see chapter 5, "Resolving Conflicts in Your Home and Workplace").

UNHEALTHY QUADRANTS FOR YOUR CONSTITUTION IN THE WORKPLACE

CONSTITUTION OR DOSHA	NORTHERN HEMISPHERE UNHEALTHY QUADRANT	SOUTHERN HEMISPHERE UNHEALTHY QUADRANT
Vata / Air	Northwest (Air)	Southwest (Air)
Pitta / Fire	Southeast (Fire)	Northeast (Fire)
Kapha / Water	Northeast (Water)	Southeast (Water)

If your team is one of many teams, its assigned workspace may easily be in a quadrant other than the southeast. In this case you make two appeasements. Offer one appeasement to the element of fire and place it in the southeast quadrant. Your computer equipment, which belongs to this element and the southeast, has been introduced into a wrong quadrant. Consider hanging a brass image of Surya, the sun deity, on the wall in the southeast. Offer a second appeasement, such as an aquarium with fish, to the element of water and place it in the northeast quadrant. If your team sits in the northwest, you make your second appeasement to the violated element of air. Hang a fancy paper kite from the ceiling in the northwest. If your team sits in the southwest quadrant, make your second offering to the element of earth; in the center, the element of space (ether). (If you live in the Southern Hemisphere, follow the spiritual blueprint on page 116, which shows the correct location of the elements below the equator.)

THE PLACEMENT OF YOUR FURNISHINGS AND EQUIPMENT

Divide your team space, whether it's an entire room or in an open-floor setting, into four quadrants and note the sacred center. Try to place all your desks or workstations in the southwest so that everyone benefits from the strength and wisdom associated with this quadrant, which belongs to the element of earth and our ancestors. Encourage everyone in your team to face the north, the northeast, or the east when they look into their monitors. The north blesses them with wealth and health, especially spiritual health and wealth. The northeast is calming. It also receives the beneficial cosmic energy and spiritual power that enter this quadrant. The east brings clarity and enlightenment.

The properties associated with these directions make you mindful of your well-being. You remember to rest your eyes and give your hands a break from the repetitive motions connected to your keyboard, mouse, or touch-pad devices. You remember to stop all work occasionally to focus on your self, which helps you maintain a healthy perspective and holds back

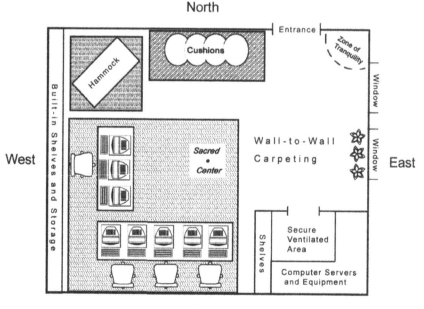

 Figure 84: Spiritual Blueprint for the Silicon Team Workroom

job-related stress. You hear your inner voice, which is connected to the self and not the ego. This voice keeps you centered, balanced, and blesses you with calm.

Try to place the monitors on your desk or workstation or any bank of monitors so that they are about thirty inches from your eyes. Monitors send out low-frequency electromagnetic emissions that diminish with distance. Do your best to put all servers and other computer hardware that isn't used daily inside the realm governed by the element of fire—the southeast quadrant of your team workspace. If possible, isolate this equipment inside an enclosed space so that it won't do any harm to your team.

Finally, add a relaxing escape inside your space that can draw each of you away from your computers and reinforce the healthy habit of periodic down-time. In your "anything goes" environment, there are so many options. A

YOGA TO RELIEVE REPETITIVE HAND MOVEMENTS

Your fingers suffer from the nonstop small movements that accompany hours of work at your computer. But if you do these two yoga exercises every hour, you can give your wrists and hands a health stretch that keeps them nimble.

Push your chair away from your desk and sit up straight. Hold your arms in front of you at shoulder height. With the palms pointing to the floor, open your hands and stretch your fingers as wide apart as you can. Then, close your fingers and make a tight fist with your thumb tucked inside. Repeat this exercise five times in a series.

Keep the original pose—arms outstretched in front of you. With your fingers straight and palms open, bend your hands so your fingers point to the ceiling, then bend them so your fingers point to the floor. Don't bend your elbows or your fingers. Repeat this exercise five times in a series.

group of employees who introduced vastu living into their high-tech environment placed a hammock in the northwest quadrant of their room. The hammock's to-and-fro motion is in consonance with the movement associated with the northwest's element of air. The restlessness connected to this element also keeps everyone from zoning out. After spending a few minutes in the hammock, the team member feels rested, clarified, and ready to go back to work.

❋ Your Soul-Filled Décor

Nature needs to assert itself in this environment that has so much artificial intelligence and plastic in the computer components. Place an area rug on the floor even if the company has wall-to-wall carpeting. Let this rug honor the sacred center and the colors of the earth. But please stay away from synthetics—don't let artificial dyes or fake materials for rugs sneak into your environment.

Bring plants into your work area if you have reasonable lighting. Plants, which help detoxify the air, connect everyone to the positive value of the diversity that runs through all creation. Or display fresh or dried flowers on your workstation or desk. If there isn't enough room, place a handsome tapestry, woven from natural fibers, on your workstation surface and cover it with glass to protect the material. The tapestry brightens up your space. Or bring in a wood coatrack and hang a mix of nature from each hook—a garland of dried flowers, a string of garlic bulbs and gourds, a collection of silk scarves or ties entwined together. Introduce lots of nature into your stressful yet permissive environment.

If the team works in a room, try to have soft colors on the walls that continue the rhythm of serenity and calm. Use pale shades of blue (with its night-time complement of yellow) and greens, which balance the fiery nature of all the computer equipment, which is connected to the element of fire. Stay away from stimulating colors, such as orange and red, unless your workspace is in the northeast quadrant of water, which provides an abundance of serenity. Even then, keep warm colors soft and muted. You don't want to irritate your overtaxed eyes.

You and your team may not have any control over the lighting in your space if it is in an open area of the company. But if your team works inside a room, lower the overhead lighting and attach small lights to each workstation or desk. Small directional lights are gentle on the eyes, which suffer already from staring into the display monitors. If your work area has windows, use window treatments that block out the sun's glare, but not its energy. Use filmy, natural fabrics or grass-fiber blinds that filter in the sunlight.

Finally, play quiet music in your environment. It extends the rhythm of serenity and calms your nerves. It is so good for your soul. Played softly, appealing music, such as classical music, won't interfere with your concentration either. In fact, it can effectively block out those subtle computer noises that become audio interference just when you are trying to think up a new solution to a tricky high-tech problem.

Your Zone of Tranquility

Please create a zone of tranquility in your computer-oriented workspace. If everyone on your team is into sports, celebrate your mutual passion in the northeast quadrant of the work area. In the Southern Hemisphere, your zone belongs in the southeast. Ask your teammates to donate objects from their chosen sport—a baseball, golf ball, tennis racket—something that honors their special pleasure and therefore their unique identity. Just don't let anyone introduce synthetics (see Figure 85).

Have some fun and use old-fashioned, outdated versions that have been replaced by the high-tech invasion. By honoring the old, you honor the past and, by extension, the cycle of life. Include that important identification with nature in your display. Place your objects on top of a jute mat along with a rectangular container of lush rye grass that grows inside the office. Why rye grass? If your team is celebrating tennis, baseball, and golf, rye grass honors the turf.

North   East

Figure 85: Sporting Zone of Tranquility

30

Bless Your Boutique

WELCOME TO THE VASTU LIVING BOUTIQUE. PLEASE TAKE OUT YOUR SPIRITUAL BLUEPRINT OR BLUEPRINTS IF THIS DEFINES YOUR WORK ARENA AND REFER TO THEM AS YOU READ THIS CHAPTER.

Boutique owners are quick to agree that they're in a volatile business. Their shops, which are often so pleasing to the eye, often mask a turbulence that runs just underneath the surface. Success is tied to so many variables that I call the boutique business a vata business—subject to the properties connected to the element of air. The designers who supply the merchandise, the mandatory first step to a healthy bottom line, may unexpectedly cut off their pipeline and sell their products somewhere else or they may lose their magic touch. The customer, who has every right to remain fickle and unpredictable, may suddenly disappear—ignoring a once preferred boutique for the new competition next store. Loyalty has no meaning in the retail world. Creative pizzazz and a mysterious je ne sais quoi control a shopper's allegiance.

In this risky world known for slow success and faster failure, the practice of vastu living can calm down your nerves as well as the vata edge to your boutique business. You can steady yourself and focus on the issues within your control that affect the well-being of the boutique and, therefore, your own well-being.

Vastu living is also a natural fit inside your boutique. Its three important principles—balancing the five basic elements to mirror the harmony of the universe, honoring nature, and celebrating one's individuality—reinforce your existing goals. You already try to make people feel comfortable when they are in your shop. Your boutique, by definition, celebrates your unique interests. They are expressed in the products that you display, which you hope turn every visitor into a customer who wants to come back.

Vastu living gives a boost to these intentions. Vastu's logical guidelines introduce harmonizing aesthetics that connect to the eye. Its principles ensure the flow of positive energy that reaches into the heart and the soul. This powerful combination creates an unmistakable welcoming ambience that encourages people to linger once they step inside your vastu living boutique.

THE SPIRITUAL BLUEPRINT FOR YOUR BOUTIQUE

An entrance door in the east or the north wall near the northeast corner turns the generally open space of your boutique into a huge receptacle for the positive cosmic energy and spiritual power that enter this quadrant. The northeast, which belongs to the element of water, is serene and reflective—good qualities for a boutique. Everyone who comes inside—from the customer to the designer—is inclined to slow down and not rush through a visit.

An entrance door in the northwest fills your shop with the properties associated with the element of air, which lords over this quadrant. Visitors to your shop may be easily distracted and struggle to focus on your merchandise; your personnel may fail to focus their attention on the needs of your customers. But the properties of air can also make your inventory fly off the shelf. So offset the negative side of this element by introducing soothing colors, such as blue (with its nighttime complement of yellow) or green, or calming objects from nature that settle the mind and increase the attention span.

If your entrance door is in the southwest, this creates an easy exit for the cosmic energy and spiritual power that flow into this quadrant from the northeast. But you can place an attractive barrier, such as a carved-wood screen, near the entrance that helps retain these positive forces. The screen can serve a double purpose as an entrance display (as opposed to a window display) that is dressed up on both sides with merchandise. You convert a problem entrance into an attractive advantage (see Figure 86).

An entrance in the southeast quadrant connects to the element of fire. It brings warmth, perhaps too much warmth, into your boutique. Are you bossy? Does your temperament turn off your designers or personnel? Are your customers supercritical when they try on things in your dressing room?

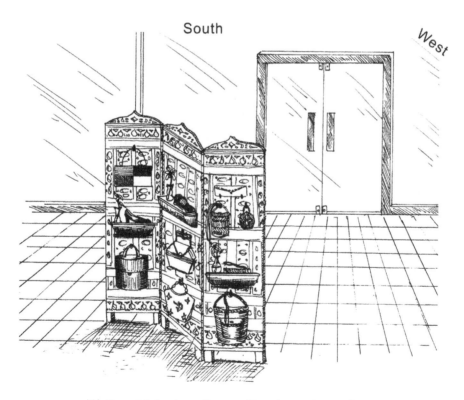

Figure 86: Southwest Entrance Turned into a Positive Barrier

You may need to add cooling colors and lots of nature to reduce the "heat" inside your shop. (If you live in the Southern Hemisphere, examine the spiritual blueprint on page 116 to see the location of the elements below the equator.)

Your Dressing Rooms

If your boutique has a substantial dressing area with several try-on rooms and an open center area with three-way mirrors for your customers, treat this area as a separate spiritual blueprint. Try to place the individual dressing rooms in the north, the east, and the west inside this part of your shop. The north brings wealth and health, including spiritual health and wealth. The east brings inspiration, and the west won't do any harm. The southwest quadrant may give too much power to your customer, and the southeast quadrant may create a critical eye where nothing is flattering to the beholder.

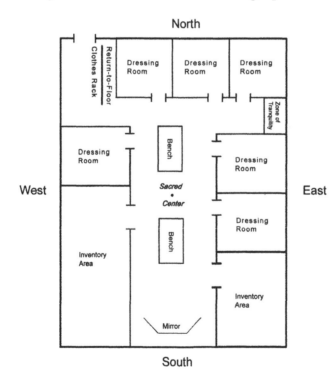

If just a couple dressing rooms are inside your boutique, be mindful of the properties associated with their location. If you feel that the prop-

✳ Figure 87: Spiritual Blueprint for the Separate Dressing Room Area

erties are not conducive to good sales, use colors and objects from the world of nature to offset the disadvantages.

⁕ THE PLACEMENT OF YOUR FURNISHINGS AND MERCHANDISE

Take advantage of the healthy forces that flow through your boutique. Do your best to keep the center of your shop uncovered so that this sacred realm can generate positive energy that circulates in every direction. Let the northeast quadrant be open and free of heaviness so that it receives an abundance of cosmic energy and spiritual power. Keep heavy and tall furniture in the south and the west so that the gifts from the northeast stay inside your shop.

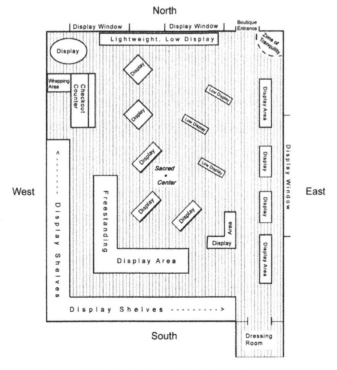

⁕ Figure 88: Spiritual Blueprint for the Boutique

Place your built-in display shelves and cabinets on the west and the south of the boutique. Put delicate displays of merchandise on the north and the east so that you establish an open and airy look in this part of the floor. This arrangement honors the vastu sense of proportion with an asymmetry that establishes a visual rhythm. The eyes of your customers won't settle on an area, but will sweep around the entire boutique. They will notice your products that are the highlight of each display and organized with care on each shelf.

Dressing Up Your Windows

Each window display in your boutique requires a separate spiritual blueprint that guides you through the beneficial placement of your merchandise. When you follow the vastu principles in your window displays, you capture the attention of window-shoppers and draw them into your shop. A boutique owner sold merchandise exclusively for young children. Her window displays, which adhered to vastu guidelines, were so winning that her customers often wanted something right from the window. She learned to keep a healthy inventory of all the items so that her window environments weren't emptied within days.

One of her most successful displays paid tribute to Santa in December. He sat in a snowdrift in the window's southwest quadrant, which introduces appropriate heaviness into the element of earth. Stuffed animals and a big metal jeep sat in front of him. In the realm of the element of fire in the southeast quadrant, a curious Rudolph, with his red lightbulb nose, peers at a "let's pretend" barnyard (see Figure 89).

Winsome dolls "floated" like angels on small, cloudlike shelves mounted in the north wall of the northeast quadrant, which belongs to the element of water. The dolls overlook a toddler's bathtub filled with aquatic toys. In the northwest, with its element of air, three crib mobiles bobbed above a rocking horse. The toys, the fat Santa, and the lightbulb-glowing Rudolph honored all the elements. Even the sacred center was left uncovered.

Figure 89: Vision of Joy

❋ Your Alluring Décor

Think about your merchandise. Doesn't it express your special area of interest—perhaps your passion? This interest, which has inspired you to run a boutique, represents a part of you, so your décor already practices part of the vastu
living guidelines for a successful décor. You just need to put more of yourself
on display and add an equal part of nature. You want your customers to connect to you and the personal world that you create inside your boutique.

KEEP UNWANTED CRITTERS AWAY

DO YOU HAVE TROUBLE WITH MOTHS?
Take whole cloves and stick them into the skin of an orange, then hang this pretty moth repellent in the corners of your shop. The moths go away.

BOTHERED BY MOSQUITOES?
Put a few decorative displays of dried eucalyptus inside your shop and rub some eucalyptus oil mixed with warm water on a few of the leaves. This creates a fragrant and powerful insecticide that also pleases the eyes.

A young man who had lived in the country and now lived in a Northeastern city took over a factory space in an up-and-coming commercial area. The former company had a northwest entrance and huge window that faced the sidewalk on the north. A receiving area for trucks had been built on the west side of the building. The young man sells city gardening supplies from plants, preserved trees, and cut flowers to an array of statuary, tiles, and indoor fountains.

His entire floor became a garden, and periodically he showcased a different example of a natural urban environment in his window—terrace garden, atrium garden, balcony garden. One month he turned the factory display window into an apartment window with lacey curtains that peeked into a mock library. Plants hung from the inside of his stenciled fake panes. A terra-cotta window box with pansies sat on its interior ledge.

Inside his shop, the young man arranged tall plants, including preserved palms and rubber trees, on the west side of the floor. Near the wall behind the tall plants, he put redwood bins, which contained packages of potting soil, compost, and other organic foods. He placed an old worktable, where he created displays and small container gardens for his clients, in the southwest. This quadrant gave him strength and wisdom, and he always faced into his shop toward the north, the northeast, or the east, which were beneficial directions.

Lovely, garden statues stood amid reeds of dried grasses and stalks of dried wildflowers that extended across the south of the shop. The checkout counter at the northern edge of the southwest quadrant was close to the shop entrance in the northwest quadrant, which enabled his salesperson to greet people as they entered the store. The products in the store eliminated the distraction attached to the element of air. The store was a natural oasis that drew customers who loved to escape the noise and gray of the city.

Every touch of the interior resonated with the young man's artistry and love of nature. In the northeast, he celebrated water with an indoor pond, which he surrounded with an assortment of stone, wood, and bronze garden critters that poked out from between small plants and ferns. Outdoor garden fountains decorated this quadrant along with handsome plant containers.

His most charming detail called attention to the sacred center of his factory space. First, he placed a thin layer of sand on this part of the brick floor. Then he celebrated the creative energy that circulated from this area with a delicate sundial placed in the direct center, which he surrounded with sample tiles that were available to his customers, which were, in turn, surrounded by stepping-stones. His square "sand paintings" were natural mandalas, which kept customers from walking on the sacred center. They also celebrated his talent and the earthy colors and textures that contribute to nature's diversity and beauty (see Figure 90).

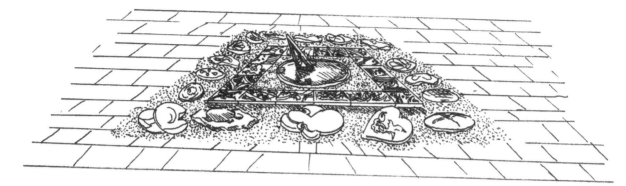

Figure 90: Creative Sacred Center

YOUR ZONE OF TRANQUILITY

Your zone of tranquility in the northeast quadrant of your boutique calms down the turbulence of your vata-prone business. Your display also appeals to your customers. As they examine your merchandise, they discover the peaceful display, which gathers power from the stillness of the element of water, which rules this quadrant. In the Southern Hemisphere, place your zone of tranquility in the southeast quadrant.

Your successful display makes a meaningful distinction. Your visitors recognize that the objects that you sell in your boutique represent your passion, but the objects that you display in your zone represent your essence—the fabric of your being.

Let the display in your boutique be understated and cohesive, so that it clearly connects to your décor. Less is more in this environment. If you sell women's clothing, create a statement that draws from the world of nature and fashion. Perhaps, you can recycle three articles of baby clothes that belonged to your mother, you, and your child—three generations that commemorate the past, present, and future (see Figure 91).

You can place each article on a hanger and mount them on the wall near the northeast corner. Add a sprig of dried baby's breath and a single rosebud tied together with a violet ribbon around the neck of each hanger. Violet is the complementary color of red, which is auspicious and wards away evil. This is such a simple display, but it reaches deep—reflecting the undistinguishable light of life and the everlasting nature of the soul.

✳ Figure 91: Creative Zone of Tranquility

31

Consecrate Your Medical Suite

WELCOME TO THE VASTU LIVING MEDICAL SUITE. PLEASE
TAKE OUT YOUR SPIRITUAL BLUEPRINTS IF YOU WORK IN THIS
SPECIAL ENVIRONMENT AND REFER TO THEM AS YOU READ
THIS CHAPTER.

This book began with a discussion of a doctor's waiting room, which
painted an all-too-familiar picture of an environment where the spirit of
holism was forgotten and everyone sitting there suffered from its absence.
Generally, these rooms are impersonal and devoid of nature. They rarely speak
of interconnection and interdependence or celebrate the divinity of the soul.
So it seems fitting that this book should conclude with the practice of vastu
living incorporated into this environment—specifically the patients' waiting
room and the examination room, where so many of us have passed so much
time in uninviting spaces.

Doctors take the Hippocratic oath when they complete their medical
training. It includes this wonderful line: "With purity and with holiness I will
pass my life and practice my art." Just imagine if the medical profession used
the message of this line in the reception room so that it celebrated the purity
and holiness of the soul. Or imagine if we found ourselves sitting in one of

those skimpy paper garments on a paper-covered examination table surrounded by an ambience that warded off the chills in a deep, internal way?

The practice of vastu living supplies guidelines that can help you create environments that support your Hippocratic oath. Your waiting room and examination room become positive retreats that benefit your patients when they feel out of sorts. Visual reminders, which are expressed through your décor, reinforce your commitment to practice the art of healing with purity and holiness. You offer nurturing environments. Your waiting room and examination room help calm the mind and soul, and this helps heal the body.

Your Waiting Room

The Spiritual Blueprint

Try to place your waiting room in the north or the northeast quadrant of your medical suite or practice. These two areas offer antidotes that can assuage the worries that bubble over or simmer just below the surface of your patients. The north showers everyone with health and wealth. Spiritual health and wealth offer comfort to everyone who sits here—wondering how much longer he or she must wait before hearing good or bad news from you. Few enjoy a visit to the doctor. The northeast is a great source of inner peace and deep calm. It also receives the gifts of the gods: beneficial cosmic energy and spiritual power that enter this part of a space. (If you live in the Southern Hemisphere, follow the spiritual blueprint on page 116, which shows the correct location of the elements below the equator.)

Honor Your Constitution

If members of your staff who work in your waiting room discover its location is governed by the same element that dominates their own constitution, ask them to observe how they feel (see chapter 2, "Personalizing Vastu Living"). If they find that their constitution is overstimulated and exhibiting the negative consequences of the principle of like increases like, they should make an appeasement for themselves to restore the balance in their body (see chapter 5, "Resolving Conflicts in Your Home and Workplace").

UNHEALTHY QUADRANTS FOR YOUR CONSTITUTION IN THE WORKPLACE

CONSTITUTION OR DOSHA	NORTHERN HEMISPHERE UNHEALTHY QUADRANT	SOUTHERN HEMISPHERE UNHEALTHY QUADRANT
Vata / Air	Northwest (Air)	Southwest (Air)
Pitta / Fire	Southeast (Fire)	Northeast (Fire)
Kapha / Water	Northeast (Water)	Southeast (Water)

The Placement of Your Furnishings

Two sets of important people, your patients and part of your medical staff, generally occupy the waiting room. Each group has distinct needs. Your patients require emotional, mental, and physical relief, and reassurance. Until they see you, anxiety and impatience can eat away at their defenses. Your staff needs to remain calm and keep everything organized in the face of nervous patients. So you need to arrange your waiting room so that it works against all this negativity.

Use comfortable, lightweight chairs and place them in the north, the northeast, or the east. The north gives a lift to the health and wealth of your patients, including spiritual health and wealth. The northeast quadrant surrounds them with calm and provides beneficial cosmic energy and spiritual power. Patients who sit in the east area are blessed with clarity, inspiration, and enlightenment (see Figure 92).

Your staff typically sit behind a workstation, where your patient records are organized on shelves or in files within their reach. These furnishings, which are generally the heaviest objects in your waiting room, belong in the southwest quadrant where they hold in the cosmic energy and spiritual power that flows here from the northeast quadrant. The southwest, which belongs to the element of earth and Lord Pitri, who watches over all ancestors, empowers your staff with strength and wisdom. As soon as your patients enter your office, they know they're in good hands. Your staff is prepared and organized. The southwest is also a safe location in which to work—it helps protect everyone's constitution.

Water dispensers in your waiting room ideally belong in the northeast quadrant, which is governed by the element of water. But try not to place your waiting room bathrooms in this quadrant, which is also called the gateway to

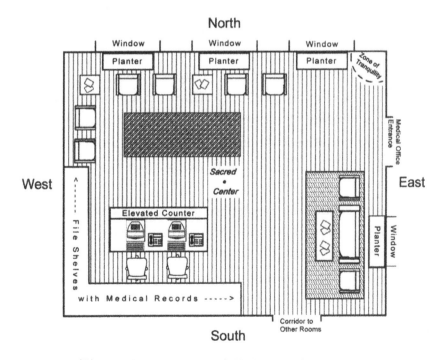

Figure 92: Spiritual Blueprint for the Medical Waiting Room

the gods. The bathroom is connected to ritual acts of purification, but human wastes pollute the water. Instead locate your bathrooms to the west, the northwest, the southeast, or the south of your waiting room.

Normally, it's easy to honor your waiting room's sacred center so that its positive energies can circulate freely. But in this particular environment, where patients come for care, try to enhance this special realm that belongs to Lord Brahma so that it is not just spiritually potent, but visually appealing.

Your Healing Décor

The focus on sterility, a prerequisite in every medical practice, often wipes away more than germs in the waiting room. Sterility wipes out an inviting ambience and creates a décor that is impersonal, monochromatic, synthetic. Vinyl coverings or hard plastic chairs re-create the atmosphere of a waiting lounge at an airport or bus stop. The medical practice waiting room feels crowded and transitory. Some medical literature even calls the waiting area the "holding area"—a term connected to the slaughterhouse.

Of course, you can't compromise cleanliness. It is part of the purity that defines your art. But your décor should respect your noblest intention—healing—and offer a nurturing and calming ambience. The presence of plants, in all their diversity, does not interfere with your waiting room's sterility. Plants help purify the air.

If the room's lighting doesn't support plants, introduce organic objects so that everyone sitting here receives nature's positive messages. The interconnection that binds together all existence and endows everything with meaning and reason will speak to their souls. In turn, the soul's quiet voice speaks to a troubled mind and releases healing energy into the body. Consider having wood furniture with a high-gloss finish that is easy to clean. Use natural fiber covers for comfortable seat cushions and seat backs that are easy to remove and wash.

Amplify the importance of the sacred center. An internist who practiced vastu living in his medical suite asked an artist friend to paint a white square in the center of his waiting room. The artist added the word *peace* in violet, which extended from the north to the south and again from the east to the west. Each rendering of the word made use of the same letter *A,* which fell on the exact center of the square and the room. Then the internist put dried cuttings into four urns and placed one on each corner.

The square shape honored the five basic elements and the symbols attached to each cardinal direction. It represents the perfect universe, and its static energy is relaxing to the body. The letter *A* is potent. It begins the words *amen* and *aum.* It symbolizes creation and honors Lord Brahma, the Hindu god of creation, who governs this sacred space. The colors added more meaning. White speaks of purity, so important in this space. Violet is the nighttime complementary color to red, which gives the strength and power to ward away evil.

Express your personality in your waiting room. Let it celebrate your self, not only your degrees. If you love to take pictures, hang up some photographs

Figure 93: Sacred Center of the Waiting Room

Healthy Colors

Incorporate soothing colors into your waiting room—blues, greens, and white. Use the nighttime complement to blue, which is yellow, as a bright touch. Consider a bold blue wall surrounded by lighter shades of blue on the other walls. Spell out "To Your Health" in green on a creamy northern wall.

Break up the monochromatic cold of your examination room with warm shades of yellow, which help lift the chill that brings such discomfort to this room. Surprise your patients with appealing wallpaper that is associated with an English cottage—tiny-flower patterns or country motifs—which are rich in yellows, blues, white—and create a cheery and cozy ambience.

that you've taken or some copies of prints taken by great photographers whom you admire. Do you collect pottery or china or Asian art? Do you collect folksy roadside Americana? Do you love the opera or chamber music? Share your CDs with your patients and let them hear uplifting music in the background. Don't be afraid to tickle the funny bones of your patients either. A good sense of humor cheers them up. Your patients feel more comfortable waiting in a room that gives clues to your identity. These clues, which personalize the room, establish a link and a connection that binds you to them. It says that you are approachable and open, not reserved and distant.

Don't forget that the reading material in your waiting room also says a lot about you. More to the point, the reading material says a lot about your attitude toward your patients. Unless you are displaying a great collection of old periodicals, such as *National Geographic* or *Saturday Evening Post* or *Collier's*, out-of-date issues do not age like vintage wines. A six-month-old issue of *People* or *Time* isn't an "absorbing" read.

Because patients are preoccupied with their personal concerns and worries, show your care by offering them positive distractions that help them get through the wait to see you. The waiting room should be your welcoming room. It should be patient friendly and reassuring.

Your Zone of Tranquility

Your waiting room zone of tranquility helps calm your patients while they wait to see you. Create a special display that reminds everyone of the everlasting nature of the soul and the beauty of the universe. Since your zone is placed in the northeast, let your display enhance the serenity that belongs to this quadrant's element of water. (In the Southern Hemisphere, place the zone of tranquility in the southeast quadrant.)

The internist who fixed up the attractive sacred center in his waiting room added a small, bubbling fountain on a low table in the northeast quadrant. Its rhythmic play of water was so pacifying that everyone felt its effect and took the time to look closely at the fountain, where white pebbles glistened on the bottom and three white blooms, which express the cycle of life, danced around the water's surface. On the nearby wall he placed a small bulletin board, and every month he and his staff honored a town resident who had done something positive for the community—the picture promoted selflessness and the good that people do for one another.

Your Examination Room

The Spiritual Blueprint

There are many positive locations for examination rooms that work for you and your patients. The north inspires health and wealth, the northeast reinforces calm and contemplation, the east brings clarity and enlightenment, the south is a reminder of your duty and responsibility, and the southwest gives you strength and wisdom. The west is manageable, but you need to be careful with the orientation of the furnishings since this direction represents darkness and the unknown. The southeast, which reflects the properties of fire, and the northwest, which has the characteristics of air, need an infusion of calm to guard against a fiery temperament and an overcritical impulse that accompany the element of fire and the indecision and distractions that accompany the element of air. (If you live in the Southern Hemisphere, follow the spiritual blueprint on page 116, which shows the correct location of the elements below the equator.)

The Placement of Your Furnishings

The most important object inside your examination room is the examination table, and its placement should be determined by the vastu guideline relating to height and weight. If your examination table is heavy, it belongs in the south or the west, but not the southeast, where the element of fire can turn up the heat on your bedside manner. You want warmth to prevail, not fire. If your examination table is relatively light, try to place it in the north, which belongs to the lord of health, or in the east; but avoid the northwest, where the property of air can cause distractions (see Figure 94).

Try to orient yourself at the examination table so that your body is positioned toward the north, the northeast or the east when you examine your patient. These calming directions improve concentration, and the north, in particular, promotes good health for you and your patient—meaning, as always, the health of the body, mind, and soul. Your orientation is especially important if your examination rooms are located in the west of your practice. You want to turn your back on the darkness and the unknown that come with this direction so that you can live up to that line in your oath: "With purity and with holiness I will pass my life and practice my art."

If possible, place your medicine cabinets against the north wall in the northwest quadrant of your examination room. The healing properties associated with this direction protect your fragile drugs, and the element of air keeps them from hanging around beyond their expiration date. Heavy cabinets normally belong in the southwest quadrant, so this adjustment requires two appeasements. You need to offer an appeasement to restore the harmony of the element of earth, which has been introduced into the quadrant of air. You also need to offer an appeasement to the element of air, whose quadrant has been violated by the cabinet, which belongs to the element of earth (see chapter 5, "Resolving Conflicts in Your Home and Workplace").

The sinks or watercoolers inside your examination room belong in the

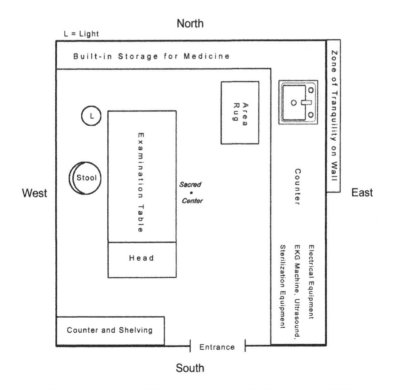

Figure 94: Spiritual Blueprint for the Medical Examination Office

northeast quadrant, which belongs to the element of water. Machinery that requires electricity, such as an electrocardiograph or ultrasonic device, belongs in the southeast with its element of fire. Finally, try to keep the absolute center of your examination room free of heavy weight so that the positive energy generated here can move around the room to everyone's benefit.

Your Healing Décor

Look around an examination room that is part of your practice. Imagine how your patients feel when they sit in a disposable gown on the crinkly disposable tissue paper pulled over your leatherette examination table. Wouldn't you also feel vulnerable and trapped here, more like a specimen about to be poked and probed rather than a unique individual with special needs?

Yes, good hygiene legitimizes your need for a sterile environment in this room. But sterility shouldn't become the license to create a cold, inhospitable space. Your typically windowless, cell-like rooms require a healing "touch" in their ambience. After all, this is where your patients often wait—alone—a few minutes before they meet you. You want this small room to speak positively of you in your absence.

Plants often don't make sense inside this environment, which rarely exceeds eight by ten feet and has only artificial lighting. But the vastu living emphasis on nature and the celebration of your personality are invaluable here. A décor that honors these principles helps put nervous patients at ease and adds the comfort that is so much a part of the concept of holism—the sense of personal worth and uniqueness.

Your Zone of Tranquility

The doctor who created the welcoming waiting room invited his artist friend to paint a mural on the east wall in the northeast quadrant of his two exami-

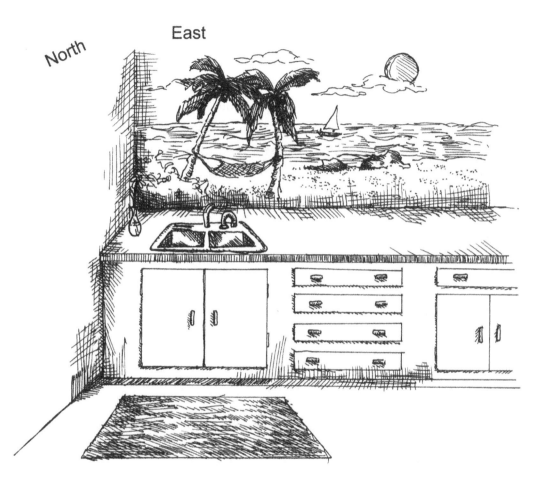

North

East

✳ Figure 95: Tropical View in the Examination Room

nation rooms that served as zones of tranquility. The doctor loved spending time at the seashore, so one mural showed off a cove where frothy waves pounded against a rocky outcrop. The other mural showed off a tropical vista with palms lining a beach. His zones of tranquility successfully diverted the eyes of his patients from the medical paraphernalia and appealed to their minds and their souls. These scenes also personalized the doctor, and his patients felt more comfortable in his presence.

Your successful zone of tranquility in your examination room can be a simple tackboard filled with pictures of your patients, which is placed on the wall in the northeast quadrant. These pictures bring life into the room and all the faces become a happy distraction for your patients. Just add an organic border around the tackboard, such as small decorative tiles or thin wood edging, to honor nature. This is all you need to create an effective contemplative zone.

CALMING YOUR NERVES

The next time you sit alone in an examination room waiting for your doctor, use the time to calm down your mind and body. Sit with your back straight in a comfortable meditation pose on the examination table. Place your knees about eighteen inches apart on the edge of the table so that the rest of your legs hang down toward the floor.

Relax your arms and place your hands on your knees with the palms facing down in the *gyana mudra,* where your index finger is folded to touch the inside of your thumb and your remaining three fingers are relaxed and held slightly apart. Close your eyes and keep your head straight and motionless. Inhale slowly. Then say "aum" as you exhale—the primordial sound that is so sacred. Repeat this breathing exercise until the doctor arrives.

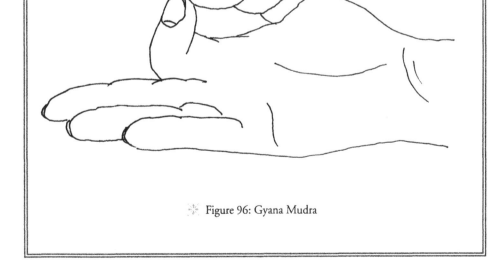

Figure 96: Gyana Mudra

Spiritual Blueprints

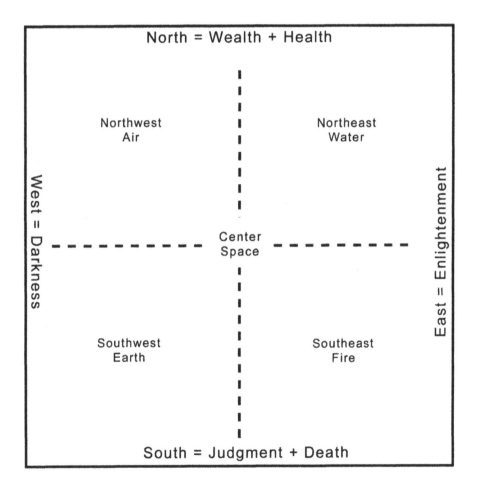

North = Wealth + Health

Northwest
Air

Northeast
Water

West = Darkness

East = Enlightenment

Center
Space

Southwest
Earth

Southeast
Fire

South = Judgment + Death

❋ Square Spiritual Blueprint

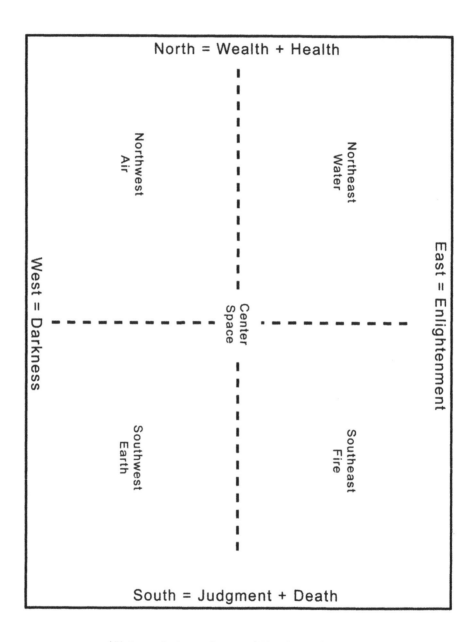

❖ Rectangle Oriented East-and-West Spiritual Blueprint

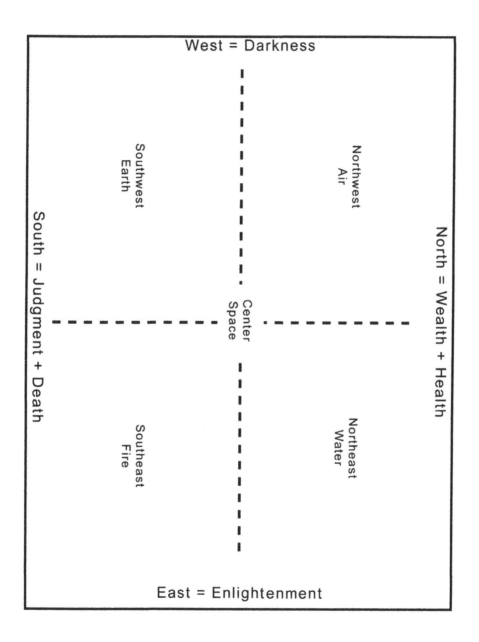

West = Darkness

South = Judgment + Death

North = Wealth + Health

Southwest
Earth

Northwest
Air

Center
Space

Southeast
Fire

Northeast
Water

East = Enlightenment

Rectangle Oriented North-and-South Spiritual Blueprint

Glossary

ASANA: posture or pose performed in the practice of yoga

AYURVEDA: Vedic science of life and longevity that emphasizes disease prevention and wellness

BRAHMASTHANA: place of God, name for the sacred center of every vastu space

DHARMA: duty or responsibility to follow ethical and moral behavior

DHURRIE: woven rug usually of wool, cotton, or camel hair

DOSHA: ayurvedic term that relates to our constitution or specific configuration of the elements of air, fire, and water in our body, which unfolds at the time of our conception—dosha balance or imbalance determines our health

JYOTISH: Vedic science of astrology and astronomy

KAPHA: dosha (constitution) in the body dominated by the element of water

KARMA: law of cause and effect that operates on the metaphysical plane that states every action ultimately produces an equivalent reaction

KILIM: woven tapestry rug

MANDALA: spiritual diagram or grid

MOKSHA: liberation of the soul from the recycle of birth that leads to its reunion with the divine

MUDRA: symbolic hand gesture

NAMASTE: Hindu blessing expressed with hands held together at the chest and used to greet or say good-bye to someone. Accepted translation: I bow to the divine within you

PITTA: dosha (constitution) in the body dominated by the element of fire

PRANA: life force or energy within the body

PUJA: Hindu prayer service

PURUSHA: unseen energy or life-giving force—the soul or essence

RAGA: Indian classical music

SOMA: juice of immortality

TAT TVAM ASI: Sanskrit phrase that means "Thou Art That"

THANGKA: religious wall hanging

TORAN: Indian hanging mounted above the door that showers blessings on anyone who walks under it

VASTU: Vedic science of design and architecture; *vastu* is Sanskrit for "site" or "dwelling" or any built form, including the human body

VASTU PURUSHA MANDALA: spiritual blueprint in vastu that depicts the cosmic spirit of the land on a grid; used to determine healthy organization of a dwelling or site

VATA: dosha (constitution) in the body dominated by the element of air

VEDAS: spiritual texts that provide the foundation to Hinduism and its way of life; *veda* is Sanskrit for "knowledge"

YOGA: Vedic discipline that includes a series of practices to lead one to the realization of the self; *yoga* is Sanskrit for "to join"

About the Illustrators

RACHEL EVANS, who created the drawings, is a graduate of the School of Visual Arts, where she earned degrees in illustration and art education. She teaches art in the New York City public school system and at Amherst College during the summers.

ADAM CHARLES LEE, who created the computer diagrams, received his bachelor's degree in information technology from Queensland University of Technology in Australia. Lee has been working with computers and computer technology since the 1980s. He currently lives in New York City, where he is a successful computer programmer, Web designer, and network administrator.

Index

Agni, Lord, 16
air, 13, 14, 15–16
　fresh, in the bedroom, 227
　guide to placement of appease-
　　ments, 81–82
　location in vastu living, 15–16
　psychological properties of,
　　15–16
allergies, 32
alterations, care with, 113–15
anxiety disorders, 4
apartments, special issues for,
　　147–54
　absence of sunlight or view of
　　nature, 153–54
　cramped space, coping with,
　　148–53
　entrance, 147
appeasements, 79–100, 271,
　　287, 289
　in the bathroom, 251
　in the bedroom, 230
　color's healing power, 39, 44,
　　67, 83–90
　in conference room, 315
　for conflicts between two ele-
　　ments, 80
　for covered sacred center, 81,
　　188, 315, 317
　in the dining room, 188–89
　guide to placement of, 81–82

impossibility of physical solu-
　　tions, 79
　in the kitchen, 80, 178, 180
　in the living room, 203–04
　in medical suite examination
　　room, 357
　nature's healing power, 39, 44,
　　90–100
　with object that represents the
　　divine, 99–100
　as offerings, 79
　in pod area, 299–302
　for "Silicon" workspace, 331
　sincerity of, 99–100
　for threatened constitution,
　　81
appliances, placement of
　　kitchen, 156, 179, 180
　in company dining area,
　　322–23
aquariums, 238
area rugs, see rugs
ashes, sacred nature in
　　Hinduism of, 64
ayurveda, xvi, 28–32
　five basic elements and, 28
　as holistic health system, 28
　like increases like, principle
　　that, 38–39
　order and harmony as central
　　to, 11

relationship to vastu, 5, 8,
　　28

backache, waking with a, 227
bad breath, 183
balconies, see transitional areas
basic elements, see five basic ele-
　　ments
bathing, 255
　to aid sleep, 226
bathroom, the, 249–55
　appeasements, 251
　care for your physical body in,
　　249
　clutter free, 249–50
　décor for, 252–53
　in dining area at work,
　　322
　honoring the elements of fire
　　and water, 250–51
　natural materials used in, 250,
　　252–53
　spiritual blueprint for, 251–52
　toilet, orientation of, 251, 269
　workplace:
　　company guidelines,
　　　269
　　medical suite waiting room,
　　　351–52
　zone of tranquility in, 250,
　　253–54

bedroom, the, 218–41
  avoiding clutter in, 229
  child's, 219, 220, 234–39
    décor for, 237–38
    furnishings, placement of,
      234–36
    orientation of, 234
    zone of tranquility, 238–39
  color, use of, 222, 228
  décor for, 226–28, 230–32, 240
  dual-function, 148–53
  furnishings, placement of,
    223–26, 230, 234–36
  general guidelines for all bed-
    rooms, 219–29
  guest bedroom, 239–41
  healthy quadrant for:
    kapha (or water), 42, 70, 222
    pitta (or fire), 40, 70, 222
    vata (or air), 41, 70, 222
  healthy sleep, guidelines for a,
    224–26
  master bedroom, 229–34
    décor for, 230–32
    furnishings, placement of,
      230
    orientation of, 229
    zone of tranquility, 232–34
  natural materials, use of, 227,
    232, 237–38
  as personal, private space,
    218–19, 228, 237
  room swap, 70–76
  sharing with person of differ-
    ent constitution, 223–24
  spiritual blueprints for,
    220–21, 231, 235, 236
  unhealthy quadrant for:
    kapha (or water), 42, 60, 70,
      152, 221
    pitta (or fire), 39, 60, 70,
      152, 221
    vata (or air), 41, 60, 70, 152,
      221
  waking with sore back or neck,
    227
  zone of tranquility, 228–29,
    232–34, 238–39, 240–41
bee stings, 183
birdbaths, 168, 171
birdfeeders, 168, 171
blinds, 123, 131

blue, 62, 63–64, 65, 84–85, 214
body, human, as example of
  vastu, 7, 14, 45, 321
book collections, guidelines for,
  132
boutiques, 337–47
  décor, 343–45
  dressing rooms, 340–41
  dressing windows, 342–43
  entrance door, 338–39
  furnishings and merchandise,
    placement of, 341–42
  spiritual blueprint for, 338–40,
    341
  zone of tranquility, 346–47
Brahma, Lord, 15, 157, 168,
  188, 189, 271, 287, 302,
  306, 315, 353
Brahmasthana (place of God), 15
breath, focusing on your, 293
building interior:
  spiritual blueprint of, 58
burnout, 4
business travelers, tips for, 274

calming your nerves, 350
candles, 123, 168, 187, 215
  in zone-of-tranquility room,
    246, 247, 248
canteen, company, *see* dining
  area, company
cardinal directions, *see* directions, cardinal
career, expressing worthiness of
  your, 259
carpeting, 132, 310
CD collections, 132
centerpieces, dining room,
  188–89, 192–93
  edible, 193
CEOs:
  conference room seating, 317
  spiritual blueprint for office of,
    279
chamomile tea, 318
chief operating officer, spiritual
  blueprint for office of, 279
child's bedroom, 219, 220,
  234–39
  décor for, 237–38
  furnishings, placement of,
    234–36

orientation of, 234
zone of tranquility, 238–39
Chinmayananda, Swami, 312
circular furniture, 131, 226–27
cleanliness in the kitchen,
  176–77
clutter, avoiding, 128–30, 140
  in the bathroom, 249–50
  in the bedroom, 229
  in cubicles, 291
  in the dining room, 188
  in home office or study, 208
  in the kitchen, 176
  in the living room, 205
  in pod area, 301
coffee machines, 322
colds, 32
color, 62–67
  absence of natural light, to
    overcome, 153
  in the bedroom, 222, 228
  in boutiques, 340
  complementary colors, 66,
    66n, 67, 83–86, 170, 353
  in the conference room, 318
  contemporary research on,
    66–67
  in dining area at work, 324
  in the dining room, 188, 189
  in efficiency kitchen, 157
  in home office or study, 214
  in the kitchen, 178, 179, 182
  in the living room, 197, 205
  nighttime complements, 66,
    66n, 67, 83–86, 353
  properties of each, 83–86
  rhythms in, 122–23, 197
  in "Silicon" workspace,
    334–35
  using the healing power of, in
    vastu living, 39, 44, 67,
    83–90
  assessing the problem's effect
    on your well-being, 86
  example of, 87–90
    kapha (or water), 87, 170
    pitta (or fire), 86–87, 170
    vata (or air), 87
  Vedic awareness of, 63–66
  vibrations of, 62–63, 66, 83
  in the workplace, 276
    cubicle, your, 286

office, your, 283
    pod area, 297, 298, 302
    reception area, 308
    in zone of tranquility, 173
    in zone-of-tranquility room, 246
    see also specific colors
company, general workplace guidelines for the, 264–77
    appeasements, 265
    bathrooms, 269
    corridors, 268
    décor, 273–76
    doors, 267
    drinking fountains and coolers, 268
    entrance, 266–67
    furnishings and equipment, placement of, 269–73
        desk or workstations, 270–72
        seating arrangements, 272–73
        television, 273
    inventory exit, 268
    rented space, 265
    seating arrangements, 272–73
    spiritual blueprint, 265–70
    transitional areas, 267–68
    unhealthy work environments, 264
    windows and outdoor areas, 267–68
    zone of tranquility, 265, 276–77
complementary colors, 66, 67, 170
computers, placement of, 135
    company guidelines, 272–73
    in conference room, 316
    in the living room, 200–01
    in "Silicon" workspace, 331–33
conference room, 313–19
    atmosphere fostered by, 313–14
    décor, 317–19
    furnishings, placement of, 315–17
    spiritual blueprint for, 314–15, 316
    zone of tranquility, 314, 319

conflicts, resolving, *see* resolving conflicts
constipation, 31
constitution, *see dosha* (constitution)
cooking:
    reclaiming the joy of, 174–76
    rhythms in meal preparation, 177, 185
corridors, workplace, 268
cramped apartment space, coping with, 148–53
creativity, nature as catalyst for, 24
cubicle, your, 286–94
    attitude toward, 286–87
    color of, 286
    décor for, 291–92
    furnishings, placement of, 289–90
    spiritual blueprint for, 287–89
    zone of tranquility in, 292, 293–94
curtains, 131

dark and light, dualities of, 123, 161
décor, *see specific rooms*
depression, 4
desks, 210
    in child's bedroom, 235–36
    in the workplace:
        company guidelines, 270–72
        cubicle, your, 289–90
        office, your, 280
        "Silicon" workspace, 331–32
diabetes, 4
diarrhea, 30
diet, 177, 320–21
    dosha (constitution) and, 40, 41, 43, 326
    see also cooking
digestion, 30
    problems with, 31, 39
dimmer switches, 123, 187, 246
dining area, company, 320–28
    décor for, 324–26
    furnishings and appliances, placement of, 322–23
    spiritual blueprint for, 321–22, 323, 324
    zone of tranquility, 326–28

dining room, the, 186–95
    ambience of vastu living, 187
    centerpieces, 188–89
    clutter in, 188
    color use in, 188, 189
    formal, 186, 187
    furnishings, placement of, 188–92
    nature in the, 192–93
    as part of larger space, 191–92
    rhythms in, 188
    spiritual blueprint for, 188, 191
    warmth of, 187
    zone of tranquility, 193–95
dining tables, 180–81
    circular, 131
    square, 130, 181, 187
directions, cardinal, 20–22
    chart of five basic elements and, 22
    in Southern Hemisphere, 106
dishwasher, 179, 322
divinity, 243
    acknowledging your divinity, 259, 261–62
    in all creation, 12–13
    appeasement with object that represents the divine, 90–100, 178, 188–89
doctors' offices, *see* medical suites
doors, workplace:
    boutique, 338–39
    company entrance, 267
    interior, 267
dosha (constitution):
    creating harmony for different constitutions sharing a space, 43–44
    five basic elements and, 28–29
    honoring your, 39–43
    seasonal changes and, 39
    threatened, appeasements for, 81
    tridoshas, 29–32
    Vastu Living Ayurveda Test, 32–38
        evaluating your answers, 37–38
    see also kapha (or water); *pitta* (or fire); *vata* (or air)

drapes, 123, 131, 160, 267
dressing rooms, boutique,
340–41
drinking fountains, workplace,
268
dryness inside your body, 30,
31
dualities, 20
creating rhythms with, 123–24
of the four cardinal directions,
20–22
dual-personality rooms, 148–53

earth, 13, 14, 17–19
guide to placement of appeasements, 81–82
location in vastu living, 17–18
east, the, 20, 266
dining room in, 188
orientation of entrance to, 142
transitional areas oriented
toward the, 164
see also spiritual blueprints; specific rooms
ego, 313, 319
Emerson, Ralph Waldo, 1
entertainment systems, placement of, 135
in home office or study, 210
in the living room, 200–01
entrances, orientation of,
141–43, 147
of boutiques, 338–39
company guidelines, 266–67
equipment, office:
company guidelines for placement of, 270–73
conference room, 315–16
in "Silicon" workspace,
331–34
ether, see space (ether)
examination rooms, see medical
suites, examination room
executives:
conference room seating,
279–80
spiritual blueprint for offices
of, 279
eyes, soothing your, 300

fabrics, natural, 23
family heirlooms, 134

feng shui, 8
fickleness, 31
"fight or flight" mechanism, 4
financial officers:
conference room seating,
316–17
spiritual blueprint for office of,
279
fine-tuning over time, 112
fire, 13, 14, 16, 250–51
guide to placement of appeasements, 81–82
location in vastu living, 16
psychological properties of, 16
fireplace, 123
holder, 167
placement of, 202, 203
five basic elements, 13–19, 164
chart of cardinal directions
and, 22
guide to placement of appeasements, 81–82
predetermined locations in
vastu living, 14–19
chart, 18
in Southern Hemisphere, see
Southern Hemisphere,
location of basic elements
in
rhythms created with, 122
see also air; earth; ether (space);
fire; water
floor coverings:
guidelines for, 132
in the workplace, 274, 310
see also specific types of floor coverings
flowers, 215–16, 274, 302, 308,
312, 324, 326, 334
focal point, 248
food, see cooking; diet
function of room, décor following, 124
furnishings:
asymmetry of arrangements,
125
care in shifting, in an enclosed
space, 114
circular, 131, 226–27
distance from the wall, 130,
226, 271
drawing in cosmic energy and

spiritual power, 125–27
lightweight-vs.-heavy guidelines, 114–15, 124, 126,
181, 190, 199, 223,
234–35, 248, 271, 341
moving to a new space, mapping out arrangements
when, 114–15
natural materials, use of,
139–40
overloading a room or space
with, 129
placement of:
in the bedroom, 223–26,
230, 234–36
in boutiques, 341–42
company guidelines, 270–73
conference room, 315–17
cubicle, your, 289–90
in dining area at work,
322–23
in the dining room, 188–92
examination room of med-
ical suite, 356–58
in home office or study,
210–13
in the kitchen, 179–81
in the living room, 199–204
office, your, 280–82
pod area, 298–99
reception area, 306–07
in "Silicon" workspace,
331–34
waiting room of medical
suite, 350–52
in zone-of-tranquility room,
244–46
shuffle, 76–78
square, 130, 131, 181, 187
symmetrical arrangement of,
114–15

Ganesha, Lord, 64, 94–96
gardens, kitchen, 183
ginger tea, 318
glossary, 367–68
green, 62, 65, 84, 182, 214
guest bedroom, 239–41
guest cottage, home with,
145–46
guidelines of vastu living,
125–40

book collections, 132
computers, 135
draw in cosmic energy and
    spiritual power, 125–27
entertainment systems, 135
flexibility of, 110–11
floor coverings, 132
making space at least 51 per-
    cent vastu-correct,
    111–12
mirrors, 135
for money, jewelry, and other
    valuables, 136
musical instruments, 133–34
music collections, 132
nature, respecting, 136–39
organic products, 138–39
paintings, 134–35
pictures, 134
plants, 137–38
sacred center, honoring the,
    127–28
treasures from the past, 134
unique identity, celebrating
    your, 139–40
window treatments, 131
gyana mudra, 361

hammock, 334
harmony, 25
    order and, 9–11
headaches, 285
heart attack, 4
heirlooms, family, 134
holism, 25, 358
    humanity included in, 25
    spirituality and, 12
home, 119–255
    apartments, see apartments,
        special issues for
    the bathroom, see bathroom,
        the
    the bedroom, see bedroom, the
    the dining room, see dining
        room, the
    entrances, orientation of,
        141–43
    with guest cottage, 145–46
    ideal property, 143–44
    the kitchen, see kitchen, the
    living room, see living room,
        the

multistory, 144–45
resolving conflicts in your, see
    resolving conflicts
rhythm, power of, see rhythm,
    power of
studio or loft, see studio or loft,
    special issues for
transitional areas, see transi-
    tional areas
zone-of-tranquility room, see
    zone-of-tranquility room
home office or study, 207–17
    avoiding clutter in, 208
    color, use of, 214
    décor of, 214–15
    dual-function room, 148–53
    furnishings, placement of,
        210–13
    spiritual blueprint for, 209–10,
        211, 212
    zone of tranquility in, 213,
        215–17
honey in bath products, 255
hotel rooms, tips for business
    travelers using, 274

immortality, 21
immune system, 29, 31
incense, burning of, xvi
indecision, 31
indigo, 62, 65, 83–84, 85
individual room, spiritual blue-
    print of, 58–59
infertility, 4
inner voice, listening to your,
    104, 333
insomnia, 31
inventory exit, 268
Isa, deity, 17

jewelry, place to keep, 136
jyotish (Indian astrology), 8,
    27–28

kapha (or water):
    characteristics of, 31
    color, using healing effect of,
        87, 170
    diet and, 43, 326
    excess, 31–32
    healthy quadrant for, 42, 70,
        222

home office or study and,
    178
unhealthy quadrant for, 42,
    60, 70, 152, 221
in the workplace, 275–76,
    279, 280, 289, 298, 331,
    350
weather, 43
karma (law of cause and effect),
    10
kitchen, the, 174–85
    appeasements in, 80, 178,
        180
    appliances, placement of, 156,
        179, 180
    avoiding like increases like,
        178–79
    cleanliness in, 176–77
    color in, 182
    cooking, reclaiming the joy of,
        174–76
    drawing nature into the,
        182–83
    furnishings, placement of,
        179–81
    rhythms of meal preparation,
        177
    spiritual blueprint for, 177–78,
        180, 181
    in studio or loft, 156–59
    windowless, 183
    zone of tranquility, 179,
        184–85
Krishna, Lord, 64
Kuber, Lord, 21–22, 142, 198,
    231, 266, 279

Lakshmi, goddess, 96–97
lavender oil for headaches, 285
lethargy, 32
light and dark, dualities of, 123,
    161
lighting, 123
    absence of natural light, over-
        coming, 153–54
    apartment, 153
    in the bathroom, 253
    dining room, 187
    in "Silicon" workspace, 335
    in studio or loft, 160–61
    in zone-of-tranquility room,
        246

like increases like, 38–39, 275
  avoiding, in the kitchen,
    178–79
  home office or study and,
    209–10
  master bedroom and, 230
  pitta dosha and, *see pitta* (or
    fire), avoiding like increases
    like
  restoring harmony based on,
    79
listening to your inner voice,
  104
living room, the, 196–206
  avoiding clutter in, 205
  color, use of, 197, 205
  décor, 205–06
  furnishings, placement of,
    199–204
  grouping related objects,
    205–06
  hospitality as focus of, 197,
    198
  orientation problems, 202–04
  personalizing the, 196, 197
  seating arrangements, 197–98,
    199–200
  spiritual blueprint for, 198–99,
    202
  zone of tranquility, 206
lofts, *see* studio or loft, special
  issues for
L-shaped space, spiritual blueprints for, 51–52

managing director of a company,
    spiritual blueprint for,
    279
mandala, 45
Mansara Series, xvii
master bedroom, 229–34
  décor for, 230–32
  furnishings, placement of, 230
  orientation of, 229
  zone of tranquility, 232–34
Mayamata, xvii
medical equipment, placement
    in examination room of,
    358
medical suites, 348–61
  examination room, 355–61
    décor, 358

furnishings, placement of,
    356–58
  spiritual blueprint, 355–56,
    357
  zone of tranquility, 358–61
waiting room, 349–55
  décor, 352–55
  furnishings, placement of,
    350–52
  honoring your constitution,
    349–50
  spiritual blueprint, 349, 351
  zone of tranquility, 355
meditation, xvi, 8, 242, 243,
    277, 303
mirrors, 157–58, 212
  guidelines for, 135
miscarriage, 4
mistletoe, 171
moisturizing mask, 255
moksha (liberation), 10
money, place to keep, 136
mosquitoes, 344
moth repellent, 344
moving, mapping out new fur-
    niture arrangements when,
    114–15
multifunctional rooms, 148–53
multistory home, 144–45
music, background, 325, 335,
    354
musical instruments, guidelines
    for, 133–34
music collections, guidelines for,
    132
music system, *see* entertainment
    systems

namaste, Hindu greeting, xv–xvi
natural materials, use of, 23–24,
    139–40
  absence of natural light, to
    overcome, 153–54
  in the bathroom, 250, 252–53
  in the bedroom, 227, 232,
    237–38
  in the dining room, 188,
    192–93
  guidelines for, 138–39
  in the kitchen, 182–83
  in transitional areas, 165, 168,
    171

in the workplace:
  boutiques, 345–46
  company guidelines, 268,
    273–75
  conference room, 318
  cubicle, 292
  dining area, 324–25
  medical suite waiting rooms,
    352
  office, your, 282
  in pod area, 300–02
  reception area, 308, 312
  in "Silicon" workspace, 334,
    335, 336
  in zone of tranquility, 173
nature:
  in the conference room,
    317–18
  in the dining room, 192–93
  healing side of, 39, 44,
    90–100, 164, 222, 358
  rhythms created by, 122
  in the workplace, 276
  in home office or study, 214
  in the kitchen, 182–83
  laws of:
    color and, 63
    order and harmony and,
      9–11
  respecting, 23–24
  workplace, presence in the,
    262–63
  see also natural materials, use of
neck pain, waking with, 227
nerves, calming your, 350
new and old, duality of, 123–24
north, the, 21–22, 266
  living room in, 198
  orientation of entrance to, 142
  transitional areas oriented
    toward the, 164
  see also spiritual blueprints; *spe-
    cific rooms*
now, being in the, 260–61

obesity, 32
office, your, 278–85
  décor for, 282–83
  furnishings, placement of,
    280–82
  spiritual blueprint for, 279–80
  zone of tranquility in, 283–85

see also home office or study;
  workplaces
old and new, duality of, 123–24
orange, 62, 64–65, 83–84, 85,
  170
order and harmony, 9–11
organic food, 177
organic materials, *see* natural
  materials

paintings:
  conference room, 319
  guidelines for, 135
  see also pictures and pho-
    tographs
peppermint oil for headaches,
  285
peppermint tea, 318
personalizing your space,
  108–10, 139–40
  failure to claim your space, 26,
    109–10
photographs, *see* pictures and
  photographs
pictures and photographs,
  205–06
  in the bedroom, 226, 228, 231
  in dining area at work, 327
  guidelines for, 134
  in home office or study, 215
  in the kitchen, 179
  in medical suite examination
    room, 351
  in medical suite waiting room,
    353–54
  in the workplace, 274, 282,
    292, 294, 304, 319
  see also paintings
Pitri, Lord, 17, 18, 351
pitta (or fire):
  avoiding like increases like:
    in the bedroom, 220
    in home office or study, 178
    in the kitchen, 178–79
    in the workplace, 275–76,
      298, 330, 331
  characteristics of *dosha* of,
    29–30
  color, using healing effect of,
    87, 170
  diet and, 40, 326
  excess, 30, 39

healthy quadrant for, 40, 70,
  222
honoring your *dosha,* 39–40
unhealthy quadrant for, 39,
  60, 70, 152, 222
in the workplace, 275–76,
  279, 280, 289, 298, 330,
  331, 350
weather, 40
plans, carefully considering, 113
plants, 23, 136–38
  as appeasements, 179, 203–04
  in the bedroom, 237–38
  in boutiques, 344–45
  in dining area at work, 324
  in the dining room, 192
  to divide space in studio or
    loft, 161
  in home office or study,
    214
  meaningful display of, 137–38
  in medical suite waiting
    rooms, 352
  music's effect on, 201
  in transitional areas, 166–67,
    168–69, 170
  in the workplace:
    company guidelines, 267,
      274
    reception area, 308
pod, your part of a, 295–305
  color, 297, 298, 302
  the décor, 299–302
  furnishings, placement of,
    298–99
  spiritual blueprint for,
    296–98
  zone of tranquility, 302,
    303–04
porches, *see* transitional areas
potpourri, 217
Prabhakar, Sudesh, xvii
prana (life force), 15
private space, ambience for, 124
property:
  ideal, 143–44
  orientation of entrances,
    141–43
  spiritual blueprint of the,
    57
public space, ambience for,
  124

puja (prayer service), xvi
purusha, 45

quiet space, ambience for, 124

raga (Indian classical music), 8,
  200
reading materials in medical
  suite waiting room, 354
reception area, 305–12
  color in, 308
  décor for, 308–11
  furnishings, placement of,
    306–07
  spiritual blueprint for, 306,
    307, 309
  zone of tranquility, 312
rectangular spiritual blueprints,
  51, 364–65
red, 62, 64, 83, 85–86, 170,
  353
refrigerator, 156, 179, 322
renovations, care with, 113–15
resolving conflicts, 68–100
  appeasements, *see* appease-
    ments
  furniture shuffle, 76–78
  with room swap, 70–76
respiratory illnesses, 32
rhythm, power of, 121–24
  color and, 122–23, 197
  in cooking, 177, 185
  in the dining room, 188
  dualities and, 123–24
  three vastu principles and, 122
  in work, 261
room swap, 70–76
rugs, 132, 168, 179, 302, 318,
  334

sacred center:
  appeasements for covered, 81,
    188, 315, 317
  in boutique, 346
  of conference room, 315, 317
  of dining area at work, 323
  of home office or study,
    210
  honoring the, 127–28, 165,
    334
  of medical suite waiting room,
    352, 353

sacred center *(cont.)*
  workplace furniture and equip-
    ment, placement of, 271,
    272
sacred center, honoring the:
  clutter, avoiding, 128–30
screens, Japanese rice paper,
  160–61
seasonal changes, 39
self-esteem, 262
self vs. ego, 313–14, 319
senior executives, spiritual blueprint for offices of, 279
sexual dysfunction, 4
shades, 131
sharing a space with person of
  different constitution,
  43–44
Shiva, Lord, 17, 46, 92–94
"Silicon" workspace, 329–36
  décor for, 334–35
  furnishings and equipment,
    placement of, 331–34
  spiritual blueprint for, 330–31,
    332
  zone of tranquility, 335–36
sincerity of appeasements, 99–100
sink:
  kitchen, 156, 179, 322
  medical suite examination
    room, 357–58
sinus problems, 32
skin cleanser, 255
skin rashes, 39
soma, 21
Soma, Lord, 21, 142, 198, 231,
  251, 279
south, the, 22, 266
  orientation of entrance to, 143
  transitional areas oriented
    toward the, 164
  see also spiritual blueprints; *spe-
    cific rooms*
Southern Hemisphere, 117
  bathroom location, appease-
    ment and, 251
  cardinal directions in, 106
  child's bedroom, location of,
    234
  flow of cosmic energy and
    spiritual power in, 107
  kapha dosha in, 42, 70

kitchen location in, 177–78
location of basic elements in,
  15n, 19–20, 105–06
  chart, 19
master bedroom location in,
  229
pitta dosha in, 40, 70
placement of heavy and dense
  furnishings in, 107
placement of lightweight and
  delicate furniture in, 107
spiritual blueprints for, 56, 69,
  116
vata dosha in, 41, 70
workplaces, unhealthy quadrant for, 275–76, 279, 280,
  289, 298, 331, 350
zone of tranquility, 102, 173
southwest, adding weight in the,
  126–27, 128
space (ether), 13, 14, 15
  guide to placement of appease-
    ments, 81–82
  location in vastu living, 15
spiritual blueprints, 45–61
  for the bedroom, 220–21,
    231, 235, 236
  for boutiques, 338–40, 341
  choosing the correct shape,
    49–51
  company guidelines, 265–70
  conference room, 314–15, 316
  creating your own, 56–59
  cubicle, your, 287–89
  determining the appropriate
    number of, 54–56
  for dining area at work,
    321–22, 323, 324
  for the dining room, 188, 191
  for home office or study,
    209–10, 211, 212
  interpreting your, 59–61
  irregular shapes, 51–54
    L-shaped space, 51–52
    odd-shaped building or
      property, 53–54
  for the kitchen, 177–78, 180,
    181
  for the living room, 198–99,
    202
  materials needed for creation
    of, 57

medical suites:
  examination room, 355–56,
    357
  waiting room, 349, 351
  office, your, 279–80
  pod, your part of a, 296–98
  problems, fixing, 61
  reception area, 306, 307, 309
  rectangular, 51, 364–65
  for "Silicon" workspace,
    330–31, 332
  square, 47–49, 363
  for transitional area, 164
  using your, 125
  of zone-of-tranquility room,
    243–44, 245
spiritual health, 24
sports zone of tranquility,
  335–36
square:
  furnishings, 130, 131, 181,
    187
  spiritual blueprint, 47–49,
    363
stillness, taking a journey
  toward, 312
stove, kitchen, 156, 179
stress, 3–5, 303, 329, 333
strokes, 4
"Studies in Geobiology:
  Colours-Man-Building
  Interrelationship," 66n
studio or loft, special issues for,
  155–61
  breaking the flow, 159–61
  kitchen compressed into one
    wall, 156–59
  lack of walls, benefit of, 155
study, *see* home office or study
suicide, 4
Surya, Lord, 20, 63, 142, 182,
  266
swing, porch, 167

Tat Tvam Asi (Thou Art That),
  12–13, 24, 282
teas, 318
television, placement of,
  200–01
  in child's bedroom, 236
  in home office or study, 210
  in the workplace, 273

terraces, *see* transitional areas
threatened constitution, appeasements for, 81
toilet, orientation of, 251, 269
toran, 171–72
transitional areas, 162–73
  balcony or terrace, 167–70
  benefits of, 162–63
  company guidelines for, 267–68
  orientation of, 164
  porch or veranda, 165–67
  removing shoes before entering home from, 163
  shared terraces, 170–71
  spiritual blueprint for, 164
  symbolic, 171–72
  zone of tranquility, 172–73
tridoshas, 29–32
  see also kapha (or water); *pitta* (or fire); *vata* (or air)

unique identity, celebrating your, 25–26, 164, 358
  in the dining room, 188
  in the living room, 196, 197
  in medical suite waiting room, 353–54
  personalizing your space, 108–10, 139–40
  failure to claim your space, 26, 109–10
  in the reception area, 308–09
  rhythms created by, 122
  in the workplace, 274–75, 276, 282–83
  in zone-of-tranquility room, 248
U-shaped table for conference room, 315

vacillation, 31
valuables, placement of, 136
Varuna, Lord, 20–21, 142, 266
vastu:
  defined, xvi, 7
  five basic elements, *see* five basic elements
  history of, xvii, 5
  human body as example of, *see* body, human, as example of vastu

personal environment as focus of, 8
  principles of, 13–26
  sister sciences, 5, 8, 28
  Western adaptation of, *see* vastu living
vastu living, 5
  ayurveda and, *see ayurveda*
  guidelines:
    flexibility of, 110–11
    making space at least 51 percent vastu-correct, 111–12, 265, 287, 310
  in the home, *see* home
  time to reap benefit of, 112
  web site, xviii
  workplace, *see* workplaces
Vastu Living: Creating a Home for the Soul (Cox), xviii, 133n, 141n
Vastu Living Ayurveda Test, 32–38
  evaluating your answers, 37–38
vastu purusha mandala, 45–47
  diagram, 47
  see also spiritual blueprints
vata (or air):
  characteristics of *dosha* of, 30–31
  color, using healing effect of, 87
  diet and, 41, 326
  excess, 31
  healthy quadrant for, 41, 70, 222
  home office or study and, 178
  special note for *"vata"* people, 38
  unhealthy quadrant for, 41, 60, 70, 152, 221
  in the workplace, 275–76, 279, 280, 289, 298, 331, 350
  weather, 42
Vayu, Lord, 15
Vedas, 8
Vedic civilization, 8–9
Vedic philosophy, 9, 110
  divinity in all creation, 12–13
  order and harmony, 9–11
veranda, *see* transitional areas

vibrations, 46
  color and, 62–63, 66, 83
  keeping furniture four inches from wall to protect your, 130
  meshing your, with your environment, 112
  power of, 11–12
  religious significance of, 133
  renovations and alterations, changes resulting from, 113
violet, 62–63, 65–66, 83, 85–86, 170, 353
Vishnu, Lord, 63
voice, speaking in a soft, 133–34, 326

waiting room, medical suite, *see* medical suites, waiting room
wall-to-wall carpeting, 132
washing machine, 179
water, 13, 14, 17
  bathroom, honoring element in the, 250
  in conference room zone of tranquility, 319
  guide to placement of appeasements, 81–82
  location in vastu living, 17
  in the northeast, adding, 126, 127, 172
  source of, on property, 143
watercoolers, workplace, 268, 322, 351, 357–58
water fountains, 322, 355
weather:
  kapha, 43
  pitta dosha and, 40
  vata, 42
west, the, 20–21, 266
  dining room in, 188
  orientation of entrance to, 142
  transitional areas oriented toward the, 164
  see also spiritual blueprints; *specific rooms*
white, 64, 66, 86, 182, 286
window displays, boutique, 342–43

window treatments, 123
  bedroom, 226
  conference room, 318
  guidelines for, 131
  reception area, 308
  in "Silicon" workspace,
    335
workplaces:
  boutiques, *see* boutiques
  celebrating your divinity, 259,
    261–62
  the company, guidelines for,
    see company, general work-
    place guidelines for the
  conference room, *see* confer-
    ence room
  cubicle, your, *see* cubicle, your
  dining area, *see* dining area,
    company
  failure to personalize, 26,
    257–361
  home office, *see* home office or
    study
  medical suites, *see* medical
    suites
  nature's presence in, 262–63
  new work world, vastu living
    in, 259–63
  now, being in the, 260–61
  office, your, *see* office, your
  pods, *see* pod, your part of a

reception area, *see* reception
    area
resolving conflicts in your, *see*
    resolving conflicts
rhythm of work, 261
"Silicon," *see* "Silicon" work-
    space
workstations, placement:
  company guidelines for,
    270–73
  cubicle, your, 289–90
  in medical suite waiting room,
    351
  office, your, 280–81
  in "Silicon" workspace,
    331–33

Yama, Lord, 22, 214, 266
yellow, 62, 64, 65, 84–85, 182,
    214
yoga, xvi
  group, in the workplace, 277
  relationship to vastu, 5, 8
  to relieve repetitive hand
    movements, 333

zone of tranquility, 101–04
  in the bathroom, 250, 253–54
  in the bedroom, 228–29,
    232–34, 238–39, 240–41
  boutique, 346–47

company guidelines, 265,
    276–77
conference room, 314,
    319
cubicle, your, 292, 293–94
of dining area of company,
    326–28
in the dining room,
    193–95
in home office or study, 213,
    215–17
kitchen, 179, 184–85
in the living room, 206
in medical suite:
  examination room,
    358–61
  waiting room, 355
message of, 103–04
office, your, 283–85
pod area, 302, 303–04
reception area, 312
in "Silicon" workspace,
    335–36
in transitional area, 172–73
zone-of-tranquility room,
    242–48
  décor of, 246–48
  furnishing, placement of,
    244–46
  spiritual blueprint of, 243–44,
    245

Lightning Source UK Ltd.
Milton Keynes UK
UKOW06f1614020315

247136UK00003BA/139/P